MW01640007

For Joan

Looking for Eulabee Dix

The Illustrated Biography of An American Miniaturist

By Jo Ann Ridley

The National Museum of Women in the Arts
Washington, D.C. 1997

Cover: Eulabee Dix
Me, ca. 1899, 2½ x 2⅛ in. oval
The National Museum of Women in the Arts
Gift of Mrs. Philip Dix Becker and Family

Frontispiece: Getrude Käsebier
Portrait of Eulabee Dix, ca. 1907
Platinum print, 8 x 6⅛ in.
The National Museum of Women in the Arts
On loan from Joan Becker Gaines

Miniatures illustrated throughout the text are watercolor on ivory. When dimensions are given, height precedes width. Unless otherwise credited, archival photographs featured in this book are located in the Archives on Women Artists in the Library and Research Center (LRC) of the National Museum of Women in the Arts. These materials were generously donated to the museum by the family of Eulabee Dix.

Editor: Laureen Schipsi
Copy Editor: Deborah Phillips
Designer: Polly Franchine, PrimaryDesign, Washington, D.C.
Printed and bound in England by Balding + Mansell.
We wish to thank Amanda Nelson, Elyse Buxbaum, Neala Shiralkar, and Cameron Smith for their editorial assistance. We also wish to thank Lee Stalsworth for photographing many of the miniatures and archival photographs that appear in this book.

Library of Congress Cataloging-In-Publication Data
Ridley, Jo Ann, 1925–
Looking for Eulabee Dix : the illustrated biography of an American Miniaturist / Jo Ann Ridley.
p. cm.
Includes bibliographical references.
ISBN 0-940979-36-5. -- ISBN 0-940979-37-3 (pbk.)
1. Dix, Eulabee, 1878–1961. 2. Miniature painters--United States--Biography. I. Title.
ND 1337.U6D5837 1997
759. 13--dc21
[B] 97-29794
CIP

ISBN 0-940979-36-5 (hard cover) ISBN 0-940979-37-3 (soft cover)

Contents

Foreword

In 1989 the National Museum of Women in the Arts was fortunate to receive a generous and important donation of paintings and sketches from the family of the American miniaturist, Eulabee Dix (1878-1961). The gift was received with much appreciation, for it is significant to have in the museum's collection works by an artist who played an instrumental role in the revival of miniature painting during the late nineteenth and early twentieth centuries.

With the advent of the more accessible medium of photography in the mid-nineteenth century, the long-esteemed tradition of miniature portrait painting began to fade, until it was eventually crowded out of the mainstream of the fine arts. To those who relied on cameras to record or interpret a likeness, miniatures became an unfamiliar medium. Dix, during her lifetime, successfully maintained the integrity of this medium and fostered appreciation for its special qualities. Today, a growing group of enthusiasts keep the art alive with societies of miniatures existing in various cities of the United States.

This authorized biography and the accompanying essay provide a look into the history and technique of miniature painting. It will serve as an important resource for those interested in and appreciative of the skill involved in creating detailed portraits that fit easily into the palm of one's hand. However, the book is more than a discussion of a technically sophisticated art form. As with many artists, Dix's dedication was intense; but unlike most, she chose a medium that presented challenges many other artists eschewed. She mastered the painstaking process of painting in miniature on ivory. Dix's technical skill was matched by her ability to capture not only the likeness of her subjects, but their often formidable personalities as well. She reveled in the glamorous lifestyle of the "high society" clientele she so boldly sought.

Looking for Eulabee Dix: The Illustrated Biography of an American Miniaturist is the story of an artist whose personal and professional pursuits were firmly intertwined. It is the biography of a woman whose encounters provide a unique glimpse into the likes of Mark Twain, Robert Henri, and John Butler Yeats. At the same time it reveals Dix's strength and courage in pursuing art as a divorced mother, raising two children under the scrutiny of a society entrenched in Victorian mores. Reading about Eulabee Dix allows us to understand that singular devotion to art involves both loss and triumph. She triumphed by living her life doing what pleased her most, making art, but in the process was forced to make many sacrifices. Losing family approval and financial security necessitated living a meager existence. It was a challenge to secure commissions for portraits in a dwindling market. Now, many years later, we are the fortunate beneficiaries of Dix's singular perseverance, which helped to keep miniature painting alive in America and abroad.

We are tremendously gratefully to the family of Eulabee Dix. Without their constant commitment this project would not have been possible. Our deepest thanks go to Joan B. Gaines, Samuel M. Dix, Mr. and Mrs. L. William Lisle, Mark Dix, and Peter Becker for their generous assistance in funding the publication. We are also extremely indebted to Joan B. Gaines and Mrs. Philip Dix Becker and her family for their donations of works from the Dix oeuvre to the National Museum of Women in the Arts. Because of these gifts, the museum now has the largest collection of miniatures by the artist. In addition, the family's donation of the Eulabee Dix Papers has come to fruition with the publication of this book, and these materials will continue to be an important resource for researchers and scholars.

We are also thankful to Joan B. Gaines, Mrs. Philip Dix Becker, Horace P. Dix III, Samuel M. Dix, and Mr. and Mrs. L. William Lisle for endowing the beautiful small Eulabee Dix Gallery at the National

Museum of Women in the Arts. It provides an intimate setting in which to showcase Dix's miniatures and works by other women artists and is a special place to share with visitors. The late Lewis Hoyer Rabbage, a prominent collector of revival period miniatures, deserves special acknowledgment as an early facilitator of the Eulabee Dix collection.

It is with great pride that the National Museum of Women in the Arts presents *Looking for Eulabee Dix*. Jo Ann Ridley spent ten years researching Dix's life. Her efforts have produced a vivid narrative, told with thoroughness, directness, and compassion. The book not only enhances our understanding of Dix's works by providing insights into the life of a fascinating woman who helped to keep an art form alive, it advances one of the founding purposes of the National Museum of Women in the Arts: to recognize women artists who have made significant contributions to the history of art.

Wilhelmina Cole Holladay
Founder and Chair of the Board
The National Museum of Women in the Arts

Acknowledgments

WHEN I FIRST BEGAN MY SEARCH FOR EULABEE DIX ALMOST TEN YEARS ago, I was not fully cognizant of my responsibilities to this complex woman. It was only as the scattered and often contradictory pieces of her story began to fall into place that they emerged. It would be imperative for the biography to portray with unerring accuracy her life, times, and art, to be truthful about her foibles, and cushion her fragility with understanding. Above all, I had to tread the narrow path of fact while accomodating the biographee's fiction, which she often presented as fact. Finally, it was important to secure acknowledgment of her elegant legacy to the art of miniature painting. The challenge was of immense proportions, as were the rewards. If that challenge has been met, it is because the Dix-Becker family and countless others have been extraordinarily generous with their support and assistance.

Two special women head this list. First in the chronology of the undertaking was Mary Randlett, the gifted Pacific Northwest photographer who introduced me to Eulabee Dix's daughter, Joan Becker Gaines, in 1988. Mary steadfastly encouraged us to forge ahead, and then stood by at the difficult bends in the road to publication.

Joan Gaines also stands alone, as an unfailing collaborator and provider of critical resources, including her own remarkable unpub-

Left:

Roses, ca. 1941
Watercolor on paper, 11¾ x 9 in.
Courtesy of Samuel M. Dix
Photographed by ©1996 Charles Heiney

lished autobiography, *Exhuming Eulabee*. She was a superlative first editor who asked no quarter where her mother was concerned, and gave little where writing was at stake. Our friendship is an unforeseen gift of this book, one that I shall forever cherish.

It was my great good fortune, too, that others in the Dix family withheld nothing, nor suggested changes that might have polished the subject's image. I am deeply grateful to them: Eulabee's nephew, Samuel M. Dix; his sister, Sally Dix Lisle and her husband, L. William Lisle; and two of Eulabee's grandchildren, Ayala Becker Talpai and her brother, Peter Becker. David Gaines helped to keep family perspectives in balance, and I thank him for that.

The late Lewis Hoyer Rabbage, who facilitated the gift of the Eulabee Dix collection to the National Museum of Women in the Arts, early on encouraged the writing of this biography and generously shared his own meticulous research. His untimely death in 1995, and therefore his not being here to accept the credit he richly deserves, is a sad footnote to the otherwise felicitous completion of the project.

William M. Murphy, the distinguished biographer of John Butler Yeats, brought a significant layer of scholarship to this journalist's efforts. Not only did he graciously permit the use of passages from his book, *Prodigal Father,* but he also cast a critical yet kindly academic eye on early versions of my own manuscript. I hope he will not object to being considered a bountiful and much appreciated mentor. I also thank Clark S. Marlor for initiating and passing along his Brooklyn research.

Wilhelmina Cole Holladay, founder of the National Museum of Women in the Arts in Washington, D.C., along with the museum's director, Rebecca Phillips Abbott, and Susan Fisher Sterling, chief curator, helped to bring *Looking for Eulabee Dix* to life. Krystyna Wasserman, the museum's devoted and highly creative librarian, was particularly supportive from the beginning. She opened the Dix archives for research even before the papers had been collated. She also located obscure materials about the Polish artist, Olga Boznanska, for which I am most grateful.

My warm thanks go to the scholars who responded so kindly to requests for help: the late Dale Johnson, research associate, American paintings, at the Metropolitan Museum of Art; Andrew L. Thomas, archivist, Research and Scholars Center at the Smithsonian's National Museum of American Art; Patricia Swoboda of the catalog of American portraits, the National Portrait Gallery; Lee Ann Dean, archivist, the Helen Farr Sloan Library at the Delaware Art Museum; Jeanette M. Toohey, associate curator for collections, and administrators of the John Sloan Trust at the Delaware Art Museum; Maura Haggerty, assistant curator at the Mark Twain House in Hartford; Judy Larson, curator of American art at the High Museum of Art in Atlanta; Charles Johnson, librarian, and his staff at the Ventura Museum of History and Art; Gino Francesconi, director and archivist at the Carnegie Hall Museum; Lisa Blackburn, communications associate at the Huntington Library; E. Jane Connell, curator of collections and exhibitions at the Grand Rapids Art Museum; and Carol Aiken, the Baltimore conservator whose excellent essay about the use of ivory in miniature painting is an enlightening addendum to the biography. The Albright-Knox Art Gallery in Buffalo, New York, assisted in earlier research made available to me by Lewis Hoyer Rabbage.

To Marianne Gibson, who co-authored with Susan Strickler a catalogue of the miniature collection at the Worcester Art Museum, goes my heartfelt thanks for invaluable research assistance and support, including her reading of an early draft of the manuscript. Mona Dearborn, former keeper of the Catalog of American Portraits at the National Portrait Gallery, and biographer of the early American miniaturist, Anson Dickinson, performed important research chores *in situ*, and then reviewed the manuscript. Her encouragement and excellent suggestions are reflected, with my deep appreciation, in the final version. California art historians Richard Warren and Janann Strand are valued friends whose enthusiasm and expertise kept me at work when energies flagged. Richard always was at the ready with his extensive library; Janann, the ultimate investigator, uncovered the whereabouts of the "lost" wedding portrait of Eulabee by Robert Henri, and found the ashram where Eulabee lived briefly prior to World War II.

Others who greatly assisted me were Margaret M. Sherry at the Princeton University Libraries; Michael B. Yeats and Anne B. Yeats of Dublin; and Jack Karraker, chairman of the University of Nebraska Art Department. My gratitude also goes to Mary Anderson, Dorothy Anthony, Marietta Ivanden Berg, Brooke Hayward Duchin and her secretary, Betty Walsh, and to Ann Titus and Patricia Van Mason. Inspiration and encouragement came from, among so many others, Carol and Joe Andrews, Sonya and Richard Halley, B. J. Hargreaves, Sheila Horder, Joanne Horton, William Norton, and Barbara Patten. In England, my writer friend Heather Higgins, J. L. Evans, administrator of the former Duke of Anglesey family home in Wales, and Paul Barker at Warwick Castle were of immeasurable help, as well.

Finally, my lasting thanks go to Laureen Schipsi, director of publications at the National Museum of Women in the Arts and the editor of this book, Amanda Nelson, editorial assistant, and Randi Jean Greenberg, NMWA's collections manager, for their hard work and expertise in producing this publication. My thanks also to Deborah Phillips, who gently led me through revisions without inflicting a single bruise. I ask expiation for any sins of omission regarding these acknowledgments. They were not deliberate. Indeed, I am deeply indebted to every person who was part of this fascinating, ultimately satisfying, search for Eulabee Dix, particularly my husband, John Ridley, who made it possible.

JO ANN RIDLEY
The Sea Ranch, California
May 31, 1997

I write to you, and to you, and to you. We are each other.

Eulabee Dix

Eulabee Dix, ca. 1906
LRC Archives of The National Museum of Women in the Arts

CHAPTER 1

The Circumference of My Life to Be

1878–1888

How dull a world without fools and saints and artists.

SHE WAS NOT A FOOL, nor was she a saint. But Eulabee Dix was an artist, and her world was never dull.

It was a world of her own creating. During the serious mid-forties housing shortage in New York after World War II, for example, she managed to locate a tiny storefront under the Third Avenue "El" and asked to be shown the space.

"What is your business?" inquired the puzzled landlord.

"Beauty," she replied, "I'm in the beauty business."

"A beauty parlor?"

"No, just art. I make a lot of things and they usually turn out to be beautiful."

It was true. Furthermore, if something was not beautiful in Eulabee's eyes, it was not of importance. Or it did not exist. Sometimes she would say it was beautiful because she thought it should be.

The persona, as well, must be beautiful. Her refusal to accept the aging process underlay a chronic reluctance to disclose the exact date of her birth, just as she hated to acknowledge the biological process that brought it about. Therefore she deemed the prim opening sentence of her memoirs sufficient unto the subject.

> It was in St. Louis, Missouri, in the 1870s that my newly wedded parents made their home, and a few years later I was there.

In fact, she arrived only a year and a half later. A birth certificate, recorded in the first year that Greene County, Illinois, undertook such recordkeeping, confirms that a female child, "Ula Bee" (misspelled by the clerk), was born on October 5, 1878, in Greenfield, Illinois, to Horace P. and Mamie E. Dix. While the family Bible records that she was christened "Eula B.," Southern fashion, by the time she was old enough to indulge her theatrical instincts, the child who would grow up to challenge and baffle the genteel Dix family became, in a word, "Eulabee."

Her ancestry was rooted deep in American soil, transplanted from Scotland in 1690 when the youngest son of the Earl of Mar fled service in the militia of King William III to seek his fortune in Virginia. Three brothers among his descendants settled in Kentucky in 1792 just as it became the newest of the United States, and changed their name to Marrs. One of these brothers, Henry Marrs, planted the seedling for a family tree that two generations later leafed out in Dixes when Henry's granddaughter, Sally Negley, married Henry Dix and produced Eulabee's father.[1]

Eulabee's mother, Mary Elizabeth Bartholomew Dix, "Mamie," was the only child of Benjamin Bartholomew, an English craftsman who emigrated to Davenport, Iowa, as a young man in mid-century. Mamie's mother was Mary Ann Hassett, of a well-established St. Louis family. Mamie was born in Iowa and reared in Carrollton, a small southern Illinois town. The location afforded the Bartholomews a comfortable rural lifestyle, and was only thirty miles from a thriving St. Louis with its requisite access to the Hassett social circle. There is no record of how her grandfather earned a living at the time; Eulabee's memoirs record only that Carrollton was a rich farm community where great barns stood beside double brick houses, and that her mother was a spoiled little girl who rode her pony to visit friends.

When they met at a dancing party in Carrollton, Mamie was eighteen and Horace, the handsome son of a Louisville builder of some repute, was twelve years her senior. They married in 1877 and set up housekeeping on the north side of St. Louis in what then was a modest residential neighborhood on Cass Avenue.

> Our house . . . was one of three alike. It had not pretense—a plot of green, a few steps to the front door, the hall past the parlor, the stairs leading up and the bathroom with the built-in zinc tub . . . the front room with a bed in the alcove.

By that time, Papa Bartholomew, apparently a dapper and convivial sort, had bought a small hotel in nearby Greenfield, Illinois, where Mamie went to have her first child. "Bart's House" burned down shortly thereafter, and the Bartholomews moved in with the young Dixes. As Victorian ladies were wont to do when faced with unpleasantness, Grandmother Bartholomew took to her bed. She lingered for nearly four years, then died, affording her daughter the seemingly not unwelcome opportunity to go into mourning. Due to successive deaths in the family, including Mamie's and Horace's second baby (neither Henry Bryant Dix's birth in 1882 nor his death two years later are mentioned in Eulabee's memoirs), it seemed to Eulabee that Mamie always was swathed in a long crepe veil. Mourning clothes bestowed an elegant dignity that female survivors, having acquired a taste for black, seemed loathe to relinquish.

Benjamin Bartholomew adored his daughter and granddaughter, and they him, to such an extent that Mamie lived in dread that he would remarry. Displaying an overweening, almost Oedipal, devotion, the family has said, she made sure that he lived with her until he died in 1910 at the age of eighty-four.[2]

A copy of Eulabee's birth certificate, obtained in 1994 (thirty-three years after her death), lists her father's occupation as a "drummer." Conventional family wisdom has it that, although well-born, he was an "unsuccessful businessman who dealt in harnesses and agricultural hardware."[3]

Whatever her father's deficiencies as a breadwinner might have been, Eulabee recalled her early years in St. Louis as a secure childhood hedged about with loving parents and simple indulgences. She was her grandfather's pet, and Horace was her beloved hero; Mamie relished motherhood, read light novels, and "enjoyed" delicate health when there was nothing else to do. It seemed the archetypical middle-class American household in the archetypical American city of the 1880s. What Eulabee chose to recall of that time is laid on memory's canvas with deft strokes.

> [I was] a little girl in a house of grown-ups, like giants. I played with children no one else could see. . . . The great world about me seemed tall and big and solid; time was long, distances far. My father would appear at the end of the day, after that mysterious lack of presence, with something beautiful or good to eat under his arm; tangerines, called kid-glove oranges, flowers, or red bananas or a book.

Mamie sensed early on that her daughter was not like other children. She cosseted Eulabee's artistic inclinations as best she could within the narrow perspective of a sheltered young wife with no formal education. Eulabee described her mother as conventional, though possessing "independently delightful" taste. The pivotal moment of discovery seems to have occurred when Eulabee was four years old.

> I remember one dismal rainy afternoon when my mother and a friend were cozily chatting before the upstairs grate. They sat in rockers by a soft coal fire, which sputtered and cast light and warmth into the room. I was sprawled on my stomach on a flowered Brussels carpet, curls and frilly muslin moving with the motion of my energy as I swept lines of pink chalk over

> paper laid on a lapboard brought from the sewing room . . . when the guest suddenly exclaimed "See! That child has drawn a perfect circle!"

In one of the sometimes florid ruminations that embellish her memoirs, Eulabee identifies the personal ramifications of the event.

> The symbol of consciousness, drawn unconsciously, had produced an audience. Freely expressed, the circle meant my freedom, the circle of my being, alone in a round wide world—no dent of vanity or care, no lid of prejudice or fear. Myself alone in creative joy. The spell was cast—an artist—the circumference of my life to be.

Her uninstructed but intuitive love for beauty received only ordinary stimulation in home surroundings. There were, of course, the ancestral pictures that were *de rigueur* in good Southern families. Horace had spent his first spare five hundred dollars on lifesize portraits of his Kentucky parents, which for years hung in dignified oblivion in the front parlors of the Cass Avenue house and successive Dix domiciles.

Chromolithographs, the popular if not always tasteful color prints introduced to the middle classes in 1860, adorned the upstairs rooms. Eulabee grew up with one titled *Simply to the Cross I Cling.* Downstairs, an engraved patchwork of Biblical scenes over the dining room mantel provoked lively dinner table conversation when guests came. "Even at that early age I had a feeling that never took form that the picture was not worth talking about," Eulabee recalled. "Certainly it was not art."

As a child, her first exposure to "real" art came during visits to the annual state fairs with her grandfather, who drove the family to the fairgrounds in an elegant buggy.

> It was a merchant's fair with displays of the latest products in

> a great building. Afternoon and evening concerts were led by the famous Gilmore and John Philip Sousa bands. . . . Everybody [was] eating popcorn balls wrapped in pink paper. Tired from all the walking we sat and listened to music, then traversed the fine arts galleries looking at paintings from Europe—fine great Russian, Swedish, and German paintings. One picture, well painted, the head of a girl, blond with blond eyelashes and deep violet-blue eyes, impressed me. . . . I was fascinated and did not forget her. Of course I had then not seen Velásquez's little Princess Margaret [*Infanta Margaretta*] with her blond eyelashes.

The fascination resurfaced years later when Eulabee met and married a man whose pale coloring immediately evoked for her that painting. The circumstances prompt speculation that it may have exerted some misdirected psychic influence on her decision to marry.

Similar connections seem to have linked Eulabee the child to Eulabee the artist. In those early St. Louis days, her mother's friend Meddie Fisher was receiving love letters from the not yet famous American painter, William Merritt Chase, who was studying art in Munich. Mamie knew little about art and even less about artists. Nevertheless, while the two young women pored over Chase's ardent correspondence from far off Europe, Mamie's romantic Victorian nature led her to ponder aloud the juxtaposition of Art and Love. Eulabee was to recall those discussions when she moved to New York at the age of twenty and enrolled in Chase's art school.

Then there was her serendipitous first encounter with art in kindergarten where "My hands, in time, became as useful as the wings of a bird." Although art education for children did not exist as such in the 1880s, the kindergarten movement founded by the German pedagogue, Friedrich Froebel, had gained its American foothold in the St. Louis school system before Eulabee was born. A valuable decade of experimental teaching preceded her enrollment in kindergarten in 1883 at the age of five.

The experience there paralleled Froebel's philosophy of early childhood education: Under the guidance of a "mature maternal figure," it employed set routines of creative play through organized stories, songs, and games. Children were to express themselves through the manipulation of Froebel's "gifts"—colored forms and shapes—and develop both cognitive reasoning and affective understanding.[4]

> Ours was a separate building in the yard of the Divoll public school—a single long room with windows to the floor. . . . Such creative activity as folding glossy paper in intricate shapes, sewing cards, modeling clay, and weaving colored narrow strips of paper to make patterns were tasks for apt fingers. We also had games that made blindfold tests of smell and taste. . . . We had one unusual game . . . pieces of marble we crushed to make white sand. . . . With empty cigar boxes and colored inks we would put a little sand in a box, add a few drops of ink, shake well, put it in the sun to dry—and behold beautiful pink, blue, green, purple or lavender sand. Then, with a plank on chairs or the ironing board, we would go into business in the yard with spoons to measure and pins for money.

Eulabee remained in this garden of self expression for three years before entering regular school as a second grader, to her educated father's great relief. Here, the didactic lessons of *McGuffey's Eclectic Reader* replaced creative play. Nevertheless, her teachers soon learned to utilize the gifted 8-year-old's artistic talents. On special holidays she was sent around to the blackboards of various rooms to copy drawings of famous people and events from a booklet that came with Clarke's O.N.T. cotton thread. Eulabee took these assignments seriously and wept over every misplaced line in her drawings.

During play time at home, Eulabee and her friends cut paper dolls from *Delineator* fashion books. She had no patience with the careless ones who left white space around the cut-outs. But she was fascinated by her mother's ability to cut silhouettes and would sit quietly while a little "Chinaman" with pigtail and flat shoes emerged from scissors and letter paper. She learned this quaint talent for herself; today a number of her own silhouettes are in private and museum collections.

When Eulabee was nine, Mamie gave birth to her third child, Horace Philip Dix, Jr. He was a sickly infant, and needing to give him their undistracted attention lest they lose yet another baby, Horace and Mamie sent Eulabee to Louisville to stay with her father's older sister. Because the family had spent many happy summers in Kentucky, the little girl welcomed the prospect of visiting her beloved Aunt Eliza again. Nowhere else do her memoirs bestow such affection on a childhood interlude that had nothing to do with the nurturing of her creative genius.

> In the lives of grown-ups there is a particular spot, or time, that seems the very woof and web of one's youth. To me this spot and time were my Kentucky summers. They hang like a moving picture in the background of my past.

Over the years, the Dix family tree had sprouted an unconventional twig or two. Eulabee's father was still a child when his four older siblings were grown. His sister Kate married, but less than a year later died giving premature birth to a daughter, who was named Sally. His younger sister, Eliza, carried the infant about the house on a pillow until her survival was assured, then married the widower to become the second Mrs. Matthew Neill. Eliza raised Sally as her own, bore Matt Neill two more children, lost them, then nursed her husband for thirty-five years after he suffered a debilitating stroke.[5]

Sally married John G. Roach, a Kentucky gentleman of means (he owned three sour-mash whiskey distilleries) and stern devotion to family, good horse flesh, and, like his wife, the Baptist church.

Cousin Jack and Cousin Sally were the stuff of family legend. In 1882, at twenty-three, Sally Roach wrote and sold to J. B. Lippencott a 215-page epic poem entitled *Theon, A Tale of the American Civil War.* When the publishers requested a promotional photograph of the author, her husband's Southern sense of chivalry was so outraged that he forbade her to send it. Instead, he bought up the entire edition of his wife's book, and stored it in the attic.

Sally next turned to the study of Biblical texts in their original Hebrew and Greek, and heroically translated the King James version of the New Testament into modern Greek. Academia failed to reward her, but Jack did, sending Sally and their two sons on an extended trip to the Holy Land. While they happily lurched about the Middle East on camelback, Jack redecorated the house and acquired a fancy two-wheeled vehicle and tandem horses to celebrate their return.

It was to this generously endowed mènage, where she had complete charge of the household, that Eliza Neill brought her young niece in 1887. Although the war between the states had been over for twenty-two years, the effects of Emancipation had lingered long in Louisville.

> My father was born on Chestnut Street near Aunt Eliza's house. The family owned some slaves. He, being much younger than the other children, had a slave named Kitty to watch over and play with him. She was in our family, off and on, all her life, and would never say that my father was a bad boy, as I would tease her to do. Aunt Eliza told me that on the morning when the slaves left, she, who had never made her bed, was so tired afterward that she rolled in and took a nap.

Eliza recovered enough to learn how to make a bed, and a good deal more. With the keys to her domestic kingdom secure on a cord around her waist, she ran an efficient household that perfectly accommodated the various interests of its occupants. Possessed only of male grandchildren, she siezed the opportunity to lavish her determined taste in children's clothes on Eulabee, whose frilly custom-made dresses, with fashionable overskirts and decorative aprons, bristled with the blue and cherry-colored ribbons decreed appropriate by Aunt Eliza.

For the most part, the color-conscious child submitted meekly to being dressed up and endlessly groomed for formal calls on neighboring Louisville gentry. When the latent rebellion erupted, as was inevitable, it was not the first nor certainly the last time Eulabee would throw a temper tantrum over color.

> My best clothes were on, the pale pink sash adjusted, and I sat for the hair ribbon when, alas, I caught sight of myself in the mirror. No, I could not go! The hair ribbon! What a terrible color. It did not match the sash! I sat atop my castoff clothes, crying bitterly. No argument would comfort or persuade me, till at last my hair was simply pinned. But my face was ruined with crying. Again my dear aunt won with her gentle manner, and off we went.

The Kentucky visits were not always circumscribed by ruffles and proper deportment. Eliza Neill, understanding very well that children need time to be carefree, indulged her niece and grandsons when the family was at Clifton, the ten-acre farm they owned in south central Kentucky. Here, near Cane Valley in Green River country, Eliza repaired each spring to oversee the garden and housekeeping preparations for the summer. Eulabee and her boy cousins were allowed to roam the countryside virtually unsupervised.

Her account evokes the affluent country lifestyle that flourished in Kentucky during the 1880s and is the only really idyllic childhood adventure she ever recorded. Although written during the enlightened 1950s, today it seems archaic and flawed by unapologetic references to "darkies" and "pickaninnies."

She tells of transporting trucks, boxes, and barrels of provisions on a dusty journey of nearly a hundred miles from Louisville south to Campbellsville by train. From there they traveled by coach to Tampico

Aunt Eliza, ca. 1898
Pencil on paper, 11¾ x 9¾ in.
The National Museum of Women in the Arts
Gift of Mrs. Philip Dix Becker and Family

(since renamed Coburg) in Adair County, and, finally, by buggy late at night to the long white farmhouse. Here the adventures began.

> The early screech of peafowls awakened me. Without shoes or stockings, the fine bluegrass under my feet, I was about all day with my aunt, counting guinea hens, hunting young turkeys, and visiting the chicken house, the corn crib, ice house, and carriage house. Only the smoke house seemed always vacant. Three times a day the darkey boy went down hill to the spring-house, where milk and butter were kept cool in crocks setting in the flow of icy water. . . . Whitewashing was a spring occupation. The darkies used it inside and outside their cabins, with blue on blinds to keep the "hants" out. I must paint! I begged to paint! I was allowed a brush and bucket. My first painting lesson! . . . Peacock and polka-dotted guinea feathers dropped about were beautiful, and gathering them delighted me. We had a fly brush of peacock feathers, used by the house boy to sway back and forward over the dining table to keep the flies away. We ate peafowl—like Roman emperors!

When the Roaches arrived with Eulabee's cousins, Neill and Ethrick, social activities revolved around formal calls by carriage on the turnpike to other "gentleman farm" families. But the children were happiest in their off-pike wanderings on horseback. There were streams to wade and magical places to explore.

> My boy cousin and I on old Tilden, without a saddle, our bare legs hugging his sides, delighted in these trips. Sometimes we were visited by the neighbor children, all three bareback on one horse; then if we begged, we were all allowed to go down beyond the cornfield to play with "Aunt" Sarah's little pickaninnies. The road had no shade. The sun blazed on the deep dust and we ran fast rather than linger in the heat. Only the tumblebugs could detain us . . . large beetles ever busy rolling a ball of dirt and manure to a hole for safe deposit, for deep in

> the center of the ball was an egg for another tumblebug. . . . Between the house and the river, over the stile-blocks and down the hill was a dell—cool on the hottest of days. In its clear stream we waded. The sand and mud and the mosses and the stones became beautiful castles with gardens of wildflowers and trees of maidenhair fern. There it smelled sweet of the earth and greens; the quiet, with birds twittering and insects humming, was like music. . . . Then, in the stillness of the warm summer nights, tired with play, as I lay in bed I would hear the darkies coming down the road, singing, singing, singing; their beautiful mellow voices coming nearer and nearer, and I would fall asleep beneath the wide white mosquito netting bars.

When her baby brother was pronounced out of danger, Eulabee returned to St. Louis. She could not know that the cozy security of Cass Avenue was about to disappear in the detritus of her parents' respective difficulties. At ten, her life was about to undergo what must have seemed to her a profound change.

Eulabee in Grand Rapids, Michigan ca. 1898
Courtesy of Joan Becker Gaines

CHAPTER 2

Beginning Aright

1888–1899

Could it have been the pretty tea gowns so popular in the Eighties and Nineties, the lacy and delicately colored robes that trailed the floor and clung gracefully to reclining figures? Were they somehow responsible for the fashionable health of ladies—an excuse, perhaps, to wear them?

TO THE END of her life, Eulabee liked clothes and wore them well, whether she wheedled them from a New York couturier friend, remodeled a bargain-basement find, or, more often than not, designed and made them herself. She knew the important role clothing plays in a woman's life, so it was logical to associate the comfortable flowing negligees of the chaise longue to a Gilded-Age predilection for ill health. But she did not attribute her mother's intermittent infirmities to pretense.

> I never saw her wear a lacy, trailing thing. Her ill health was part of her energy. When nothing was on her program she would create an ailment and be ill, then bounce from her sickbed to nurse someone in need. The quiet old-fashioned women of America, strong in the making of our country, were now stirring to the cry of Woman's Rights, some . . . to stride forth in public, while others remained at home and uncovered their subdued ambitions for those about them, domestic women with little worldly knowledge but plenty of ideals. My mother was of the latter type. I became her ambition. Our

door was ever open to friends and relatives, delightful but taxing to mother. The doctor advised a change of climate.

For her father, though, more than a change of climate was at stake. It was a bitter paradox that in spite of unprecedented expansion in American agriculture during the last three decades of the nineteenth century, the Depression of 1873 pushed farm prices into a long decline. As farmers suffered, so did the businesses that served them. In 1888, Horace decided to move West and start anew, a common decision in those hard times.

Going alone to Helena, Montana, where there were relatives, he found some promising business opportunities in what was about to become a brand new state. He then sent for his family. Mamie, Eulabee, young Philip, and Grandfather Bartholomew followed by steamboat up the Mississippi River to St. Paul; from there they took a train across the Dakota Badlands to Helena.

Mamie declared Montana too remote for the good life, so they forged on to Nebraska at the urging of Illinois friends who already had moved there. The family passed that first hot summer in a Lincoln hotel, where nightly thunder and lightning storms pummeled Eulabee's fragile sensibilities like "a sort of hell."

Horace finally settled in Beatrice, a young community of about fifteen thousand people on the Blue River in southeastern Nebraska. They pronounced the town BeATrice. Here, in fertile prairie lands converted by homesteaders into vast fields of grain and pasture, he set out once more to make a living selling agricultural equipment.

Another of the odd connections linking Eulabee's early years to her later life originated less than two hundred miles, as Nebraska crows flew, northwest of Beatrice in Cozad. An artistically gifted boy named Robert Henry Cozad had grown up in the town his father founded on the North Platte. His family had left Nebraska five years before the Dixes arrived in Beatrice because the elder Cozad had been accused of murder. Moving on, the Cozads assumed new identities on

My Mother (Mary Elizabeth Bartholomew Dix)
ca. 1901, 2¼ x 2 in. oval
Courtesy of Samuel M. Dix

the East coast. Their son, who became the well-known artist, Robert Henri, years later would paint two full-length portraits of Eulabee Dix. They hang today in Atlanta's High Museum and at the Museum of Nebraska Art in Kearney.

It is unlikely that Eulabee and Henri ever discussed their mutual Nebraska experiences. Henri's real name and background were a closely kept secret until Van Wyck Brooks, also a later acquaintance of Eulabee's, published a biography in 1955 of Henri's friend and fellow iconoclast, the painter, John Sloan.[1]

Eulabee never took to the prairie, but it was a pleasant enough life and, as she recalls in quaint felicity, "There I grew taller and five years older, comfortably protected by a goodness of interest and situation." She had long talks with her father during carriage drives through fields of waving wheat and high tasselled corn as he went about business calls. "Have some style about you!" he advised her more than once, "Be somebody!"

She was to do both, but right now their 10-year-old daughter's emotional intensity concerned the Dixes. It was impossible to satisfy her passion for perfection. On one occasion, when her mother planned a trip to St. Louis, she asked Eulabee what she might bring back to her.

> From somewhere I had acquired a wide but short piece of Royal Stuart plaid ribbon which delighted my eye. Mother said perhaps she could find some material like it. . . . The piece had crimson red in it, but the length of silk my mother thoughtfully and kindly brought from St. Louis was Royal Stuart with vermillion red. The instant I saw the silk it was wrong. I could have wept. To my parents it was the same plaid. So slight a difference in color meant nothing to them. I hated it. I could not look at it. Father tried to make me see my ingratitude and unappreciativeness. . . . I kept trying to make them understand. . . . If my parents saw my point they did not let me know. The silk was made up and I wore it.

Eulabee's memoirs neither allude to nor explain her father's long absences during those Nebraska years. "He would be gone for a month," Mamie later told her granddaughter, "and I didn't hear from him. Finally I'd put on my bonnet, go find him and bring him home."[2] Drink? Women? Trouble at home? Whatever personal demons were giving chase, while Horace Dix the Southern gentleman struggled with Horace Dix the salesman, young Mamie happily flowered in the social and charitable interests of their local Episcopal parish's comparatively sophisticated congregation. Preoccupied as she was with church work and two demanding children, though, she never stopped looking for ways to advance Eulabee's gifts. Art teachers knocked at their door to no avail. Mamie insisted she must begin "the right way," not sure exactly what it might be.

> There were discussions of my artistic talent which seemed a

> superior thing, which people said I should be proud to possess. My mother and others made me feel that it was something precious, something of outstanding value. Thus it was that ART, like a garment, clothed my youthful dreams of fame and fortune. Truly I had a bird in my bosom and Mother helped to make it sing.

But Eulabee felt different, separated. "A child whose eye is arrested by rays of light from a window, or the form of a vase, or the folds of a garment, or the color of a flower, is an odd child." Even at that early age she was developing her improvisational talents.

> I seemed never to be lonesome, my hands formed somethings out of nothings: dolls' furniture out of chips of wood, dolls from clothespins with tissue paper dresses, hats, parasols; piano lamp shades of Dennison's crepe paper.

Growing up, Eulabee was a voracious reader of the classic histories and biographies she found on her father's bookshelves. She wept over *Abbott's History of Lady Jane Grey*, went into battle with Napoleon, ventured into the essays of Bacon, Montaigne, and Emerson, and even "strayed around the East with Josephus." Tales of kings and queens and their royal lives fed her childhood fantasies. The resplendent elegance of the miniature portraits she later painted of Edwardian court beauties, and her obsession with knowing "the right people," preferably with titles, originated in these bookreading retreats from the arid realities of life in Beatrice.[3]

Nebraska seemed to Eulabee one long series of fierce snowbound winters, summer dust storms that drove them into root cellars, depressions, and droughts. But it gave life to learning.

> Those years of vivid constant summer sun and wind taught me to love clouds and the quiet of a rainy day. The winds that blew and blew, going and coming, coming and going, gave me

High school photo of Eulabee ca. 1893
LRC Archives of The National Museum of Women in the Arts
Photograph by Canova Studio, St. Louis, Missouri

a sense of distances. Beyonds! Life seemed unsettled, tormented.

In 1893, when she was fifteen, the way opened at last for her to "begin right" as Mamie determined she must. After only two months in the Beatrice high school, Eulabee returned to St. Louis to live with her mother's wealthy uncle, George Hassett, and his wife. She was to attend classes at Washington University and study art at the St. Louis School of Fine Arts, which recently had been joined to the university.

But Eulabee was not there for book learning. Her heart was set on absorbing everything she could get from art school, and she readily took to a strenuous curriculum that provided the sound academic training of the day. She labored with charcoal over plaster casts of classical sculptures, and by the end of the first semester had won a medal inscribed "Art Is All That Remains Of Men." After receiving another medal for a drawing called *Nike Tying Her Sandal*, Eulabee, never one for false modesty, had to agree with the judges that it had "lovely drapery." Weekends were not free. In Saturday morning classes they sketched, without erasing, a model in costume, and afternoons they worked at portrait heads.

Access to life classes during Eulabee's second year in St. Louis reflected hard-won gains for women artists of the Gilded Age. The Pennsylvania Academy had crept toward liberation in 1856 when they abolished "ladies day" and permitted women to join the men in drawing classical figures wearing a "close fitting but inconspicuous fig leaf." American women generally had been allowed to draw from live male models only since the 1870s. It was worse in England, where women were barred from life classes until 1893. Determined females sneaked into class disguised as men.[4]

If it was difficult for the sheltered girl of sixteen to confront a nude male model for the first time, she didn't say so. On the contrary, this fully focused art student simply reports in detail the excellent teaching.

> Mr. Wherpel, our instructor, said "First get 'placement'—then the figure established on the paper within one-half inch of top and bottom. Second, 'movement.' Get the swing of the figure. Third, 'character.' Get the character of the model." Difficult for beginners, but perfect instruction. . . . An art student's interest in drawing or painting the nude figure is as serious as the scientific interest of a medical student in dissection. In a fine drawing, line and spot are like sound. They must have relation, expression, volume. It takes years to understand drawing.

As the year progressed she began to work in oil—"I could get a likeness even of a pumpkin"—and honors accumulated, among them the offer of a scholarship for her third year. It provided living accommodations and the opportunity to teach in a private school. But she would be only seventeen, younger than some of her pupils. Too young, her father said, so Eulabee returned to Nebraska.

Once at home, she learned that Horace had more critical matters on his mind than her education. Defeated by three successive years of Nebraska drought, and lacking the proprietary interests that kept prairie landowners in place, he decided to find new employment. The family moved to Grand Rapids, Michigan.

It was 1895. Now representing a Chicago firm, Horace finally was in a position to put down roots. He purchased a two-story house in a respectable neighborhood at 220 Paris Street, and this time they stayed. Eulabee would be leaving home in a few years, but her younger brother settled there and married into the affluent Morman family of Grand Rapids, where the Dix name still is prominent.

The town rather bemused her, although Eulabee probably was unaware that Grand Rapids was home to Michigan's most active art community outside of Detroit.[5]

> A place tied up in ribbons and bows, all by itself in the middle of Michigan. What other city comes popping into the news more often with events and personalities? The city has sent out ambassadors, notable senators, ecclesiastics, and provided the nation with furniture and the world with Bissell carpet sweepers. . . . People scatter everywhere from Grand Rapids.

She was going to scatter, too, but for the present she simply wanted to use her art school training. There was money to be made drawing pen and ink pictures for Grand Rapids furniture catalogues. No! She thought it too prosaic and commercial. Instead, she gathered up all her St. Louis art school drawings and paintings and entered them in the county fair.

Not only did she win prizes; she also won the attentions of a gentleman she dismisses in one sentence as "my first beau." He was older than she, and Mamie, who "as chaperone bubbled with Southern gaiety," seems to have enjoyed the man far more than her daughter did.

Encouraged by friends to organize a class, Eulabee collected some children and a few adults and "from the depths of my silent self began to give out something of Art." Mamie wept when she sent out the announcement cards; whether it was for her own higher ambitions for Eulabee or for the prospect of losing her, is not clear.

The aspiring art students received useful instruction. All they would ever draw or paint, she told them, was either a modified sphere, cube, cone, or cylinder.

"And where did I get this basic idea?" she asks, without answering her own question. Did she know Cézanne's famous quote, or perhaps hear it at art school in St. Louis? "The painter should treat nature in terms of the cylinder and the sphere and the cone."[6]

Social life in Grand Rapids centered on a group of young friends who read serious books and discussed John Ruskin's writings on the relationship between art, morality, and social justice. A well-worn copy of George du Maurier's *Trilby,* in those days considered slightly scandalous for nice young ladies to read, came into Eulabee's hands. She read and remembered it. Edith Wharton's novels "played another, more polite role." Gibson Girls were in tremendous vogue; Eulabee and her friends critiqued the drawings by Charles Dana Gibson, never dreaming that some day she would be a studio neighbor of the famous illustrator.

Horace "came and went," often absent but providing well for his family. Mamie once again plunged into church work, and for a while Eulabee followed her example. She taught Sunday school and performed altar guild duties with a zeal born either of religious enthusiasm or her youthful energies. It ended when the rector's attentions became what Eulabee, by now a strikingly attractive young woman, intuitively felt were unseemly.

But her memoirs mirror a growing frustration with a lack of opportunity to use the skills she had learned in art school.

> I should have died. My life should have ended but I was to go on like a paper doll blown by the wind. My portraits were good enough and I knew people of position and wealth. Why did I

> not ask them to sit, or my friends and family? Was I shy? No, I just did not know enough. . . . That was the usual thing . . . to be the polite daughter of the house. Quite normal. But why be normal? Be super normal with my ability. And have someone to help beside me. No, not for me. I must blow on!

It was about to happen. The adopted daughter of the local Episcopal bishop was working in portrait miniatures, "between spells of exhaustion over them," and urged Eulabee to take up miniature painting. She disliked the "overly-stippled, pale things" the bishop's daughter did and felt sure she could paint better ones. But it was an old and technically demanding art form; she knew she needed help.

There was another problem. Parental apron strings were fraying under the strain of frequent arguments between Eulabee and her mother. Providential intervention appeared when a neighbor's daughter, the wife of the English artist, Sidney Starr, saw Eulabee's work and was impressed enough to persuade her parents that she should go to New York for further study. The Starrs would keep watch over her there.

If Horace and Mamie had any misgivings about sending their daughter alone to a big city still vibrating with the high spirits of the Gay Nineties, it's unlikely that they could have dissuaded her.

> Plans were made. I had saved some money, and with some from Father, it seemed logical that if I could paint miniatures, I would make money and study later for large canvases.

Family members have suggested that Eulabee, extremely slender when she was young, lacked the stamina for long sessions standing at an easel, and so chose the less physically taxing art of miniatures. The evidence, however, indicates otherwise. Eulabee always possessed boundless energy; in middle age, when finally she was able to study oil painting, she had enough stamina to climb several flights of stairs to her Paris garret and tramp all over Montparnasse in search of cityscapes to paint. It would seem the choice was based on circumstance, not delicate health. Becoming a painter of miniatures, she had determined, simply was the means to an end, which was to earn money for further studies in oil painting.

Mamie accompanied Eulabee as far as Buffalo to visit her own mother's sister, "Aunt Amanda," née Hassett. From there, Eulabee and a large flat-topped trunk entrained for New York on the round-trip ticket bought at the insistence of her skeptical parents. Leaving the comfort of home and family "seemed undisturbing," even welcome.

> Art had been my dream and effort, mediocre as it was. Now it was off for my life's desire. At twenty, this is serious—profoundly me. Though as I look back, nothing had a mundane reality. I was a bird flying out of the nest.

Eulabee loved her Victorian metaphors and garnished remembrance with wry humor, if not candor. She was, actually, on the cusp of twenty-one.

> I was pretty. My clothes were tasteful. I wore them well. I was graceful. But I was very dumb about the world.

Eulabee in her studio ca. 1902
LRC Archives of The National Museum of Women in the Arts

CHAPTER 3

Attending to Art

1899–1902

To paint, draw, accomplish something worthwhile was a passion. No plan, no definite idea. My art had to be attended to and I was there to do it.

PERHAPS SHE THOUGHT she was dumb about the world, but the very day after her arrival in New York City, Eulabee found her way to the ticket scalpers on lower Broadway and sold the return ticket to Buffalo. Now to attend to Art!

She was approaching her twenty-first birthday in that autumn of 1899. A self-portrait, entitled simply *Me*, shows us a pretty young woman with a confident, direct gaze and a slightly defiant tilt of the head. It reveals almost as much about its subject as does the young artist's written perception of herself.

> I was five-foot-six, my neck so long one wondered where my sloping shoulders began. A large mouth, nose that seemed too big to me when I looked in the glass, but its bigness might help me through life. My reddish brown hair tumbled into order without much care. Terribly sensitive to my attire, all must be harmonious—then forget myself and feel good and kind and generous.

Such high aspirations! Well, let her have them. Life was too exciting not to feel good and kind and generous, at least for awhile. She had caught the heady scent of New York.

> I was there, there to walk the streets, ride the horse-drawn streetcars, know the blocks and blocks, rows and rows of four-story brownstone houses. It was a brown town, here and there brown churches with aspiring steeples. The elevated structure, binding transit up and down and crosswise like a spider's web, and over all a gust of energy and wealth and smugness. . . . The West Side was popular and flourishing, West End Avenue and Riverside Drive fashionable, while Park Avenue had factories, livery stables and butcher shops; with smoke and steam from the New York Central trains rising through large apertures in the middle of the street.

Eulabee was accepted in a boarding house on West Fifty-seventh Street, between Eighth and Ninth Avenues, run by "one of those middle-aged women with large bosoms and good clothes [who] presided like queens over their homes for other people and appeared to have seen better days." She enrolled at the nearby New York School of Art founded three years earlier by William Merritt Chase. He had turned the administration over to a more business-like director, but for several years remained at the school as its leading faculty member.

Chase was an influential figure in New York's art establishment from 1878 to 1916. Trained in Europe, he is recognized for still-lifes and portraits that combine impressionistic brushwork with realistic detail. As a teacher, he influenced a number of important painters of the next generation, including Marsden Hartley, Georgia O'Keeffe, and Edward Hopper.

Whatever attracted Eulabee to the school—Chase's immense popularity (people still called it "the Chase School") or its proximity to the boarding house—she found it not at all to her liking. She even presumed to critique the painterly "fast brush" of one of the day's leading American artists.

Me, ca. 1899, 2½ x 2⅛ in. oval
The National Museum of Women in the Arts
Gift of Mrs. Philip Dix Becker and Family

The Chase School on 57th and Sixth Avenue was up a flight and sprawled over the corner. Nothing seemed to make me feel at ease and this was the Chase who wrote long letters to my mother's friend. When Mr. Chase painted for the class, I was fascinated and repelled. William Merritt Chase was a good painter and won much praise. He was a short man with Van Dyke beard, pinz-nez glasses with a wide black ribbon guard hanging down. Always white spats. He was very pleased with himself as he painted with sweeping strokes from his huge palette laid with some ten or thirteen colors. The crowd of students watching in adoration. He did not impress me. This was a good painter but not a great artist.

She abandoned Chase and went to the Art Students League to work at drawing for a brief time with the well-known George Bridgman, whom she thought wonderful. Then, "I must get on with the miniature painting. Make some money. Then into oil." This time her more fortuitous choice of teacher was the noted miniaturist, William J. Whittemore, one of the founders of the American Society of Miniature Painters.

In Grand Rapids she confidently had exclaimed, "Orders for miniatures seem to fall into the lap of the bishop's daughter. Why not into mine?" But there was so much to learn. Even the most gifted artist seeking to become a miniature painter carried an extra burden: centuries of a demanding aesthetic tradition from both sides of the Atlantic; a difficult and exacting technique unlike conventional portraiture; and ultimately a struggle for survival of the art itself.

Although excellent male miniaturists like Whittemore were working at the turn of the century, a sisterhood of established American women artists more or less dominated the revival of miniature painting in the United States. Among them were Theodora Thayer in New York, Laura Coombs Hills in Boston, and Emily Drayton Taylor in Philadelphia. The revival coincided with a backlash in art against the country's fascination with technology, an attempt to counteract the ugliness and misery of the burgeoning industrial society. The renewed interest in handwork inspired by England's John Ruskin and William Morris, essayist and designer respectively, culminated in the Arts and Crafts movement, which flourished for three decades at the end of the nineteenth century. Americans followed, for a time shunning the realism of photographic portraiture for the more profound likeness possible in painted miniatures.

More women than men constituted the group that was in the process of founding the American Society of Miniature Painters when Eulabee Dix came to New York City. Modeled after similar English societies, the American miniaturists set out to re-establish "painting in little" as an art form separate from imitative photographs and deserving of its own exclusive venue in museums and galleries. Eulabee eventually joined this distinguished sisterhood and became one of the last and loudest champions of the medium.

The burden of the technique she sought from Whittemore at the Art Students League was the manipulation of vulnerable watercolor on tiny sheets of slippery ivory. The unforgiving material, despite all its fragile shortcomings, had been the miniaturist's support of choice since the early 1700s. Although it was imported legally at that time, ivory was expensive and required careful preparation. Yet in the hands of an expert, no life-size portrait in oil could capture as exquisitely the flesh tones, the sheen of a garment, the background of sky and clouds, as those translucent leaves glowing through delicate color applied with a small sable brush. For good reason, miniatures are called the "jewelry" of portraiture.

Whittemore, who taught in the YMCA building on West Fifty-seventh, gave Eulabee what she was looking for, and she diligently recorded his instructions in her journal: "From Mr. Whittemore—Careful of masses. Careful of little niceties. Careful of too much yellow. Be careful not to get darks in shadow too dark." One of her class exercises was a miniature of the ubiquitous Chief Thundercloud. A nineteenth-century symbol of the noble savage, he frequented art schools and posed for a number of well-known painters. Eulabee's miniature was given to the National Portrait Gallery in 1989.

She worked hard, to the exclusion of nearly anything else but weekly dinners with Hatsie and Sidney Starr, who kept their promise to watch over her. Doubtless she was more serious about her work than most of her classmates, socialites who leashed their pet lap dogs to the work tables and chatted aimlessly over their painting. "Dilettantes!" Eulabee contemptuously labeled them. They, in turn, made a point of ignoring the intense Midwesterner.

Once the excitement of stimulating new surroundings receded, life in New York became lonely. To conserve her dwindling funds she moved to less expensive quarters in a rooming house at Fifty-fifth Street at Broadway. It was only a hall room, but the more important consideration was that it had a north window for good painting light and cost just three dollars a week.

Dinner with the Starrs was a welcome change from the skimpy meals Eulabee prepared for herself on a lamp stove in her room. More diverting, though, were the Starrs themselves. "Theirs was a love nest, themselves and art. . . . Sydney talked art to me as I had never heard it." She found a kind of dizzy happiness in these weekly visits and sought out little other company. Nor did she answer the affectionate but worried letter from her father, written in a neat Spencerian hand during a business trip to Traverse City on September 24, 1899.

> My dear Daughter,
> Your leaving home has given me no little trouble. Not that I have any doubt but that you will take care of yourself and use your best efforts in your school, but on a/c of your over-abundance of self confidence and disposition to rush, or as we say in the commercial world, a plunger. I would suggest that you don't be too hasty about your conclusions before taking someone's advice about seemingly trifling matters. When you are away from home you should remember that other eyes are upon you and not those who love you and know your disposition and ways. Do not be discouraged if you fail to meet with success and remember you can always find a home with Mama if you fail. This is a dreary rainy day and I suppose I have written as I feel and the weather looks. Try and keep well and write to your, Papa

Eulabee responded only to herself. "Terribly lonely at times, I missed my parents and my brother, but would not tell them or anyone else."

Whittemore had advised her not to read after working all day on miniatures, so "for company" she began to keep a diary.

> November 12, 1899: The noise of cabs and wagons and steps is as alive as at noon, but the clock tells a different tale, and

> the stars are beginning to blink at the rays of the sun. But what does it matter to a little girl who lives all alone whether it be noon or night, with God for guidance and self for company? That bothersome, interesting *self* I have been pondering, but cannot seem to begin. Is it because . . . of its minuteness, or because I cannot find a beginning in its immensity?

This was the beginning of Eulabee's lifelong struggle with her sense of self. She was certain she had an ally in God, but not certain where to find Him, writing in her journal "My heart longs with a dark sweet yearning for that near and dear affection of your presence." From family Episcopalian beginnings, once in New York she attempted to practice a highly selective version of the relatively new religion, Christian Science. She borrowed chunks of what she perceived to be its theology in order to claim a kind of bodiless spirituality. Later on, she dabbled in positive thinking, East Indian philosophy, numerology, and, finally, came full circle when she requested an Episcopal funeral service. Alas, her assertions of spirituality inevitably fell *hors de combat* to a strong-willed "self."

In the best of those lonely times, the noisy rhythms of the city kept her amused and even cheerful.

> December 3, 1899: I am perfectly happy because, firstly, a street piano is jingling all the popular airs just beneath my window. Yes, I love them. My dear old friend the street piano, what company to have the thing tune up amid the jingle and rattle and buzz of the world. It plays the tune of the rag man, of the pampered babe, and of the ballroom, and yet it seems to play wholly for me.

But as Eulabee's first Christmas away from home drew near, the diary reflected a frenetic despair.

> December 23, 1899: I have relit the gas to record the events

of today. Came near being run over by a street car. Bought some shoestrings (five cents), half pound butter (fourteen cents), salmon (fifteen cents), colored tissue paper (five cents). . . . Noon, [I] called on Bishop and Mrs. Worthington (formerly of Beatrice, Nebraska), [at the] Manhattan Hotel. They told me that Mrs. S. C. Smith, the banker's wife, of Beatrice, had called to see them and asked about me. . . . 1:20—Bought trimmings for grey dress. . . . 2:00—Went to Siegal & Coopers, Eighteenth and Sixth Avenue. Wrote to mother and all a Christmas letter. Had some bread and tea and walked to dressmaker, Forty-fourth Street. Then called on Mrs. Smith. She was out, rode back. Mended my summer nightgown and took hot bath. Tired out, would like a square meal. But shall have one tomorrow and turkey the next day. . . . People. I liked people. Everyone seemed so busy. Everyone seemed important to themselves, certainly none stopped beside me long. I wrote:

I climb the stairs and ring the bell
But no one seems to hear.
How dark the way and silent, too.
Though deep within the light shown bright
And beauty was within me there.
But the people did not know.
With a heart of leaden hope I went.
The people did not know.

The youthful angst could be expected from one so sensitive, but it sprang more from self-imposed isolation than the neglect of others. In fact, there were people who did care. They praised her miniatures and invariably asked *who* she had painted. She was too naive still to understand that "who" was important. Art, alone, was all that mattered to her.

Even so, recognition came remarkably early. The memoirs claim that two of her miniatures were accepted by the American Society of Miniature Painters for their first exhibition at the Knoedler Galleries in January of 1900, about three months after she arrived in New York. Her involvement in the first ASMP exhibition is questionable, as reviews don't mention her submissions. But subsequent exhibition notices do confirm frequent participation in ASMP shows from then on. Among the miniatures produced during the first two years in New York City were *Woman with White Hat* from a model, *Dottie Cox*, also a model, as well as undated portraits of her mother, *My Mother*, painted during a visit to Grand Rapids, and *Aunt Amanda*, painted in Buffalo.

She found another mentor in the well-known American miniaturist, Isaac A. Josephi. He came to Eulabee's attention through the bishop's daughter in Grand Rapids, who had studied with him. Josephi was a founding member and first president of the American Society of Miniature Painters. She must show the great man her work!

> I made an appointment, and went to his studio at Twenty-eighth Street and Fifth Avenue—up an elevator—down a hallway to his door. He was a plump little man with a Van Dyke beard, nice eyes and a quiet pleasant voice. A short hall led past two small rooms to an ample studio with comfortable furnishings, pictures and miniatures in large cases. . . . He saw my miniatures, some done with Whittemore and some, more recently, by myself. He seemed surprised and liked them. . . . [He] showed some of his and gave me some instructions. He did not have a class but said by all means come when I needed help. I had not shown him the beginning, on a large ivory, of Mrs. Gale and her two daughters—a commission, a difficulty in composition, indeed quite an ambitious undertaking for me.

Eulabee carefully penciled his instructions into her journal: "From Mr. Josephi: Cover all the ivory with color. Use color to model lights over greys in shadows. Flatter! Flatter! Flatter! (Be careful with

Dottie Cox, 1900
3 x 2¼ in. oval
Worcester Art Museum, Worcester, Massachusetts
Gift of the family of Philip Dix Becker

spotty masses.) Use different techniques for different textures."

She consulted Josephi several times before returning with the finished miniature. He liked it, and invited her to come for dinner, which he would cook, for "cooking was as interesting an art to him as painting."

> And what should we have to eat? What did I like? Pink roses is all I could say or think of—we laughed. I went to the dinner—pink roses, of course—delicious food, but more, far more, a proposal of marriage.

Marriage! How could this happen on such short acquaintance? Had she not thought about the propriety of accepting an invitation to

Aunt Amanda, ca. 1900
2 in. dia.
The National Museum of Women in the Arts
Gift of Mrs. Philip Dix Becker and Family

dine with him alone in his apartment? The memoirs reveal little of this first New York romance with a man eighteen years her senior, except for the personal anguish it caused her. Either Josephi truly was smitten, or he had succumbed to a quasi-fatherly interest in a beautiful, young supplicant. How easy it might have been for the inexperienced girl to think she was in love with a man who possessed the talent to which she so intensely aspired.

> I had felt that this very delightful person, and our relationship, were getting on too well. It was precious. I wanted all of it. He did not capture my romantic ideals; he seemed so well balanced, and intellectual, much older and Jewish, but I had no prejudice about Jewish people. . . . He was so quiet and wise, like God. It seemed natural for me to go to him.

Overwhelmed and confused, she looked in vain for a sea anchor in the emotional storm. Hatsie and Sidney Starr were too absorbed in themselves to offer either comfort or advice. She tried to talk to a

Isaac Josephi, ca. 1928
1¾ x 1⅛ in. oval
The National Museum of Women in the Arts
Gift of Joan Becker Gaines

Jewish friend, who only warned her against marrying a Jew. "In time you will realize that his people are not your people and your people not his people." Eulabee was miserable. "But it was not over. I loved him more than ever."

Whether or not she actually saw Josephi while she anguished over his proposal, Eulabee hovered like a teenager suffering her first crush. She wrote letters to him and anxiously waited for replies. She walked his apartment neighborhood and went to places where she thought he might appear. In the memoirs she is a lovesick heroine, but we are not to know how Josephi played out his role in the little drama. We do know that a close friendship between Eulabee and Josephi endured until his death in 1954.[1] She painted a miniature of him in 1928, but he does not reappear in the memoirs.

Again, Art had won out over Love. The incident seems not to have broken her heart, but it did leave its mark.

I was at an age to cling to someone but there was not one to

Eulabee boating on the Grand River
Cyanotype ca. 1900
Courtesy of Joan Becker Gaines

> cling to. The days and nights of loneliness turned my thoughts from people to potential forces and basic ideas. Something was happening to me, I was so miserably alone. . . . In my agony, God seemed near enough to talk to. . . . My lonesome struggle had established contact with an inner self. I felt rich and self-sufficient.

Finally secure in her new life after a year or so in New York, Eulabee went back to Grand Rapids to visit her family and see old friends. She was photographed perched in a skiff on the Grand River with a smiling young man in a high round collar and straw boater. Surely there had to be men in the life of this exciting and beautiful young woman. She speaks of several suitors during her twenties, none of whom seems to have impressed her despite their ardent protestations of undying love. Two of these, penciled on now-crisp scraps of paper, are still tucked into the pages of her journal.

The journal also offers a dark side to the relationship with her mother, who was known to peck away at Eulabee's shortcomings, including her long neck. That Eulabee herself might have provoked a few family contretemps is, of course, not indicated.

> Mother this morning declared me crazy and proceeded to scold. It came about through probably some misdemeanor of mine. Even though I longed to reply to the scolding I did not. Remained full of antagonism. I will not remain home long and will not return again soon.

On the return trip to New York Eulabee stopped in Buffalo to see her great-aunt Amanda. There, a family friend told her that if she would visit Saratoga Springs, she was sure to meet wealthy guests who would commission portraits. The aging but still-fashionable upstate New York spa continued to attract prosperous racing fans and socially prominent families bent on netting husbands and wives for their offspring.

It may have taken some courage to storm these formidable battlements, but by now Eulabee was up to it. Not long after returning to New York City, she struck out for the famed resort with a letter of introduction to a couple named Woolley, proprietors of the Grand Union Hotel. One of the first people she encountered there was the Woolleys' little boy, Monty, a bored youngster with little to do but hang around watching the hotel guests. Monty Woolley's childhood in those artificial surroundings may have prepared him for his successful acting career that included playing the haughty and somewhat disagreeable lead role in *The Man Who Came to Dinner*.

Eulabee found the historic old Grand Union Hotel, dripping with the extravagant decor of the Nineties, quite diverting, but art must be attended to!

> Two old ladies took an interest in me. They introduced me to

> Mrs. Louis V. Bell, the most lovely and bejeweled woman in Saratoga, who commissioned a miniature. I was enchanted with Mrs. Bell, but knew she would tax my talents. Painting a beautiful woman in the morning, who wished to look as glamorous as she did at night, would certainly be a problem. This was the beginning of my realization of the Art of portrait painting.

She spent two weeks on a head and shoulders portrait of the beautiful Mrs. Bell, working on a what she described as a "large" ivory oval. The lady chose to wear a white dress with pearls, ("What a trouble pearls are to paint!"), against a background of clouds and blue sky.

The specific instructions for how her client must be painted were not the only test of Eulabee's talent. Louis V. Bell was himself a connoisseur of miniatures whose own collection was to go to the Metropolitan Museum of Art. He would have to approve of the portrait.

> Saturday night I put some last touches on the picture. It filled me with joy. I could not control myself and went for a walk in the rain, having no congenial nook to expand my joy. This morning I took the miniature to Mrs. Bell, wishing her husband to see it. She had to send for him.

And while she waited, the defensive young artist furiously faced down a critic.

> A lady friend came in. She walked to the picture, looking at it several seconds then at me standing on the other side of the table rigidly defiant of her coming criticism. I felt her opinion. She looked at the picture again, at me. "It is beautiful, free and lovely, but not like her. The mouth is a rosebud mouth not like hers; it is very pretty." "Pretty!" I said with hatred, hatred at this pretty remark of a woman so shallow. She wore a colored photo of her husband set in diamonds and pearls. How

> could she know all that I suffered, for indeed this is a judgment before which I will stand. I will battle it out!

When at last shown the miniature of his wife, Bell wisely told Eulabee that he could not possibly make a judgment without studying the portrait. Eulabee might not be able to deal with a woman who wore a jeweled photograph on her bosom, but she could deal with a real expert. Nonetheless, she was fidgety about his verdict.

> August 7: How kind it seems for him not be hasty. He is a great critic and I hope will be just. He will have a criticism but I shall be just with him. The wait is trying. I wish I knew my sentence; it means much to me. . . . August 8: Miniature accepted with no criticism and check received. I am supremely happy. . . . The tears have made deep tracks down my cheeks. Their scalding heat . . . is because of the flame in my heart.

Buoyed by the successful completion of the Bell commission, Eulabee completed two other miniatures before departing Saratoga Springs. One was of a child recorded only as *Master Ellis*, whose grandfather was a "power" in Schenectady. The other sitter was not so anointed by society: when the wife of a bookmaker approached the young artist in the hotel park one morning, pulled four hundred-dollar bills out of her stocking, and asked to be painted, Eulabee agreed to do it.

> Race horses cheered my Kentucky spirit! She was fun to paint, but was conscious of her mouth and kept saying "Make my mouth beautiful." When her husband saw the miniature, he said "It is excellent, but for the mouth."

It was becoming clearer with each painting that the challenge in miniature portraiture involved more than simply getting a likeness.

CHAPTER 4

To The Tower!

1902–1904

The magic of getting a likeness, a combination of all one's knowledge of painting and the consciousness of the personality and the expression of a face, is absorbing.

EULABEE RETURNED to the little room on Fifty-fifth Street with renewed aspirations. Lessons had been learned and her professionalism acknowledged; she had even made some money. She enjoyed being introduced to new people as "a miniature painter," but like an uncertain moth, she continued to flutter around a flame of self-doubt. "Who was I?" she mused, wondering if an artist without social position, absorbed only in good painting, would attract clients.

The answer already was at hand. Not only had she attracted clients; she had gained a real patron in Mrs. Louis V. Bell of New York society. Now that she truly was a professional artist, friends urged her to find a studio.

The gallery system had yet to emerge as a major exhibition venue in New York. Artists who could afford it often lived in one of the studio buildings peculiar to the city—the Tenth Street Studios, the Van Dyke, the Sherwood Studios (New York's first artists' cooperative), or the Carnegie Hall towers—where they exhibited their work to friends and clients during regularly scheduled "at homes."

Andrew Carnegie chose to build his magnificent concert hall—

a gift to New York in 1891—on West Fifty-seventh Street at Seventh Avenue, although lesser visionaries than Carnegie considered it too far uptown. Only two years later, a twelve-story tower was added to accommodate the growing demand for studios and offices. In 1896, another eight stories topped off part of the original building.[1] In the fall of 1903, Eulabee leased studio 152, a small, skylighted studio on the fifteenth floor of the Fifty-seventh Street side of the tower. Although it was a significant financial commitment for one so precariously employed, she managed to pay the rent for the next seven years.[2]

Living out of a trunk, as she had since coming to New York, Eulabee knew exactly how her new studio should look. Her mastery at creating silken surroundings out of sow's-ears quarters began in that barren little Carnegie Hall room.

> A high screen was made, which gave some privacy when the door opened. My Saratoga patron, Mrs. Bell, contributed a net drapery, embroidered in gold threads and beetles' wings, to throw over the screen. To avoid the homely look of the studio-couch, a platform was built for it to stand on. A sofa for the other end of the room, two chairs, and a table were gifts. Screen to go around wash basin and little gas stove, completed my studio home.

Her formal debut as a Carnegie Hall tenant was sponsored by a neighbor, Miss Louise Karr, whose engraved invitation requested the pleasure of the recipient's company at her studio to meet Miss Eulabee Dix. Another Carnegie Hall resident, Miss Mabel Lyon Sturgis, would sing Scotch-Irish and English folk songs at half-past four in the afternoon on November 15.

An unidentified photographer recorded the artist dramatically posed at her easel in a Watteau gown amid her exotic studio furnishings. Aside from its being possibly the most beautiful photograph of Eulabee Dix ever taken, it exemplifies her growing gift for theatrical

Eulabee Dix in her Carnegie Hall studio, ca. 1904
Albumen print, 7½ x 9⅜ in.
The National Museum of Women in the Arts
Gift of Joan Becker Gaines

flare. She seldom missed an opportunity to put either herself or her sitters on stage.

Another of the fortuitous connections in Eulabee's life was the discovery that the noted illustrator, Frederick S. Church, lived in the front studio next door. Church (not to be confused with the Hudson River landscape artist Frederic E. Church [1826-1900]) was born in Grand Rapids, a proudly claimed famous native son whose symbolic art is more appreciated today than it was during his lifetime. Eulabee's description of this fey and gentle artist echoes what one reads about him elsewhere.[3]

> Frederick S. Church painted subject canvases of ladies in flimsy attire quietly seated beside lions or flamingoes, with trees and water. He must have had a great sense of love, for his canvases expressed peace. He seemed as removed from the world as a child. Mr. Church painted a large picture for the nursery of John Jacob Astor's children—white polar bears having a tea party.

Church took the talented girl from his hometown under a paternal wing, and although she fails to acknowledge any assistance on his part, undoubtedly he was responsible for connecting her to a number of useful New York art circles. He knew everyone. A close friend of William Merritt Chase, Church had introduced the painter to Eulabee's friend, Posie Gerson, who became Chase's wife. Church stood as godfather to their first child.

It's conceivable that the 60-year-old bachelor was no more immune to Eulabee's charms than were other men. One of his illustrated notes to her has a puckish cupid hurling "K. . . . s" across the page. "My dear Miss Dix," he writes. "Hope you'll get that." He closes with another cupid throwing "K. . . . s" while a bird in the corner chirps "Oh, my!"

Living and working in the resonating ambience of New York's studio center for music, art, and theater, Eulabee developed a new sense of self-worth, and along with it a great sense of style. "It was fun to design my own clothes," she recalls, adding "and I had an elegance far beyond my station." With serene self-confidence, she fulfilled fashion's demand for the full-bosomed, ruching-trimmed gowns that swept the floor (and, unfortunately, the streets), or, increasingly, the shirtwaist-and-skirt Gibson Girl look. And if she couldn't afford to buy exactly the right hat to go with an outfit, she scrounged for scraps and made one.

She had to look her best, always. Eulabee comments that Victorian mothers (or was it just her own mother?) were too Puritanical to tell their daughters that they were beautiful or charming. But Eulabee was too concerned about her appearance not to be aware that she was beautiful, and she used her attributes to advantage. She did, however, take great care about her behavior. Following one unhappy experience with a gentleman friend's disapproving mother, she remarked that "people thought of artists as immoral or queer." Independent and morally pure, Eulabee reflected the turn-of-the-century's ideal New Woman.

When she ventured out, it was into streets vibrating with life. Rapidly growing Manhattan rang to the sounds of construction, horse-drawn carriages, and streetcars. As she walked the "slummy" streets among the moving masses whose divinity she had pondered in her first lonely, introspective months in New York City, Eulabee wondered, "Where are their ideals, their divine spirit?" The controversial new Flatiron Building towered three-hundred feet in the air, its triangular mass bisecting Broadway and Fifth Avenues at Twenty-third Street. The Broadway subway would open soon, and the city was almost completely electrified. A few automobiles chugged along the avenues. It was an exciting time for a 24-year-old artist to be sharing a prestigious address with famous neighbors at Carnegie Hall.

Among them was Edward MacDowell, America's beloved composer of "To a Wild Rose," who was close to the end of his career but still teaching music at Columbia University. Church, of course, was quietly successful as an illustrator. And Charles Dana Gibson, of "Gibson Girl" fame, had just signed an exclusive contract with *Colliers* magazine. Theater legend David Belasco lived there, too, and would leave his name on a famous Broadway house. Gertrude Käsebier, already a prominent photographer, portrayed Eulabee, and in turn was painted by her. It is, alas, among the artist's "lost" miniatures.

Especially significant in our artist's particular context was the

Portrait of Eulabee Dix by Gertrude Käsebier, ca. 1907
Platinum print, 8 x 6⅛ in.
The National Museum of Women in the Arts
On loan from Joan Becker Gaines

presence in Carnegie Hall of another and better known painter of miniatures, Theodora Thayer. She is one of the few contemporary miniaturists Eulabee spoke of, however briefly, in her writings. It is a sympathetic account of the discouragement that must have haunted Thayer, whose death at the age of thirty-seven was rumored to be a suicide. Possibly because Thayer's brother, who had been dean of the Harvard Law School, also suffered from depression and eventually committed suicide, the Thayer family succeeded in concealing the cause of her death.[4] Eulabee, who may or may not have been privy to the truth, is not so delicate.

> After she killed herself I was at a dinner party and a young man sat next to me. He had spent some years in Paris, where his grandfather was ambassador, and liked art. He admired the Thayer miniatures and wished his mother painted by her. He went to see her and made arrangements, and as he was leaving said "But Miss Thayer, about the price. What is your price?" She said "$250." "But," he said, "that is not enough." She said "I [have] tried to get more but was not successful."

Miniature portraits were back in fashion when Eulabee, never to become as discouraged as Thayer, charged into her career with an aggressive resolve that people tolerated, up to a point, because she was charming and lovely to behold. The renewed vogue was spilling over into the middle class populace, who once preferred the "real likeness" of a photograph. But America's upper class families, natural heirs to the tradition of miniature ancestral portraits dating back to renowned English and American artists of Colonial times, undoubtedly sustained the medium's revival.

Like her neighbors, Eulabee began to hold Friday afternoon "at homes" in the Carnegie studio and soon attracted visitors. There were few commissions, but she painted constantly, often using models; it was important to have work ready for exhibit. She rented costumes from the Art Workers Club, which had been organized by a group of prominent New York women to provide artists and models with beautiful period clothing, much of it rescued from their own attic trunks. Many of Eulabee's fine early miniatures were beneficiaries of that generosity.

While she looked out of her east windows at the pretentious city mansions of the people she yearned to meet and paint—the unreachable Vanderbilts, Oelrichses, and Whitneys—Eulabee had to be content with the subjects who walked through her studio door. She was commissioned to paint from a photograph a memorial portrait of a baby who had died in some remote region of Canada. She also paint-

Bishop Gillespie, 1903
3 x 2¼ in.
Courtesy of St. Mark's Church, Grand Rapids, Michigan

ed a bride-to-be, and then a self-conscious girl whose mother insisted on hanging about, to the great detriment of the miniature. "They accepted it, but it was not my best work." Another girl brought a gown made in Paris expressly for her to be painted in. She was beautiful, but the dress was terrible and Eulabee told her, "I would rather paint you in your night dress!" No, she must wear the Paris gown. Eulabee thought the miniature was a failure. Nor was she satisfied with her 1903 miniature of the Right Reverend George Gillespie of Grand Rapids. The artist felt the "dear old" bishop's family did not like it. The portrait now belongs to St. Mark's Church in Grand Rapids, faded from constant exposure to light.

"Portrait painting is a spiritual thing," Eulabee wrote. "Today, people seem to vibrate. Perhaps Rembrandt's sitters seemed more stolid." Each sitting was a new experience in growing comprehension. She learned how to make her subjects comfortable and developed a knack for small talk to keep them from nodding off during the long sittings. If ever there was a question that painting in miniature involved fewer challenges than large portraits in oil, Eulabee's notes provide a textbook answer.

> Some people are paintable. Some have drawing, others are difficult "to get." One does not sense this at once. After deciding on dress, pose and background, I began to paint on the piece of ivory. It was my "job" to get a likeness and make as lovely a little portrait as possible. After putting in the drawing . . . never did I for one moment think of it as being small, but would paint as if it were large. Proportions and color are the same, large or small. My paints were the best of water colors (it was thought they were painted in oil when I finished); brushes not small, but with a good point from putting a little gum-arabic in the water. . . . To paint a head the size of a nickel, drawing must be firm and forms delicate, character not neglected, the actual likeness a matter of accurate, minute detail and proportions. While my subject sat before me the vitality of her being would soon become evident. . . . What I saw and felt would come to life on the leaf of ivory in two dimensional manifestation. . . . After each sitting I would work on and on for hours from memory, and for what I wanted—intensely—lost to the world, becoming one great eye. Eight hours would sometimes pass. All evening resting my eyes, I would lie in the dark. The next day at it again, then another sitting—four or five in all, over two weeks.

She would not be distracted from her work. A young Grand Rapids banker came to New York and wanted to see her, but she put him off to another day. He wrote from the Athletic Club, "I do not see why an artist's life should be equivalent to that of a nun. If so, you had better get out of the business. . . . I shall expect during the week still to be able to call and if you cannot be in a position to receive me, you ought to go home and abandon this exacting will-o'-the-wisp."

"Your note was certainly not bread for a lonely girl in a strange town," she replied. "I think as other food I can resist it."

In truth Eulabee was not leading the cloistered life she implied.

> My young men friends in New York were painters of landscapes, striving to become Academicians. Our creed was well-dressed dignity and success. We were not Bohemians, but brothers-in-arms, with paint brushes. Some fell in love with me, but I was in no mood to marry a struggling artist, nor a banker! Although maintaining a studio was a test of my resources.

Financial resources improved slightly when her affluent Hassett relative, great-aunt Amanda, died and left her one thousand dollars and a diamond pin. She almost lost the diamonds by showing the brooch to an overly attentive new acquaintance who insisted on taking it out for appraisal and, instead, pawned it. The police helped Eulabee retrieve the diamonds, and much wiser, she refrained from talking about the rest of the legacy. It was a substantial sum for those days, but not enough to allow her to give up miniatures and study oil painting as she hoped. The diamonds, on the other hand, were a source of comfort in hard times; she wore them for the rest of her life.

She now had some freedom to think about what she should do next. People still asked if she had painted someone famous or socially prominent, and until now she had not thought to ask why.

> At last the idea and its need took possession of me. All portrait painters must paint well-known persons to prove their ability to get a likeness. . . . The legacy gave me daring, possibly wings. . . . I was on the alert for a famous and beautiful lady.

One day she read in the newspaper that Minnie Stevens Paget, the daughter of Paran Stevens of New York and Newport, had just arrived from London for a visit. Since the 1870s, wealthy American girls married to impecunious scions of the British peerage often achieved the celebrity status akin to today's star system in the entertainment industry. As the wife of General Arthur Paget, a close confidant of Edward VII, Minnie moved easily in the lively new Edwardian court and was both beautiful and famous.

Eulabee says she thought about it for a while, then put on her best dress and hat and went to call on Mrs. Paget at the old Waldorf-Astoria on Thirty-fourth Street, where the Empire State Building now stands. She was prepared to be turned away, but to her astonishment the desk clerk sent her up to the lady's suite.

> The maid brought me into the presence of a very beautiful woman, who smiled and asked what she could do for me. I told her I painted miniatures and wished to do one of her.
> "But child, I am sailing for London this week!"
> "If I come to London may I paint you?"
> "Yes," was her kind reply, probably thinking she would never see me again. Two seconds earlier it had not entered my head to go to England.

Eulabee had found her famous and beautiful lady. Now she was about to take wing.

Miniature copy of a painting by Antoine Vestier, ca. 1904
4⅜ x 3½ in. oval
The National Museum of Women in the Arts
Gift of Mrs. Philip Dix Becker and Family

CHAPTER 5

The London Ladies

1904–1905

Not the hour—not the day—I remember only the year 1904; the spring I sailed for Europe, all by myself on a venture to paint a lovely lady.

"MRS. PAGET! How slight her promise was—had she remembered it?" The lady's obligation indeed was slight. Acting on strong impulse as usual, Eulabee must have booked passage for England soon after their New York encounter. In fact, the letter that she wrote ahead arrived in London before Mrs. Paget did. Her reply to Eulabee, hand-written by a secretary on discreetly embossed dove-grey stationery and hand-delivered to the Dysart Hotel, is dated May 29, 1904.

My dear Miss Dix,

Your kind letter of May 14 I found awaiting me on my return from America two days ago and I hasten to let you know that I will keep my promise to you for my miniature, but I can't quite yet. You can readily understand that after being absent for many months I hardly know where to begin to set things straight, and in addition to my many duties here I have undertaken the Menagerie at the Grand Bazaar on June 21st, 22nd, and 23rd at the Albert Hall. If you will wait until I can settle things a little and let me have the miniature done in my own time, you shall do it—but I am not feeling at all strong and am not fit for much exertion, so I cannot overtax my strength too much.

Yours sincerely,
Minnie Paget

Eulabee knew from newspaper accounts that Mrs. Paget was an important person, but she had no idea that her new patron was one of the most popular and influential women in England.

Indeed, there were several things the innocent artist did not know about Minnie Paget. To begin with, Eulabee Dix was not the first American miniaturist to paint her. That honor fell to an equally audacious artist, Amalia Kussner from Indiana. She had first met Minnie in New York while painting a portrait of her mother, Marietta Stevens. Mrs. Paget took the 33-year-old painter back to England with her in 1896 and helped to launch her triumphant career as miniaturist to English and Russian peerage and royalty. By the time Eulabee arrived in London, Amalia had married well and more or less retired.[1] We shall never know if Mrs. Paget spoke of Amalia Kussner to Eulabee, although it seems likely. Eulabee doesn't mention her in the memoirs, but their respective flamboyant lives and excellent work bore an uncanny resemblance to one another. Amalia, however, was the happier and richer of the two, which might account for the omission.

Why did Minnie Paget take up the cause of another miniaturist, about whom she knew absolutely nothing except that she was an engaging young woman? Vanity may have had something to do with it. At fifty-one, Minnie was still very beautiful, and beautiful women like to be painted while they are still beautiful. For all her privileges as a doyenne of London society, however, she was also extraordinarily thoughtful and turned out to be a kind and caring friend and patron.

Like a number of her friends, Minnie Paget, née Mary Fiske Stevens, the daughter of a deceased self-made American millionaire, was introduced to London society in 1872 at the age of nineteen.

Upon her husband's untimely death, Mrs. Stevens had joined other ambitious mothers in search of titled husbands for their daughters. While not quite as successful in securing a title as Jennie Jerome Churchill or Consuela Yznaga Mandeville had been, Minnie ran with the debutantes who helped satisfy Prince Edward's huge appetite for American girls and the good times that came with them. In 1878, she married Captain Arthur Paget, grandson of the Marquess of Anglesey and an aide to the Prince. Bright, beautiful, and capable (although thought by some to be rather brittle), green-eyed Minnie Paget became part of the old Marlborough House Set that ruled London society until her death in 1919.[2]

When finally she was summoned to the Paget house at 35 Belgrave Square, who but a wide-eyed young Eulabee, her dreams of grandeur hatched in the bookcase of a middle-class American family, would make such a disingenuous comment as "Bless me, I felt quite at home!"

> A liveried footman ushered me into the reception room off a wide hall and there I seated myself in the midst of elaborate furnishings, a profusion of beautiful things . . . all reflecting the taste of the new court. . . . Edward VII brought cheer and gladness, a gladness sprung from the long thrifty reign of Victoria, and England was now in the full bloom of her tremendous empire, with rich dividends flowing in from every corner of the earth.

A more realistic appraisal of Edward's high-flying England is offered by one of the king's biographers. "More money was spent on clothes, more food was consumed, more horses were raced, more infidelities were committed, more birds were shot, more yachts were commissioned, more late hours were kept, than ever before...[and] the doors were open to anyone who succeeded in titillating the monarch's fancy."[3]

The handsome woman who welcomed Eulabee to her Belgravia drawing room on that bright June morning had succeeded in titillating the monarch's fancy to an extent that would have shocked Eulabee had she been privy to London gossip. At the moment, though, Mrs. Paget was simply her beautiful patron saint. They made an appointment to select a dress for the sittings, and Eulabee floated off on a cloud of euphoria. "Enchantment! I was in fairyland." Crossing into Hyde Park on the way back to the hotel, she stopped for her first look at the London Season ritual just getting under way.

> It was late morning, one of the season's fashionable hours, which brought friends and admirers to crowd the paths alongside the beaten dirt of wide Rotten Row, there to promenade and view the horses and riders—men and women, side-saddle and astride, in the smartest tailored habits. There, formality and style of grace, a sense of royalty, pervaded the scene.

Some days later she was called again to Belgravia and shown up to Mrs. Paget's pink boudoir, where the maid threw open closet doors to reveal rows of magnificent gowns from the great houses of Paris, all in readiness for the Season. *Haute couture* of the day wrapped the wealthy in lace, mesh, satin, taffeta, padded hems, tucks, flounces, drapes and folds, trimmings of gold and silver thread, chenille and ruching. The richness of the famous Paget wardrobe rendered Eulabee nearly speechless, but she knew that her subject must be clothed effectively within the small circumference of a miniature portrait. She selected a romantic décolleté white chiffon dress that called for a romantic hat.

> I spied on the floor a white and shiny hat box, big and new. "But in that box?" Would they? They hesitated, but off came the lid and in the box lay a large white plumed hat with pink rose. Perfect. Just what I wished. Out it came. "But another plume like the one on it. Could I have another?" "Perhaps, my

> dear, we can find one." I left Mrs. Paget and Anne, whirled off, full of the joy and vision of what I hoped to do.

Eulabee found a room in an upscale residential hotel near Stanhope Gardens in Kensington, smoothing her introduction with mention of the purpose of her London stay, which was to paint Mrs. Arthur Paget. She didn't know how difficult it would be to get Mrs. Paget to remain at home long enough to be painted.

Sittings were arranged, sometimes kept, and often postponed. Even then, her subject would not hold a pose. When she wasn't dictating social correspondence to her secretary, Minnie was busy issuing instructions to her maid, Anne, who bustled about the boudoir with strings of her mistress's pearls bulging under her bodice. Their lustre must be preserved, so faithful Anne wore them when Mrs. Paget did not. Trying to execute the tiny painting of her peripatetic subject under these conditions was a challenge, but such splendid circumstances did not warrant complaint.

Nor did anything else. When she wasn't working on the miniature, there was all of London to see, art to be looked at, people to meet, plays to attend. "I was like a dolphin racing through a summer's sea. The long hoped-for opportunity, the life I had dreamed of had come in abundance."

> We could see the King and Queen, singly or together, driving at the fashionable afternoon hour, when streams of carriages rolled by filled with distinguished people, leisurely seated, quite conscious of being on view. Ladies in the latest and finest gowns, hats laden with flowers, plumes, ribbons and veils; their plump feather boas, and their parasols of delicate colors glowed in the sun. Pushed by engagements all were alert every moment from June to August. London was on parade. Then a grand exodus from the city. "Nobody would be seen in London" after the first of August.

She spent hours at Manchester Square studying the Wallace Collection of eighteenth-century French miniatures installed only four years earlier. At the National Gallery she gained permission to make miniature copies of famous paintings she had only read about until now—a Van Dyke, a Vestier, several Gainsboroughs, including the head of his daughter, Mary, and Romney's *Mrs. Fitzherbert.*

She took tea with the English poet and essayist, Alice Thompson Meynell, whom she greatly admired, and who with her publisher husband Wilfred had sheltered the troubled poet and addict, Francis Thompson, author of *The Hounds of Heaven*. She also acted on a New York friend's introduction to the London correspondent for the *Boston Herald*. The "amusing and capable Mrs. Granville-Ellis" hustled the pretty young artist off to a theatrical garden party in Regent's Park, where she met some of London's stage notables, among them Olga Nethersole, who had scandalized New York two years earlier with her performance in *Sappho*.

Eulabee soaked up London like a thirsty blotter. Canadian acquaintances took her to see George Bernard Shaw's favorite, Mrs. Patrick Campbell, and Sarah Bernhardt in *Pelleas and Melisande.* She found the two strong stage personalities interesting, but was repelled by the love-making scene in which Bernhardt was required to caress the long ropes of Mrs. Campbell's artificial hair that hung over a balcony. "Most unpleasant," Eulabee sniffed. These theater contacts ignited her smoldering interest in acting that would be fanned into flames, albeit briefly, during a subsequent trip to London.

Another, quite different, sightseeing jaunt almost caused her to reconsider her choice of career. During a tour of Bethlehem Hospital, the modern annex to Old Bedlam in Lambeth, a well-meaning hostess stopped several times to speak to women among the inmates, then turned to Eulabee to announce "*She* used to be a miniature painter!"

> Five of them. Each time was one too many and I wondered, I wondered if I were going mad, or perhaps was it madness to paint miniatures?

As August approached and the London Season almost at an end, Eulabee was finishing up the miniature of Minnie Paget in her Kensington room. They had just talked of meeting for one more short pose, but the next day Mrs. Paget accidentally stepped into an empty elevator shaft at her home and fell fifteen feet to the basement, breaking her hip and both legs. It was a terrible injury from which she never fully recovered, and a great shock to London society. Heartsick and sad for her kind patron, Eulabee returned to New York at once.

She completed the portrait in her studio and that fall showed it at the annual exhibition of the American Society of Miniature Painters at New York's Knoedler Gallery. Minnie Paget was the personage Eulabee had needed to attract attention. The *New York Journal-American* devoted an entire outside color page in its Sunday edition to the painting. New commissions came. "Was this some success?" (There is a faint air of martyrdom here.) "How could I stop to know? What with the business of keeping myself in order and painting, each moment was filled with effort. . . . I kept at my brush and could always be found in the studio."

For the time being there was no more talk of studying oil painting. Eulabee's artistic vision, the "circumference of her life," broadened by exposure to the European miniature tradition, to say nothing of London's elite, made her content to linger in their good company. During that winter she corresponded with Minnie Paget and learned that Arthur Paget had been knighted. Now, *Lady* Paget suggested she return to England.

Another note from 35 Belgrave Square fixes Eulabee's return to London in 1905 as late July. That Lady Paget's correspondence consistently addressed Eulabee as "Miss Dix", despite the long hours the two women had spent together, may have reflected Edwardian formality, or possibly it was meant to keep the ambitious artist at a social arm's length.

I am delighted to hear that you have arrived at last. I had been

Lady Paget, 1904
Photographed by Peter Juley; original presumed lost
LRC Archives of The National Museum of Women in the Arts

> expecting to hear of it daily. Your lovely flowers gave me the greatest possible pleasure and I think it too sweet of you to have thought of me with such a lovely greeting. Alas, today I shall be too tired to see you, as the King dines here tonight and I must rest, but I should be delighted to see you on Sunday at 1/4 to 3 if you will come then.

Eulabee found her patron in casts and braces, lying in the pink boudoir "looking wan and beautiful and helpless." She presented her with the completed miniature, which so delighted Lady Paget that she insisted on showing it to everybody who came to call. Those callers often included their Royal Highnesses Edward and Alexandra.

We can be grateful that Eulabee was assiduous about having her finished work photographed by Peter Juley, the New York photographer of choice for most artists of the day. In 1995, the current Lord Anglesey reported that the family no longer possesses the miniature of his beautiful forebear, so it is presumed lost. Today we must settle for a black and white photographic reproduction of the work, which nevertheless testifies to the artist's progress as a miniaturist and the growing skill exemplified in the London portraits. Ironically, the same loss was to befall another beautiful Dix work, the miniature of Lady Paget's younger friend, the Countess of Warwick.

If the flowery account in a London newspaper is to be believed, the countess, then forty-four, saw Lady Paget's miniature and ordered her coachman to take her immediately to Eulabee's studio. However it came about, Lady Warwick commissioned a miniature portrait, and Eulabee once more walked with the aristocracy.

By now she would have acquired enough sophistication and heard enough talk to know that Frances, wife of the fifth earl of Warwick, formerly the notorious Lady Brooke (known to her friends as Daisy), numbered the Prince of Wales among her alleged fourteen lovers. A determined contributor to the dazzling superficiality of the late nineteenth-century London scene, she had turned about in 1895 to become an ardent and lifelong Socialist. Her espousal of views that must have appeared unseemly in her circle had little effect on her position in London, although ultimately she was admonished by the Court when her Marxist soliloquies became too "tiresome" even for the King.[4]

> She was tall, with a fine head set on perfect shoulders, large blue eyes, a lovely nose, small mouth, and reddish golden hair. Her dazzling personality, wit, and keen intelligence, made her one of the most conspicuous figures in Edwardian England. Her appearance at Court bedizened in a diamond tiara and necklace, wearing Worth black velvet, was remarkable. John Singer Sargent painted her several times.

The commission garnered an invitation to Warwick Castle. Eulabee's good London friend, Flora Baker, insisted on providing a magnificent lace gown for the occasion, one that Flora had worn at Court. It was a great success, causing the richly attired countess to say it was not at all too dressy for Warwick. In that great sixteenth-century pile of masonry on the Avon River, the fairy-tale turrets and crenelated walls of Eulabee's childhood fantasy castles came to life. She gazed in awe at candle-lit master paintings hanging in her bedroom and inspected signed photographs of royalty massed on the tables. It all quite amused the 25-year-old artist. "I rolled into the great canopied bed with a sense of the long ago, keeping one eye open—hoping for a noble ghost."

For the actual sittings, Lady Warwick took Eulabee off to the comparative quiet of her country house at Dunmow in Essex, northeast of London. At Easton Lodge, Eulabee painted the countess in a soft white dress and Alice-blue hat against a cool cerulean sky and clouds. Having sat for John Singer Sargent, Daisy was a practiced model and neither moved about nor talked during the sittings.

After ten days, Eulabee left for London to finish the miniature.

Countess of Warwick, 1905
Photographed by Peter Juley; original presumed lost
LRC Archives of The National Museum of Women in the Arts

She was surprised when her hostess, who was known for not paying her bills, sent a note asking how much she owed for "the charming portrait of my ancient self." A check lay beside her plate at luncheon before train time; Eulabee does not tell us how much it was for.

She had the finished portrait photographed and framed and showed it to Lady Paget, who approved, although she thought "the mouth is too set." Eulabee wrote to the countess suggesting another sitting, but received a two-page telegram begging her not to touch it.

In autumn, Eulabee was invited to Craigengillan House in southwestern Scotland to paint Minnie Paget's good friend, Mrs. McAdam, whose husband's inherited fortune originated in the macadamized, or blacktop, road surfacing material. The two women often travelled together to Monte Carlo, where Mrs. McAdam had earned her friend's admiration by breaking the bank to the tune of forty thousand dollars. Lady Paget's letter to Eulabee in Scotland calls attention to difficult traits that impede the artist's ability to gain commissions. Otherwise, it is chatty about a gift from Mrs. McAdam, and her own slow recovery from the fall. She writes on October 5, 1905:

> I was so pleased to receive your letter this morning and to hear you are getting on well with Mrs. McAdam's miniature. Mind you make the most of her beautiful features, and there should be a great deal of simplicity about it, as anything fussed up is not her style. I will try and get you somebody else to sit before you return to America but as you must realize it is a very difficult thing. I have written to Mrs. Avery three times and she does not answer the letters. So I can only imagine she does not wish her miniature done. I am afraid if you told Mrs. Avery the miniature would be 60£ that is what put her off. I warned you that you would never get that price from her and you could not be advised by me. It is an impossible price for England. 40£ is the absolute limit. . . . They have neither the fortune of Americans nor do they really wish to have a miniature done. Had you told her

> 30£ or 40£ I am quite sure she would have sat to you. Tell Mrs. McAdam I received the snipe and enjoyed them immensely. I have one for dinner every night. My progress is slow and I am now approaching the month since my operation. Hoping that your present miniature will be a tremendous success, I remain, yours sincerely, M. Paget.

On October 18, Minnie's secretary wrote, "Mrs. Paget has begged me to write and say she would like to see you tomorrow at 3 o'clock, but please be very punctual as she wants to see you alone. It makes her head ache talking to more than one person at a time. Mrs. Paget has had a letter from Mrs. McAdam wildly enthusiastic about her miniature, perfectly delighted with it. So of course you must not touch it. She has Mrs. Belmont's letter ready for you, so you will only have to present it on your arrival." (This would be Mrs. Perry Belmont of New York, an American socialite and prospective sitter.)

Eulabee had enjoyed the misty country high life on Lake Doon while she worked on Mrs. McAdam's portrait. But a nearing sailing date—and a man!—called her back to London.

> Confidence and success, won by work, confirmed me in the happy impression that I was an artist, not just a painter, and now I met a gentleman who became my admirer—Harvey Judson, an artist. He studied with Burne-Jones and I looked to him like the "blessed damozel"—or did Rosetti paint her?

Flora Baker again proved to be a good friend, often inviting the lovers to her Chesterfield Street house. She was "so fond of us that she would have murdered the wife at a word." Not only a wife, but a child, neither of whom Judson ever saw (according to Eulabee), cast a long shadow on the romance. It doesn't seem to have been a particularly clandestine affair, if it was an affair at all. There is little doubt, however, that Judson had fallen madly in love.

The leaves fell from the trees in the parks of London and the

> days were growing colder and darker, so time to go home. Flora was ill; she didn't want me to go. To detain me, Harvey got his sister to order a miniature. Here is a note, the only saved from many which were delivered by messengers, as was the custom. "November 10, 1905. Beautiful darling: A little line to say good morning, and to go with the few flowers I am sending you. My sister is about as merry as myself, which seems odd to me, seeing that she is going to have an hour or two of you all to herself. H. J."

How neatly Eulabee wraps it up. "My dear English beau and now my second year in London was ending."

Eulabee sailed for New York on the *S. S. Arabic*. Susan B. Anthony was among the passengers. She "walked and walked around the deck, straight and slender, her hair parted severely in the middle of a fine forehead and coiled at the back of her neck... her figure enveloped in a fine old camel's hair shawl, folded point down." Eulabee's critical observation of the pioneer suffragist came during a customary benefit concert for sailors' widows and orphans at which "handsome Lord Euston" presided. Anthony rose from the audience to disparage both the cause and English charitable efforts, at which point her co-worker, Anna B. Shaw, stepped in to apologize to Lord Euston. Her "delightful remarks, [smoothed] out the cry of Militant Women's Rights."

If Eulabee thought she had left love behind in London, she was mistaken. "At my table there was a man who looked at me and made himself agreeable. Very agreeable. I had tried to avoid one of those ship's intrigues but what was this?"

Yet another letter from Minnie Paget, dated November 27, 1905, reached Eulabee (still "Miss Dix") in New York City soon after she returned. Although discouraged by the slowness of her recovery, she continues to express a warm maternal interest in her young friend.

> So very glad to get your letter, but extremely sorry to hear that Mrs. Belmont has not yet begun her miniature. I cannot imagine what is the matter with her. I am afraid like other ladies it is lazi-

> ness and she dreads the bother of sitting. She was so very keen about it over here, and I wrote her such a nice letter about you. I am so glad to hear that you are busy. After all it is the pleasantest thing in life to be occupied and I feel certain you will end by getting a lot of work. You have amused me with your quaint humour of the man and the roses. I am too sorry to hear he is not the right man! Unfortunately that is the perversity of life as they never are the right ones somehow or other. It is one of the few things that makes life unsatisfactory. . . . I do hope you will have a great success this winter.

Lady Paget was more than qualified to observe that "they never are the right ones somehow or other," and she was closer to the truth than she knew. Eulabee's admirer on the ship had something else in common with Harvey Judson. He, too, was married.

Eulabee never did hear from Mrs. Belmont.

CHAPTER 6

Filling the Circle

1905–1908

Somehow the perfect circle of my childhood had become a straight line, a point from where I started with Art, to another of what I had accomplished. Now should not the two ends be picked up and put together again, and the circle filled with more wisdom and stable elements of life?

WHILE METICULOUSLY recalled events seem to rush headlong through Eulabee's memoirs of the years 1905 to 1908, they become disorderly in their arrangement. Exact chronology, however, may not be critical to a view of her busy life. Eulabee was performing on a crowded stage, and the *dramatis personae* are far more fascinating than the precise moment of their appearance.

It is clear that during her travels between Europe and America through 1910, she was forced to divide her attention between a burgeoning career and challenging personal relationships. She was beginning to acquire an international reputation as an artist, and having worked so hard for it, she was not pleased to confront once more the classic conflict between Love and Art. Where Love was concerned, moral rectitude probably saved her from the role of home-wrecker.

> My intriguing friend of the ship could not be put off quickly. He seemed to have lost his head as well as his heart. Was this love or madness?. . . [There were] a wife and children, [he was]

(left) Detail of image on page 92.

a man of position. I wanted none of this. He was willing to break with his past, which was horrible and unthinkable to me. How could anyone be happy while making others unhappy? I wanted to fly, not to influence, not to become enmeshed but never had a man appealed to me so much: sympathetic, congenial. . . . Now, even my transitory life with art suddenly seemed substantial.

The end of the affair seems to have occured about 1908 in Eulabee's memoirs, but it is impossible to determine how long it lasted or exactly when it ended. "Each time he called must be the last and soon there was a last time." It is tempting to infer that the meetings took place in her studio. The degree of intensity of the relationship is no less puzzling. Comments about sexual advances from the few men she allowed into her life usually were couched in arch metaphors, but they indicate that she consistently adhered to the chaste Victorian standards she had been taught.

Summers in England took her also to Paris for a "vacation from hard work in London." She liked to stay at the American Girls Club, former home of the Duchesse de Chevreuse, where she could hang out of the mansard window of her third floor room to survey the city and smoke a cigarette in defiance of her carefully preserved "nice girl" image. The memoirs never make clear exactly what she did with herself during those trips to Paris. But she was young, and she must have made a fetching figure, for Paris was for clothes!

One could be giddy with delight just walking around Paris. I bought a pair of champagne-colored high button shoes from the Bon Marche; they overjoyed me. They fitted exactly, all twelve buttons fastened perfectly to the top. Very chic. And French shoes were said to be impossible! Not a button had to be set over. With the shoes a green cotton dress made by Miss Knight of London—full trimmed skirt to my ankles, pretty bodice with yoke and high collar of ecru net, and a wine-col-

> ored straw hat with soft large silk roses of the same color around the crown. An English hat always seemed to frame the face with some love woven into the brim, while Paris hats are so subtle in design and color they take your breath away; or they become part of the face, enhancing it.

The Paget and Warwick miniatures received excellent notices in London when they were shown in February of 1906 by the venerable Royal Society of Miniature Painters, where Eulabee became an associate. A full-page story in London's *The Gentlewoman* noted that "Miss Eulabee Dix, a famous American miniaturist, gives a fine impression of style in her 'Mrs. Arthur Paget'; this work is at once grandiose and modern, as our reproduction shows, and is a noteworthy development of the art." A New York paper reproduced the Paget miniature and mentioned "one of the most popular American women in London" having been painted by "Miss Eulabee Dix, whose charming work in this line is well known."

The two miniatures were shown again that winter at the Fine Art Society on New Bond Street. It was Eulabee's first invitational exhibit in England. Her noted amusement at watching sandwich board men advertise the show indicates that the 1906 trip to England extended at least into November.

Among the twenty-three miniatures included in the show, the portraits of Ladies Paget and Warwick were joined by a miniature of a third famous London beauty, *Countess Fabricotti.* The countess had been introduced to Eulabee by "Princess Hatzfeldt, with whom I occasionally lunched."

Usually eager to talk about the pedigrees of her titled friends, Eulabee says nothing else about Princess Hatzfeldt. She fails to mention that her given name was Clara and that she was an American married to a German nobleman. A London society writer listed her as the adopted daughter of the late Collis P. Huntington, the California railroad magnate who left his three-million-dollar art collection to the

Leda, 1906, 3⅛ in. dia.
The National Museum of Women in the Arts
Gift of Mrs. Philip Dix Becker and Family

Metropolitan Museum of Art. Actually she was Huntington's niece, whom he and his first wife, Elizabeth, had raised as a daughter.[1]

Clara's English friend, now the countess, had married into an old Florentine family, only to return to England alone and in reduced circumstances. This prompted the princess, who had inherited a million dollars from her uncle in 1900, to establish her friend in the millinery business.[2] The countess sat twice for Eulabee in the luxurious living quarters above her shop.

> Countess Fabricotti, languidly beautiful, resting and sitting for me, came to life on my ivory, a very glowing likeness of

Ethel Barrymore, 1905
2⅜ in. dia. set in lid of an ivory box
The National Museum of Women in the Arts
Gift of Mrs. Philip Dix Becker and Family

herself, fair skin, dark hair, sweeping black lashes shading blue eyes. What marvelous relaxation and elegance shone in every attitude of this English woman.

When the hat business failed to thrive as anticipated, the princess introduced the countess to yet another wealthy Italian, whom she married. As the wife of Baron Charles Allotti, she subsequently retired with her new title to a villa on the shores of Lake Como. Eulabee's portrait of Fabricotti turned up in the *New York Times* a number of years later in a Sunday section called "In the Social World." Unaware that miniature portraits should be shown as painted, the *Times* inappropriately enlarged it several times to fill the space. Yet even in black-and-white, the tiny portrait withstood the enlargement with grace.

Miss Morrell, 1904, 5 x 4 in. oval
The National Museum of Women in the Arts
Gift of Mrs. Philip Dix Becker and Family

Mrs. Cox, 1906, 4¼ x 3¼ in. oval
The National Museum of American Art, Smithsonian Institution
Gift of Mrs. Joan Becker Gaines

The Fine Art Society exhibition also displayed for the first time a miniature of the actress Ethel Barrymore, whom Eulabee had painted in 1905 when Barrymore appeared with her brother John in the Philadelphia production of *Alice Sit by the Fire*. And there was *Leda*, thought to be the only nude Eulabee ever painted. At that, the unidentified model's back is modestly turned to the viewer. The beautiful *Miss Morrell* in an elaborate shepherdess costume, and *Mrs. Cox* were painted in London from models.

The wife of the Cuban sugar baron, Manuel Rionda, sat for Eula-

Ella Goin Rionda, ca. 1906, 4 x 3⅛ in. oval
The National Museum of Women in the Arts
Gift of Joan Becker Gaines

bee in New York City during this period. *Ella Goin Rionda* was of several miniatures the artist did not date, but which most likely was painted in 1906. This association was an example of Eulabee's lifelong attachment to some of her clients. Her daughter vividly recalled childhood excursions to the Rionda home at the Palisades in New Jersey, years later.

Not only was Eulabee's work attracting good notices and new clients, but she, too, was beginning to sit for portraits. Among the ear-

Me, 1905, 3⅛ x 2½ in. oval
The National Museum of Women in the Arts
Gift of Mrs. Philip Dix Becker and Family

liest of these was a charcoal sketch by her Carnegie neighbor, Frederick Church. Gertrude Käsebier photographed her several times beginning in 1905. Eulabee is darkly wrapped in furs in two of the photos, but another one illustrates again her preoccupation with period costumes and poses of an earlier century. Eulabee in turn painted Käsebier. A second Dix self-portrait, titled *Me*, as was the 1899 one, is signed and dated 1905.

The miniature of her friend Flora Baker, now in the Smithsonian's National Museum of American Art, was painted in London some time after Flora's involvement in Eulabee's ill-fated romance with Harvey Judson. In that connection, there is also a rectangular miniature, painted in 1906 and set in a gold pin, of *Three Heads after Burne-Jones*, inspired by *Mask of Cupid* by Judson's teacher, the Pre-Raphaelite, Sir Edward Burne-Jones.

During one of her London summers, Eulabee met the prominent British actress, Ellen Terry. She attempted to cultivate Terry's friendship, but the actress never did fulfill a promise to be painted.

Always intrigued by anything to do with the theatre, Eulabee briefly took up acting herself when Terry and her American husband, actor James Carew, suggested that she should go on the stage. "They thought my chances of success a hundred to one!" On their advice she contacted the well-known drama coach, Rosina Philippi, and confidently enrolled for acting lessons in Philippi's barn-like London studio.

> I journeyed there for two months to recite long passages from the Song of Solomon and other selections, while Philippi played at a piano in a far corner . . . with me on a platform declaiming "Come with me; come, my beloved!" Goodness, I studied the word "come" until I could have lured the stars from the sky.

The Season was over and everybody was leaving town, so the lessons ended. Philippi told Eulabee to come back in a month because "You may be another [Mrs.] Patrick Campbell!"

Eulabee didn't quite believe her. Nevertheless, when American critic James Townsend of *Art News* provided an introduction to the theatrical producer, Dion Boucicault, she went to see him in his Picadilly Circus office. She was by now equipped with a modicum of worldly wisdom, if not judgment.

> Thin as a rail, wearing a tight black dress with a train, my old

Flora Baker, ca. 1906, 5 x 3⅞ in. oval
The National Museum of American Art, Smithsonian Institution
Gift of Mrs. Joan Becker Gaines

> fascinating French thing around my long neck and a turned up basket hat with flowers, I did not expect Mr. Boucicault to admire me or my clothes. . . . He was handsome and gentlemanly. I cannot remember a thing that was said, but while sitting there talking to him I became more and more conscious of having less and less clothing on. Of course, he was probably undressing me with his eyes and dressing me for different possible parts, for he finally said, "Come the first of September and I'll give you a part."

It is unlikely that Eulabee would have recorded any gesture toward the casting couch on Boucicault's part. She simply ends the episode with "I could act . . . but I never did nor did I see Mr. B. again."

Eulabee could act, and it served her well, but a hairline crack was creeping into her confidence. "Possibly I was tired—tired of myself. Life was crowded, complicated. Men were disturbing. . . . My painting had to go on and it was taxing. I decided to clear the deck for a while. No more men." The possibility that she had resumed her relationship with Judson is not otherwise suggested in the memoirs.

Lady Paget, ever looking out for her American friend, introduced Eulabee to Mrs. George Gould, the wife of the American railroad tycoon. She commissioned a portrait of her 16-year-old daughter Marjorie. Eulabee was supposed to paint the younger daughter, Vivian, as

(above and left) *Three Heads (After Burne-Jones),* ca. 1906
½ x 1 in. oval set in a gold pin
The National Museum of Women in the Arts
Gift of Mrs. Philip Dix Becker and Family

well, but the Goulds were about to depart for the Continent and there was no time. Mrs. Gould gave Eulabee, who was going to France, a letter of introduction to her sister-in-law, the former Anna Gould, now married to a French count, Boni de Castellane. Unfortunately, the well-intentioned act of kindness resulted only in a humiliating encounter with the count.

> Yes, I sent the letter of introduction to the Countess de Castellane and asked if she would allow me to come and show her my miniatures. And she graciously replied and set a day. Joyously I started, but missed the train. However there was another soon, which I took and arrived, a lone figure, at a small station in wide flat country. But a horse and carriage was there and took me to a beautiful chateau in a great park. As I arrived, this countess and her husband were mounted for a ride. She suggested I go to the nursery to wait. . . . The footman came to take me to the drawing room, the most beautiful

> room I ever saw, in tans and grey and pinks, a touch of lemon. And soon came the count, Boni de Castellane, slender and corseted, his blond hair high above a small face. I showed him my miniatures, and he fairly danced with rage . . . that I should dare! . . . and takes from a nearby table a beautiful Blandenburg miniature to show me. "Yes," I said, "it is beautiful." He said if I would remain seated a carriage would come to take me to the station, whereupon I walked into the hallway to stand by the door. The carriage came.

Eulabee did not always get names right. Neither "Blandenburg" nor "Brandenburg" appears in reference works about miniature painters, but "Blarenberghe" does. More likely she was shown a work by one of the eighteenth-century family of French miniaturists, Louis Nicolas van Blarenberghe, his daughter Helene, or his son, Henri Joseph. Their work, of first rank, was found in many aristocratic collections.[3] In any case, despite her matter-of-fact account of the incident, it surely must have shaken her. If the count's condescension was based on their respective positions as titled dilettante and working woman, his own credentials were hardly impeccable. He had actually worked, once, covering horse racing as Paris correspondent for the *New York American*.

For every setback, though, there were successes. In December of 1907, eighteen Dix miniatures were exhibited at the Bauer-Folsom Gallery at 396 Fifth Avenue in New York. The show was accompanied by an appropriately sized catalogue that measured only four by five inches. A favorable review in *American Art News* remarked that "the artist has been making good advances in her refined and decorative work the past two years."

Putting a fine historical point on it, the reviewer continues, "The revival of late years in the fashion and taste in miniatures has led too many who have not the artistic ability, taste, and experience into the painting of these 'pictures in petto,' and there are exhibited far too

Sketch of Eulabee Dix by Frederick S. Church, ca. 1905
Pencil on paper
Courtesy of Nonie Gaines
Photographed by Peter Juley

many weak examples of weaker painters. It is therefore all the more refreshing to see and study this little display, whose numbers are not only well drawn and painted, but are delicate and delicious in color, decorative and charming in subject and pose, and all marked by an originality which makes them each worthy of study." Frederick

Church's charcoal sketch of Eulabee rather than one of her miniatures was chosen to illustrate the article.

In January 1908, she showed at the A. R. Kohlmann Galleries in the American National Bank Building in Indianapolis. Only a month later, the St. Louis Museum of Fine Arts opened "A Special Collection of Miniature Paintings by Miss Eulabee Dix" in the Forest Park Building. Comparatively young at age thirty for such recognition, Eulabee was being honored by the city of her birth, and where also she had begun her formal art training. Other than a few recently painted American and British subjects, the Bauer-Folsom and St. Louis shows consisted essentially of the same group of miniatures. In both, the famous Paget and Warwick portraits, by now in the possession of their English owners, appeared as photographs of the originals.

In the frothy wake of the Bauer-Folsom exhibition, the *American-Examiner* in London ran an illustrated piece about the demand for Eulabee's work among fashionable women "on both sides of the Atlantic." Subtitled "The Smart Aesthetic Fad of Having One's Beauty Idealized, and Some Picturesque Examples of One of Society's Miniature Painters," as a piece of journalism it was more notable for invention than for an accurate portrayal of how some of Eulabee's commissions had come about. Nevertheless, Eulabee had truly arrived. "Have your miniature painted by Miss Dix if you want to see how lovely you might be' is a proverb of the boudoir," the writer chirped.

Nine of Eulabee's miniatures were reproduced in the full page layout, which was further enhanced by a drawing of a winged fairy hovering about an easel, paint brush in hand. Featured were Minnie Paget, Daisy Warwick, the Countess Fabricotti, Marjorie Gould, Ethel Barrymore, Mrs. Marion Cox, the Countess of Granard (wife of the Master of the King's Horses), Miss Sarah Villiers, and a child, Doris Canfield, "daughter of a member of the Lakeside set in Chicago."

As Eulabee turned thirty in October of 1908, she was by now a confident woman and an accomplished artist. Ambition and resolute dedication had given her much: travel abroad, success "in two hemispheres" as *Broadway Magazine* put it, useful social connections, and a good measure of sophistication.

> Miniature painting had brought me to a world which my mother had only read about in her novels. She could put the novels aside and forget their worldly world, but my work was in the midst of their enchantments—leisure, art, grace, wealth, fashion.

Eulabee's emphasis on the superficial aspects of the environment she most enjoyed is relieved only by an occasional meandering contemplation of where she belonged in the scheme of things, and always it was centered on self. The memoirs contain no mention of her father's death in 1907, nor of her widowed mother.

Nor does she indicate much interest in contemporary styles that were shaking up the American art establishment at the time. Although before long she would be moving among some of modern art's more prominent American exponents, Eulabee remained aloof from their impact. Caught up in her own tiny world, she was, nevertheless, aware of looming threats to the survival of miniature painting. "Alas, photography and too many amateurs spoiled the Art," she wrote.

Eulabee's lifelong efforts to secure permanency for the art of miniature painting could have led her to the "perfect circle of my childhood . . . filled with more wisdom and stable elements of life." And it might have, if she truly had comprehended the wisdom that a distinguished man of letters attempted to share with her. His name was Samuel Langhorne Clemens.

Mark Twain (Samuel Langhorne Clemens), 1908
4½ x 3¼ in. oval
National Portrait Gallery, Smithsonian Institution

CHAPTER 7

Five Sittings with Mark Twain

1908

Huckleberry Finn would have liked it.

When the Countess of Warwick visited New York City in the fall of 1907, Eulabee invited her to tea at the Carnegie tower studio. Having been the countess's house guest in England two years earlier, Eulabee of course would want to repay her hospitality in some way, and no doubt hoped to ensure her continued patronage.

We can only guess at Lady Warwick's reason for accepting the invitation. Curiosity, perhaps, or the social laissez faire of her political leanings. Whatever the inducement, the countess successfully negotiated the tower's labyrinthine hallways to Eulabee's improbably elegant little quarters. After the requisite brushing of cheeks, the two women settled at the tea table. "So, what can I do for your pleasure while you are in New York?" the artist asked the countess.

Lady Warwick thought for a moment. "I would like to meet Mark Twain! You know, I missed him at the King's garden party. A shower came up and I left, to save a pretty hat and gown."

Eulabee had no difficulty rising to the occasion. After all, it was uncommon boldness that had gained her entree into English society in the first place. Never mind that she had never met America's most renowned literary icon. "Mark Twain was a beloved name to me," Eulabee writes, "so off went a note asking if he would lunch with the Countess of Warwick and me at Delmonico's."

The acceptance came from Isabel Lyon, Clemens's devoted secretary. Eulabee took care of the publicity. Among the coming-out parties, engagements, and weddings listed in the *New York Times* "Social Notes" of October 13, 1907, is news that "The Countess of Warwick and Samuel L. Clemens were guests at luncheon yesterday at Delmonico's of Miss Eulabee Dix of 57 West Fifty-Seventh Street."

Delmonico's, then as now located at Beaver and William Streets in Manhattan's financial district, was the most elegant of New York restaurants. Gotham's finest dined there amidst gleaming silver laid on snowy table linens, fresh flowers, and the quiet bustle of an attentive staff. It was the place to be seen. The late Lewis Hoyer Rabbage, a New York collector of miniatures and one of the Eulabee Dix's most informed admirers, remarked that Mark Twain in his trademark white suit, the Countess in a stunning outfit from Worth of Paris, and the lovely Eulabee, who looked stunning in whatever she wore, must have presented a "tableaux worthy of the best genre painter of the day."[1]

Eulabee had no intention of diluting the carefully arranged historic encounter with extra guests. "I should have asked others, but that might have spoiled it for Mark Twain and the countess, who had a thoroughly good time!"

So, it seems, did Eulabee. By the time dessert was served she had asked 73-year-old Samuel Langhorne Clemens to sit for her.

Whether or not he was aware that she was a well-known portrait miniaturist isn't clear. He may simply have been amused by an attractive young woman's charming audacity, or possibly he truly wished for one last portrait. Yes, the great man would give her five sittings of an hour's duration each.

The sittings did not take place immediately, although Eulabee's gentle badgering was a constant reminder in the Clemens household that the author had made the commitment.

Meanwhile, there was some interim correspondence about books. Lady Warwick had taken to lunch her own copy of Clemens's 1886 paean to womanly courage, *Personal Recollections of Joan of Arc.* It was her favorite book, she told Clemens; she wished its writer to autograph it. The luncheon also had included a discussion about what Eulabee later would call "an odd and very unpleasant little book which Mr. Clemens seemed to feel was his great accomplishment." Soon thereafter, Clemens's secretary wrote from his country home at Tuxedo Park.

> Mr. Clemens has sent in to the Countess of Warwick the only copy that he has here of What Is Man? and he asks me to tell you that when we reach town he will send for some more of the books and that then you shall have your copy. We shall be there so soon now that it isn't worth while to have things sent out here. Mr. Clemens had a most charming time with the Countess of Warwick and yourself and he asks me to convey to you his regards. Sincerely yours, Isabel Lyon. P.S. Mr. Clemens tells me that I am to have the pleasure of meeting you and I am ever so glad.

"Spring of 1908" is as close to a specific date for the sittings as Eulabee bothered to record in her memoirs, based on a handwritten account she prepared to authenticate what was to be the last painting of Mark Twain from life. However, Clemens's inscription in Eulabee's copy of *Personal Recollections of Joan of Arc* is dated January 23, 1908, indicating that the sittings actually began during the previous winter. Some took place prior to his sailing for Bermuda in February, and the remainder after he returned in April.[2]

Isabel Lyon's letter to Eulabee from the Princess Hotel in Bermuda on April 4, 1908, reflects not only her own but Clemens's thoughtful concern for the anxious young artist.

> Dearest Child: Mr. Clemens did receive your midnight letter and put it beside his bed, so that he would be sure to tell you that it

> had reached him. But he has a dear way of forgetting to write letters, and so I suppose that is what happened. We sail from here on the 11th, and with good luck get home on Monday. I cannot make any promises about sittings, for I never know what the King is going to do next minute or next week, but I shall hope that he will want you to go on with the work.

The intuitive Miss Lyon was right, adding later in the same note: "I have just been in to see Mr. Clemens, who a moment since entered his room, and when I told him that I am sending you a note he said 'Eh, give her my very warm regards and tell her that indeed I shall hope to see her when we return to New York'."

The sittings were to be at the Clemens home (no longer standing) two blocks north of Washington Square.

> I arrived at his home on the corner of Fifth Avenue at Ninth Street. Miss Lyon greeted me and while removing my wraps we heard sounds on the stairs: Mr. Clemens gaily running down in his white suit he liked so much to wear, looking very handsome, gleeful as a child about beginning the sittings. The night before, at a banquet, one of his famous speeches had made the evening a success.We went to an unused room on the second floor, where I arranged my palette and his chair, seating him comfortably and in position to please me. His white suit was perfect, but also he must wear his Oxford [Doctor of Letters] degree robe of bright red trimmed with gray silk. Indeed he reveled in the brilliant color of this robe; he was told that it was the reddest of the reds in the procession at Yale, some months before. How he delighted in the color.

So much did Clemens delight in red that he suggested Eulabee should be married in red. Later on he would further suggest that she not marry at all, advice she was to regret not heeding.

> Soon we were at work before the window, but alas that in-

> evitable cigar must be reckoned with. His cigar was always in his mouth, or going to it, or from it; his head changing. To keep him looking at me I must interest him, talk to him, but not chatter. The conversation must be serious. He was to give me his book *What Is Man?,* a work he only parted with when he felt that the recipient would read it carefully enough to get his idea. It had been privately published and he wished to acquaint me with his views concerning it, saying that he contemplated it for many years, and having written books of so different a character, he did not wish this one to be misunderstood, and seemed to regard it as his serious life work. He feared that the world would not accept it as he meant it.

Eulabee's own religious bent was bound to reject Clemens's dyspeptic views about the Deity's contempt for mankind, but she concealed her disagreement from the author, in spite of strongly held opinions on both their parts.

At the second sitting, Eulabee thought her subject looked especially handsome. Always physically sensitive to color, she was struck by the silver-white halo around his face, and told him so.

> "Well," he replied, in response to my enthusiasm, "I've just learned how to wash it. After years of shampooing I've been doing it all wrong. Why put soap in your hair and wash it out? I now use clear water many times and it is perfectly cleansed."

As the session progressed, Eulabee told Clemens, "You are most paintable. Surely you have sat for many portraits!" Clemens drawled "No! No! I sat for one portrait—in Italy, many years ago, and I sat—I sat and I sat and I sat—and if there had been a bushel of eggs under me I would have hatched every one of them." Eulabee's notes don't indicate that Clemens identified the artist. It may be that the torpid Italian for whom he sat and sat and sat was Ugo Catani, a Florentine, described in *International Studio* in 1903 as having devoted the past five years to miniatures and garnering recognition in England for his fine work. The article is illustrated by a miniature of a Mark Twain appearing to be in his forties or fifties.

Notwithstanding the intense concentration her work demanded, Eulabee continued to engage her famous sitter in the "serious conversation" she saw as a means to keep him still.

> We talked of the independence of one's taste in dress, and Mr. Clemens and I agreed that people should wear what they pleased if they very much wished to. He liked his white suit—not because it was a white suit but because it somehow suited his fancy and he was happy in it. He believed in such individuality of taste.

In that respect, at least, the two were kindred souls. During the thirties, Eulabee adopted a style she thought suited her best, and until the end of her days she made and wore dresses with a fitted bodice and long, sweeping skirt, ignoring the dictates of fashion as hemlines rose and fell.

The "odd book" surfaced again during their third session.

> He talked of *What Is Man?,* wishing to impress me with an understanding of it, and as an illustration said "At night I was going out and there was a question as to whether I should wear my white suit or black one. My daughter wished me to wear the black suit and I did so. I did so to please myself really, for it pleased me more to please my daughter than to do as I wished—which proves that we always please ourselves."

Their fourth meeting ended on a less than ebullient note as Clemens again talked of marriage, a subject evidently on Eulabee's mind at the time. The author's own marriage had been plagued by the illnesses and subsequent death of his beloved wife, Olivia, and his daughter, Susy.

> He advised me not to marry. He spoke devotedly of his wife and his children but he seemed to see tragedy in marriages. He spoke with great sadness of [his daughter] Jean, and her having to be away from home so much because of her ill health. It was a sad hour, and this man who stirred the world with mirth seemed sad and lonely, and lonely and sad for others.

Eulabee saw Mark Twain for the last time at their fifth and final appointment. Casting about for a conversational tack to hold the author's attention, she asked him what had inspired his book about Joan of Arc. His reply as she recorded it sounds like Tom Sawyer spinning a good yarn for Aunt Polly, but Eulabee took it at face value.

> He wrote the book after years of devotion to Joan of Arc. It began when he was a long-legged barefooted boy, and the wind blowing down the village street one day carried whirling along a big newspaper, and boy-like he chased it, and having caught it, sat down and pressed the creases out. Some pictures attracted him. . . . One was there which held him for years. A girl in chains, big chains and in a prison cell. Little was told on the torn paper, but as he grew older and knew more and more of the story she became his sainted heroine, some day to write about.

When Clemens gave the artist a copy of *Personal Recollections of Joan of Arc* he wrote on the inside cover, "On the whole, it is better to deserve honors and not have them than have them and not deserve them."

The inscription was particularly appropriate for the ambitious 30-year-old, although Eulabee seemed to think she deserved some honor for her likeness of Mark Twain. "Dear Mr. Clemens, did he think I was not being appreciated? Certainly the little jewel-like portrait was good. Huckleberry Finn would have liked it and Albert Bigelow Paine, his biographer, said it was an excellent likeness."

Although the promised five sittings were concluded, the portrait continued to occupy Eulabee during several efforts to arrange one more appointment. The hands, that lurking *bête noire* of portraiture, needed more work. But there were to be no more sittings. On October 13, 1909, Clemens's daughter Jean wrote from Redding, Connecticut.

> I am sorry to disappoint you but owing to his continued ill health, father is really unable to give you the sitting for which you ask. During the last four months, father has suffered with severe pain, intermittently, 'tis true, but still sufficiently frequently to have weakened him considerably. Father wishes to be kindly remembered to you.

Clemens died the following year, but he had not forgotten why Eulabee wished to see him again. Much later, at an age when she could be forgiven for misremembering dates, Isabel Lyon recalled, "Going back to the days of 1906 or 1907 [actually 1908] when Mr. Clemens sat for you for the lovely miniature you made, and which he was quite charmed with because of his Oxford gown, I am reminded that he called to me 'don't forget that Eulabee Dix wants to make a date for the study of my hand.' He enjoyed those sittings, and your companionship." He said, Miss Lyon told Eulabee, "'Miss Dix, she is beautifully architected.' He made that word for you!"

Eulabee did not see Mark Twain again. The right hand in the portrait appears unfinished. There is no record that Clemens wished to acquire the miniature for himself.

It was shown at the Corcoran Gallery of Art in Washington, D.C., in 1933, and again at the Grand Central Galleries in New York in 1935, prompting the *New York Times* to remark that the miniature portrait of Mark Twain was the hit of the exhibition. Always in need of money, over the years Eulabee tried to sell the little painting, and even had it reproduced on postcards. She asked the celebrated actress, Cornelia Otis Skinner, to buy it for the Players Club as a memorial to her parents, Otis and Maude Skinner, Eulabee's friends in the twenties. The actress declined, albeit graciously, citing a too tenuous connection between Mark Twain and the prominent theatrical family. But, she wrote to the artist, "I remember so happily your friendship with Mother and the times we met many years ago."

Museums were not interested in buying Mark Twain in miniature. Eulabee made a large-size copy of the original and hoped it would be more marketable. In November of 1953 she took it to Hartford, Connecticut, for display at the Mark Twain Memorial during a celebration of the author's birthday. She told a reporter from the *Hartford Courant* that she had started the new portrait eight years earlier. She took some of her miniatures to show as well, and was one of the speakers during the festivities. But the Memorial had no funds to buy the painting. Eulabee took it back to New York, then in 1956 returned the portrait to Hartford on loan. After her death, the Dix family made it an official gift to the Mark Twain House.[3]

The Smithsonian's National Portrait Gallery acquired the miniature from Eulabee's daughter, Joan Gaines, in 1966. It is the only miniature among the NPG's sixteen cataloged oil paintings, sketches, cartoons, and photographs of the noted author. The autographed copy of *Personal Recollections of Joan of Arc* rests in the archives there. Her copy of *What Is Man?* was sold to a rare book dealer in Washington, D.C., and now lies somewhere in what Eulabee might have considered deserved obscurity, although the essay continued to be published and analyzed as late as 1973.[4]

Posterity has a way of refocusing the legacy of highly creative persons when personality and motivation significantly affect their creations. The lens has been turned on Samuel Langhorne Clemens and he is secure. Eulabee's legacy is not yet fully focused. She basked unashamedly in the reflected glow of the "names" she pursued for the sake of art; nevertheless, she truly earned the small niche she occupies in the Clemens chronicles. It was she who painted the last likeness from life of the most celebrated American writer of all time. It would have pleased her to know that the painting now belongs to the American people who so revere him.

A concluding short passage in her memoirs, recalled and written down more than half a century later, suggests Eulabee's awareness that the five sittings were a significant and appreciated event in her life.

> Mark Twain spoke to me, years ago: "Life does not consist wholly of facts and happenings. It is especially the constant sweep of hurrying thoughts crowding our minds that matters."

CHAPTER 8

The Crest of the Wave

1907–1910

I really needed a stage manager, someone to direct, push, pull me into a whole being, successful or not.

THE YEARS between 1907 and 1910 were good years, Eulabee said. She was "riding the crest of a wave."

Having gained the recognition crucial to making a living as a miniaturist, she continued to attract wealthy clients on both sides of the Atlantic Ocean. In addition to the portrait of Mark Twain, another important miniature of that period was a portrait of Gwendolyn Purdon Clarke, the daughter of Sir Caspar Purdon Clarke, director of the Metropolitan Museum of Art at the time.

In 1908, Eulabee met John Butler Yeats and eventually joined a stimulating new circle of friends whose later achievements would bring distinction to American art and letters. Of even more personal consequence, she had been introduced to a promising young lawyer from Buffalo named Alfred LeRoy Becker.

> Exhibitions and artistic gatherings were held at the National Arts Club, then on 34th Street, across from the old Waldorf. There were always pleasant assemblies of interesting people. One evening I was introduced to a young man whose only claim to my attention was his coloring, so extremely blond

Gwendolyn Purdon Clarke, ca. 1908, 2⅛ x 1⅛ in. oval
The National Museum of Women in the Arts
Gift of Mrs. Philip Dix Becker and Family

> and with such dark violet eyes shaded by pale lashes. . . . My fascinated gaze was probably flattering to him. He was easy to talk to and through my memory passed a picture seen as a child, the blond girl in the art gallery at St. Louis, her violet eyes shaded with long pale lashes. However, I began to see in him more than color; a serious deep sensibility.

Their meeting furthered a nagging sense of discontent as she shuttled between New York and London. She was beginning to wonder if summers chasing high society in England might well be exchanged for the security of marriage and a "stage manager."

> His visits caused me to consider. In England I had met and knew prominent and titled people, well mannered sensible beings, who had inherited great possessions and knew well how to behave with them, and I had made some good friends; warm and sincere their friendships were.

"Cheerful grate fires, good company, tea and crumpets—how could I leave?" Friendships might be warm, but come winter, London houses were cold, and she would return to New York City where "I could paint with light and comfort."

That she had spoken to Mark Twain and his secretary about Becker is clear from her account of the author's light-hearted remark about being married in red, and the later serious suggestion that she not marry at all. Clemens, reflecting on his own experience, may have sensed also that Eulabee's disposition was ill-suited to the requirements of a marriage relationship. Further affirmation that Alfred and marriage were on her mind appears in Isabel Lyon's April, 1908, letter from Bermuda: "I think of you very often and wonder what your thoughts are now, about a marriage—if that has changed."

Alfred Becker was a presence in Eulabee's life, but he did not dominate it. She continued her trips to London, and in New York made an excursion into the fashion world with Herman Patrick Tappe, whose Fortieth Street shop was dressing many a wealthy Manhattan matron.

> In 57th Street the thought of boudoir caps in Pussy's [the Countess Fabricotti] shop came to mind for a needed gift. Never had I seen one in New York. Women were wearing vast pompadours, with their hair still in curl papers before breakfast. The caps worn over were beautifiers for several hours before the toilette du jour. I made one and gave it to a friend. More flowers, laces, and net tempted me and became other caps: about twenty tucked away in a French wooden dress box.

Someone brought Tappe to see them. "I want a dozen of these, six of these, ten of these, and ten of these in different colors," Eulabee remembers him telling her. When she protested that she was too busy painting to make any more, he offered to send a French seamstress to sew them from her designs. The caps became the rage at Tappe's, some of them selling for the tidy sum (for those days) of sixty-five dol-

Alfred Becker, ca. 1910
Courtesy of Peter Becker

lars. Ethel Barrymore bought one. When department stores began to sell cheap copies Eulabee told Tappe she would do no more. Their association continued, however, as Eulabee became one of his best customers, or more likely one of his best models. She had no compunctions about walking into the shop to borrow one of Tappe's glamorous big hats to wear to luncheon at the Ritz. Having caused heads to turn as she swept through the dining room, she would return the hat to the shop, concluding a mutually satisfactory transaction.

Thus did Eulabee dally contentedly in the absorbing milieu of her own pursuits, which prolonged the courtship despite Alfred's calculated perseverance.

> The fair-complected lawyer with violet-blue eyes made trips to New York; "legal," he said, but there were teas, dinners, and theater—the theater, in which we revelled. Having taken a

> course with Baker [George Pierce Baker, a prominent drama teacher] at Harvard, Alfred knew far more than I why we liked or disliked each play. Conversation with no other man had made the sparks fly; we bewitched each other. In a few months I wore the conventional symbol on my left hand, a pearl set in prongs shaped like little hearts. I wanted all my friends to meet him, but his visits to New York were hurried.

The ring preceded the official engagement, but Eulabee was uneasy about Alfred.

> We seemed never to disagree yet something essential was missing. Was it responsibility in him? We could be serious or light and gay but in a quite knowing way he could slip hardship decisions—a clever know-how. This annoyed me. We did not quarrel, but one day, exasperated, I threw my ring to him. He caught it, calmly walked over, laid it down and said "You cannot give me back my heart." Perhaps, but I did not put it on again.

The wonder is that Alfred was not just as uneasy about Eulabee. On the contrary, he seemed quite possessed. "I had to have her!" he later said.[1] As it turned out, Alfred and Eulabee were "engaged" for three years. Meanwhile, the memoirs are surprisingly casual about her entry into an important circle of artists and writers.

> Often I joined a group of literary and artistic friends who dined at Petitpas, a restaurant in West 29th Street: John Sloan, Robert Henri, Robert Sneddon, with their wives; Alan Seeger, Van Wyck Brooks . . . and others. John B. Yeats, father of the poet William Butler Yeats, sat at the end of the long dining table, philosophizing about literature, rambling on in a fascinating way.

The elder Yeats had accompanied his daughter Lily on a visit to

John Butler Yeats on the roof of the Petitpas boarding house, ca. 1917
Courtesy of William M. Murphy

America at the end of 1907. Finding New York City rather more stimulating than Dublin, he decided to stay. After living for a year at the Grand Union Hotel, his stay subsidized by the admiring owners, the chronically debt-ridden Yeats moved to a boarding house and restaurant run by three Breton sisters, Marie, Josephine, and Celestine Petitpas. The restaurant was located at 317 West Twenty-ninth Street on the edge of Chelsea between Eighth and Ninth Avenues. Yeats remained there, nurtured by the simple French cuisine and the adoration of friends, until his death in 1922.

At sixty-eight, Yeats was widely recognized as one of Ireland's finest artists. He was also a poet, critic, and essayist, and a raconteur of warmth and wisdom. It was his misfortune, however, to be overshadowed by two sons, the poet and dramatist, William Butler Yeats, and Jack (also John Butler) Yeats, the artist. The young intellectuals and artists who gravitated to the elder Yeats's backyard table at the Petitpas establishment were happy surrogates for his own famous children, who, besides "Willie" and Jack, also included his talented literary daughters, Lily and Lollie Yeats. As proprietors of Dublin's progressive Cuala Press, they published their brother's work in Ireland.

The impecunious Yeats *père's* residence in America was supported both emotionally and financially by John Quinn, an Irish-American lawyer and collector of contemporary art. His patronage of the Yeats family had begun in the summer of 1902 when he bought Yeats senior's work after reading reviews of the 1901 Hone-Yeats exhibition in London.[2] Nontheless, W. B. Yeats would not allow Quinn to pay outright for his father's care. Over the years, he sold Quinn manuscripts he would have preferred not to part with in order to defray the costs.[3]

It appears that Eulabee began to frequent the Petitpas table as early as 1908; a note written to her by Yeats in November accepts an invitation to visit her studio. "My dear Miss Dix," he began (as he would for the next fourteen years), "Of course I shall be delighted to come November 9th. Excuse my not answering sooner. Yesterday I was busy all day sketching a beautiful girl and in the evening I escorted down Broadway Miss Isadora Duncan, the gentlest, cleverest, most captivating creature I ever met. Yours very truly, J. B. Yeats."[4]

Yeats, who always had a sketchbook in his hand, enjoyed embellishing his letters with amusing drawings. Beneath his all but illegible handwriting he shows himself with the dancer clinging to his right arm, while another man looks on in jealous pique. The canny old *bon vivant's* enthusiastic description of the flamboyant Duncan, who blazed the way for modern dance in America, may have been a mischievous jab at Eulabee's unsteady ego.

Some of the prominent Petitpas habitués joined the Yeats table a year or so after the notorious 1908 exhibition by "The Eight" (John Sloan and Robert Henri among them) at the Macbeth Galleries. The show marked the progressive artists' break with the conservative National Academy. As promulgators of the "Ashcan School" of American art, these painters presented a new style of urban realism that depicted the common man's life in blunt detail.

Sloan and his wife met Yeats at the Petitpas table in 1909 and were among his closest friends. The gatherings reached a zenith in 1910 when on August 2, his thirty-ninth birthday, Sloan began his painting *Yeats at Petitpas* in celebration of their grand evenings with the old man. His diaries suggest that he reworked the composition for several years before showing it in 1916. Appearing in the tableau are Yeats, with sketch pad in hand, and Sloan himself, as well as the future literary historian and man of American letters, Van Wyck Brooks, along with his friend, the poet Alan Seeger, both fresh out of Harvard. Seeger was killed in World War I. Next to him is Dolly Sloan, the artist's diminutive wife, and the writer and editor, Robert Snedden. The wife of a New York newspaperman, Mrs. Charles (Vera Jelihovsky) Johnston, who was the Russian niece of the Theosophist, Madame Blavatsky, is seen being sketched by Yeats. Celestine, one of the Petitpas sisters, stands nearby, and two figures to the right is Frederick A. King, who would become editor of the *Literary Digest.* Between them is Eulabee. Shown with one hand to her face, she is half-hidden by Mrs. Johnston. For almost eighty years Eulabee was officially misidentified as a woman named Anne Squire. Yeats himself described the painting as a caricature of all present.[5]

The attempted removal of Eulabee from the exclusive circle depicted in *Yeats at Petitpas* involved conscientious intrigue on the part of Sloan's wife and, sadly, Sloan himself. It was Sloan who, in his book

Yeats at Petitpas by John Sloan, 1910. Oil on canvas, 26⅜ x 32¼ in.
In the Collection of Corcoran Gallery of Art, Washington, D.C.
Museum Purchase, Gallery Fund

(left to right) Van Wyck Brooks, John Butler Yeats, Alan Seeger, Dolly Sloan, Celestine Petitpas (standing), Robert Sneddon, Eulabee Dix, John Sloan, Vera Johnston (foreground), and Frederick A. King

Gist of Art, identified Anne Squire as the half-hidden woman in the painting. Even the Corcoran Gallery of Art, which acquired the work from the Frick Collection in 1932, hesitated to accept the figure's real identity until presented with irrefutable evidence in 1988.[6]

Why did the Sloans want Eulabee removed from a potentially historic painting? The answer is more complicated than the question. Until this point in her life story, Eulabee alone has put herself on record. She was hardly a reliable witness. To posterity's gain, her name turns up several times in William M. Murphy's 1978 biography of John Butler Yeats. At last, we encounter an unvarnished view of Eulabee Dix: "Quinn called [her] a 'self-seeking, neurotic wasp of a woman' and wouldn't allow her name to be uttered in his presence."[7]

This was the same John Quinn who commissioned Eulabee to paint a miniature of his young niece, and liked it. He disliked the artist but admired her art. Quinn was not alone in his assessment. "Dolly Sloan hated me," Eulabee told her daughter some years later.[8] Dramatically beautiful, perfectly dressed, and always assertive, the artist never missed an opportunity to promote herself and her work.

It must further have annoyed Dolly that when they first met, Eulabee was unencumbered by loyalties to a husband, or for that matter anything but art. Dolly Sloan (née Anna M. Wall) is described by Van Wyck Brooks as "tiny as a hummingbird, four feet nine inches tall . . . a tempestuous little soul, mercurial, unstable, but bold as a jay in defense of her affections and beliefs. She was a manic depressive and alcoholic; and Sloan, who had no illusions about her, had much to put up with in the forty-two years of their life together."[9] Perhaps Sloan was simply worn down by Dolly's insistence that her friend Anne Squire, actually never present at the Petitpas table until several years later, be identified as the woman who in the painting certainly looks like Eulabee Dix.

Van Wyck Brooks, of course, was there. He had introduced himself to Yeats early on and was a regular at the Petitpas gatherings beginning in 1909. Shortly before his death in 1963, Brooks identified the figures in the Sloan painting for William M. Murphy, confirming that indeed Eulabee Dix had been misidentified as Anne Squire. When Murphy asked Brooks about Eulabee, "He insisted, with some agitation, that I not let her know that he had talked to me about her, as he did not wish to renew his acquaintanceship with her."[10] He needn't have worried. Eulabee had died two years earlier.

Can this be the Van Wyck Brooks Eulabee describes in her memoirs?

> Alan Seeger took me to my street car one night, but Van Wyck Brooks was my silent admirer for a time. One day he came to see me and handed me a large, very old key. I took it, looked at it well. "It is beautiful, isn't it?" and laid it on a table. Brooks was so shy. Some years later it popped into my consciousness that he meant that key as the key to his heart. I had a long time been married.

The plot thickens under the adroit pen of Conrad Aiken, the American writer, poet, and editor who was later responsible for reviving Emily Dickenson's literary reputation. Like Brooks a recent Harvard graduate, Aiken spent summer evenings of 1910 at the Yeats table and later recreated some of its participants in a short story entitled *The Orange Moth*. Yeats, Aiken, Sneddon, and Brooks, all of whom had lived at Lloyds boarding house on West Twenty-ninth Street, are thinly disguised principals in the story, along with a miniature painter named Celia Daggert. The character patterned after Van Wyck Brooks is attempting to explain to his friends why he can talk more easily to women than to men. "This afternoon I went to see Celia Daggert—you know, the miniature painter. . . . She attracts me very much, and I should like immensely to make her fall in love with me—in which case I'd fall in love with her. . . . She has a quick mind—she has a kind of tired prettiness, if you know what I mean. And really, she intoxicated me. I never talked so brilliantly before in my life."[11]

When Murphy asked Aiken if Celia Daggert was Eulabee Dix, he said that while the others in the story clearly were his friends, "I never knew who C. Daggert was. Maybe you're right!"[12] Who was Celia Daggert if not Eulabee Dix?

Eulabee's daughter, Joan, determined to restore her mother's identity to the painting, undertook her own investigation in Ireland in 1985. There, she met by chance a graduate student who was pursuing another Yeats connection. This led Joan to William Murphy at Union College in Schenectady, New York. Murphy was able to substantiate other materials Joan had gathered in the hope of persuading the Corcoran to accept the proper identification.

Why, asked a Corcoran curator, was she so intensely interested in this relatively minor matter? Joan Becker Gaines wrote to Murphy, "I must say I have asked myself the same question, and without a simple answer. To him, I said that I have six grandchildren—not to mention other probable descendants—for whom my mother's life and work will be a form of inheritance. The fact that her likeness is found in several museums, painted by notable artists, is one part of her legacy. Her miniatures, also, are beginning to find a place in museums around the country. . . . I could have given other rationales. . . . For one, the fascination of the pursuit itself. Another, a sense of debt I owe my mother because our relationship was so bad during her later years. And also my continuing bafflement about this woman who attracted and repelled, who was both creative and destructive, who was, for me, a confusing dual personality."[13]

Another lasting legacy of the Petitpas table was Eulabee's association with Robert Henri, the artist who had grown up as Robert Henry Cozad not far from the Dix's Nebraska home. A portrait and landscape painter represented today in every great American art museum, Henri was an influential teacher at both the Chase school and later the Art Students League. Today he is regarded by many as the singular force in freeing American art from Europe's domination. His friendship with Eulabee produced two full-length portraits, painted in 1910 and 1911 at the height of his career. He painted her for the first time a few days before she was married in December of 1910. Although he was not born in Nebraska, Henri's boyhood there warranted the University of Nebraska's 1979 purchase from the Henri estate of the *Portrait of Miss Eulabee Dix (Becker) in Wedding Gown* for the Museum of Nebraska Art in Kearney. The Dix-Becker family had lost track of the wedding portrait, learning of its whereabouts only a few weeks before the Nebraska museum was dedicated in 1994. The fortuitous discovery came just in time for the trustees to invite Eulabee's daughter to attend the dedication ceremonies as an honored guest.

Irene Chapellier Little, director of the Chapellier Galleries in New York, which represented the Henri estate, wrote in 1982 that the portrait is "among the most highly prized among the works of Robert Henri and also [among] the most scarce. Life-size works of this period are considered by many scholars to be the finest of the artist's career."[14]

The second portrait, *Lady in Black Velvet*, was painted in 1911 and today hangs in the High Museum of Art in Atlanta. In its discussion of this popular painting, the museum's catalogue states, "Henri believed a successful portrait was not necessarily achieved by producing a good likeness, but rather by creating an expression of the sitter's individuality. 'Realize that your sitter,' he observed, 'has a state of being [which] manifests itself to you through form, color and gesture.' "[15]

Aside from their value as examples of Henri's best work, both portraits hold clues to Eulabee's state of mind at the time. When one looks closely at those haunting faces, neither a radiant bride nor a happy newlywed gazes from the canvas.

By late 1910, the paths of Art—painting by day and stimulating evenings at the Petitpas restaurant—and Love, with Alfred in zealous pursuit, finally converged. Eulabee describes those days in an undated letter to an unnamed friend.

> Of course I am glad you are at work on the book about Petitpas's. It was a real time, for Mr. Yeats was a compact reality to

us all, and speaking from his past and well-digested thought concerning people and incident . . . we seemed to form a circle, round the table, of attention and interest, so that as I remember, it was never dull. The food was excellent, the table laid with poorish linen, plate, etc., but there was a richness of goodness about it all. Mr. Yeats' place at table seemed stationary and we of the clan always found a place. I cannot remember any of us sitting anywhere else. And after the meal no one stirred, and Mr. Yeats got out his sketch book and in his slow settled manner sketched and talked. We lingered on, not conscientiously but just because we sort of belonged. . . . I was mostly atmosphere. I'm sure had I realized the profound intelligences there I should never have ventured. It never seemed profound, but casual. What could be better? Good food, good company! And that was why we went, all of us working with the gods. In June, 1910, the New York edition of *International Studio* gave me a fine article about my art in miniatures and that to me was the peak of success. But when all I got out of it, to all appearances, was a telephone call from the daughter of Mr. Pinkerton, deceased, of Pinkerton's detective bureau, to come to Brooklyn where she wished a miniature of her father, alas from a photo—which I did—I felt the defeat of [any] fame for Art, and married in December, 1910.

CHAPTER 9

The Marriage

1910–1912

I took for granted that painting would continue, marriage a joyous part of what I had begun.

FOR ALL THE UNREALISTIC expectations Eulabee had a way of clutching to her breast, it seemed reasonable that she should take a continuing career for granted. Her miniatures were sought after and a fascinating man wanted to marry her.

In the summer of 1910, the director of the Thurber Gallery in Chicago arranged for an exhibition of Dix miniatures and asked her to go out early in the fall to supervise the installation. When Alfred heard of it, he begged Eulabee to stop in Buffalo to meet his mother.

She spent three days there in the large, comfortable home where Alfred had grown up as the only child of Minnie and Tracy Chatfield Becker. A family friend recalled Alfred, who suffered from a lifelong bronchial problem, as "a lonely little boy hanging out the window of his bedroom with thick white towels around his throat."[1]

Tracy Becker had married Minnie Alfredena LeRoy, who was from a prominent upstate New York family, in 1876. He practiced law in Buffalo from 1877 to 1907, gaining statewide prominence in several fields of jurisprudence. When their son graduated from Harvard Law School his father brought him into the firm. But even Alfred, who became a dedicated genealogist, never revealed the reason for his parents' divorce in 1907 or for Tracy Becker's move to Los Angeles that same year. It is known, however, that the New York Central Railroad was among the firm's clients and that Becker often traveled to California on business.[2] In 1908, he married Ada King Wilbur in Los Angeles and re-established himself with a new family and a new and ultimately successful practice until his death in 1935.

Although divorced, and, one suspects, considered a wronged woman, Mrs. Becker was a pillar of Buffalo society. Eulabee does not tell us if her future mother-in-law was acquainted with her other Buffalo connection, her great-aunt Amanda, but from all accounts she received Eulabee warmly. Alfred hoped the visit with his mother would settle Eulabee's indecision about marriage, which it seemed to do. A story in the *Chicago Examiner* about the miniature show revealed that Miss Dix would marry Mr. Alfred LeRoy Becker of Buffalo in December. Their engagement was announced officially in late September.

"Truly I needed someone to enjoy accomplishments with me and who wanted to give and not gather," Eulabee writes. What Alfred might have hoped for goes unmentioned, but after three years of courtship, the memoirs reveal a surprising lack of passion on both their parts.

> There had been occasional men—a bee or a butterfly—no one to consider seriously, but always Alfred, knocking on my door or writing letters . . . the most scholarly and interesting letters that ever came to me. Was this a sort of secret love affair of correspondence?. . . He was not an impressive person but his letters were impressive. There was no passion, as with other men who seemed to want to take a bite out of me, and put me to resisting. The physical disappeared in a sparkling primness. We hardly kissed each other.

Prospects for married bliss were diminished further by the conditions Eulabee imposed on Alfred's insistence that they begin married life in his mother's home. After years of travel and studio living, he suggested, Eulabee should have the comforts of the Buffalo house with its cook, laundress, and gardener "of long standing."

At thirty-two, Eulabee had lived independently for twelve years, most of them in New York City. By June of 1910, she had moved out of Carnegie Hall to a fourth floor studio in the nearby Sherwood artist's cooperative at 58 West Fifty-seventh Street. Alfred, also thirty-two and having always lived happily with his mother, pressed on, apparently innocent of any insight concerning the obstacles his maternal attachment might present in his marriage.

> "Lots of room and service. Try it. If you're unhappy, we'll come back to New York." "This is madness!" I rebelled. "Madness! No! No!" How well he argued for himself. A lawyer, then trying cases for the New York Central Railroad. What chance had I? Gradually I laid down concessions and conditions. First, we must have our own connecting rooms; I had lived in England long enough to understand "privacy," closed doors, and walled gardens. Second, his mother's consent to changes in the downstairs decoration. Third, if unhappy, back to New York at once.

"Yes! Yes! Yes! He eagerly agreed." If, as feminist Phyllis Rose contends, love is a mask used to "disguise transactions involving power . . . the ideological bone thrown to women to distract their attention from the powerlessness of their lives," the brilliant but feckless Alfred used it to propel Eulabee to the altar.[3] To be fair, Eulabee's presumptuous demand to redecorate her future mother-in-law's home is a latter-day version of childhood tantrums over mismatched ribbons and is not exactly "powerlessness."

Preoccupation with engagement and wedding plans elbows out of the memoirs any reference to the year's other happenings, including the death on April 21 of her most celebrated portrait subject, Mark Twain. Another was the passing of Britain's beloved monarch, whose trend-setting court molded the luxurious lives of her London friends. Any mention of artistic breakthroughs occurring in her own city is also absent from the memoirs. The Alfred Stieglitz 291 Gallery was showing the avant-garde works of Leger, Modigliani, Lachaise, Marin, and Stella to a puzzled public. In Greenwich Village's MacDougall Alley, Gertrude Vanderbilt, advancing on the creation of her Whitney Museum of American Art, was busy not only with her own work as a sculptor, but sponsoring, exhibiting, and buying up the work of young artists. Eulabee showed little interest in the contemporary scene except for a much later brief dismissal of abstract art.

As for her own art, in spite of bitter disappointment over lack of response to Norreys Sephson O'Conor's complimentary article in *International Studio,* she should have been encouraged by the review. It was four pages long and was illustrated with reproductions of nine miniatures. They included the portrait of Gwendolyn Purdon Clarke, and a miniature of two unnamed young ladies titled *The Sisters.* Originals of three others: *Miss Corsa, Mrs. Michael Dreier,* and *Mrs. William Wood Plankinton*, have not been located since.

Eulabee continued her visits to the Petitpas gatherings during 1910, and early in June commissioned Yeats to make a sketch of her, for which she paid him five dollars. Yeats is said to have been annoyed at the paltry fee, especially in light of the five hundred dollars John Quinn had paid Eulabee to paint a miniature of his sister Julia's daughter, Mary Anderson.[4]

On June 28, John Sloan noted in his diary that Yeats had made a brief visit and told him, "Miss Dix wants us to come to her studio tomorrow afternoon. She will read from a privately printed book of Mark Twain's, *What is Man?*, a philosophy of life." They accepted the invitation. Sloan's diary records: "At about 3 o'clock Mr. Yeats came and waited 'till we were ready to start up to Miss Dix's. She is in the Sherwood Bldg., 57th St., where we lived for four months when we first came to NY. The old building seems just the same and her place is on the 4th floor, just opposite the one Henri had. . . . Miss Dix read about half of the Mark Twain *What is Man?* Mr. Yeats thought it rather

The Sisters, 1908, 4½ x 3¾ in. oval
Worcester Art Museum, Worcester, Massachusetts
Gift of Lewis Hoyer Rabbage

Sketch of Eulabee Dix by John Butler Yeats, 1911
Pencil on paper. Photograph of original.
LRC Archives of The National Museum of Women in the Arts

elementary philosophy for beginners. True enough, but well accepted by all who know anything of such matters. . . . We all, Brooks was there, came to Petitpas for dinner and stayed and talked 'till about 11 o'clock."[5]

Eulabee began now to lecture on the history and art of miniature painting, a natural outcome of her research into the subject and her talent for dramatic visual and vocal communication. At heart, Eulabee was an actress. "Very glad your lectures were such a success," Yeats wrote on October 6. "Two of them on one day, that's more than I ever dreamed of doing, and no one ever gave me roses, and I never felt like a Prima Donna. You see, I am jealous. I am also glad about the marriage. Sneddon several days ago brought me a cutting from a newspaper with the announcement. Please accept my congratulations and good wishes. I am sorry you are going to live so far away. Between this and Dec'r you can pay us many visits. We dine outside when the evenings are warm." [6]

Sketch of Minnie LeRoy Becker by John Butler Yeats, 1911
Pencil on paper. Photograph of original.
LRC Archives of The National Museum of Women in the Arts

Felicitations came also from Minnie Paget via her secretary, who wrote from London on November 25, "Lady Paget cannot say how pleased she is that you are going to be happy and have someone to care for you."

The wedding on December 22, 1910, took up less space in Eulabee's memoirs than it did in the Buffalo and New York papers.

> We were married at St. Mary the Virgin, the Episcopalian church near Times Square. My white satin wedding dress was from Flora, Schling did the bouquet, Henri [not the artist] the catering. A little reception was held in my studio and two

days later, Christmas Eve . . . we sailed for Bermuda.

It seems a sparse account for a ceremony of somewhat theatrical proportions. The church on West Forty-sixth Street was decorated for the Christmas season in holly and white roses. The unattended bride, preceded down the aisle by a retinue consisting of vestmented choir, acolytes, and crucifers, was given away by her St. Louis great-uncle, George Hassett. Two newspaper stories listed Eulabee's brother, Philip Dix, as Alfred's best man. A third stated that Alfred's friend, Maurice Spratt, was best man. The disparity hints that Mr. Spratt might have been demoted at the last minute. At whose behest is subject to speculation.

The groom's four attendants from Buffalo more than compensated for Eulabee's decision not to be upstaged by bridesmaids, if indeed she had any close female friends to be considered for the honor. Mamie Dix came from Grand Rapids to host the reception for a hundred invited guests at the bride's Sherwood studio. Alfred's mother, as would be expected, was present, but there is no record of how many of the hundred invited guests appeared, or who they were. Frederick Church sent apologies for not attending the wedding but gave no reason other than that New York was being ruined by automobiles.

The two days that passed between the reception and their Christmas Eve sailing to Bermuda might never have existed as far as Eulabee's recollections are concerned. The door is firmly shut on their wedding night. Eulabee had come of age in a society that quashed what was quaintly called the "amative impulse" in women. The medical profession itself suggested that they should not be expected to enjoy the sexual act, which "may take place in sleep or other insensibility."[7] One wonders if Eulabee, the semi-liberated and now sophisticated artist, still subscribed to the mores of her Victorian up-

Right: Wedding photo of Eulabee Dix, New York City, December, 1910
LRC Archives of The National Museum of Women in the Arts

bringing. Women had been kicking over the sexual traces ever since suffragist Elizabeth Cady Stanton noted in 1881, "I have come to the conclusion that the first great work to be accomplished for woman is to revolutionize the dogma that sex is a crime, marriage a defilement, and maternity a bane."[8] Or is it even thinkable that Eulabee's independent nature surmounted the prescribed reticence in the bridal bed? She didn't talk about it, then or ever. Never did she bring up the subject of sex except in the context of lecturing her daughter on the importance of virginity in the marriage market. It was Joan's grandmother Dix who first divulged to her a few basic facts of life. The short honeymoon account in the memoirs is little more than a veiled complaint.

> Blue skies, blue sea, roses and strawberries, drives, and walks in the balmy air. Alfred, one night, took me walking over rough ground, regardless of my thin slippers and trailing tulle gown; a bride, accustoming herself to follow her husband.

On the way home from Bermuda, Eulabee and Alfred stopped off in Watertown, New York, to see Alfred's only relatives, his mother's sister, Lillian, and her husband, Fred Kavanaugh. The latter, a jovial and very rich clothing manufacturer, "was sweet to me, the bride, brimming over with love and pretty new clothes." Lillian drove an electric car and wore rubies, which Eulabee hoped her daughter would inherit some day. To that end "Lillian" was one of three names she and Alfred gave to their daughter four years later. It worked, but the rubies turned out to be garnets. And so to Buffalo.

> Our connecting rooms had been freshly painted and papered—my first condition met. Soon I was looking out between flowered chintz curtains at the trees and skies beyond. My possessions from the studio, wedding presents, things from the attic, a new four poster bed; gold and lavender sitting room with Grand Rapids-wedding-present-tea-table: all was ready for my new life. Alfred

> breakfasted with his mother, she and I lunched together; we three at dinner. Paint brushes and paints a million miles away!

And for the time being, there they stayed. Alfred, she said "did seem so lovingly caring for me. I was deep in the throes of love and marriage." In February, the young Beckers issued invitations for an "at home" at 403 Highland Avenue, at which Eulabee officially was introduced to Buffalo's best. She may have already met some of them in previous visits to her great-aunt's home. Although Mrs. Becker senior was active in various civic movements, it was her socially ambitious daughter-in-law who most enthusiastically took to making formal calls on "my friends and neighbors to be." But first there was something she had to do.

> Soon I would slip quietly into the downstairs parlor to consider what could be done with redecoration. Goodness, it was ugly! There must be harmony and peace. The soft olive green walls lost their value against the noisy plaid of the ceiling. A plain ceiling and no fussy overmantel, those lovely alabaster things off the hearth. Those horrid red China silk curtains in the dining room came down. . . . All else would be simple.

Mrs. Becker, unfortunately, had not been informed of Eulabee's second condition for the marriage. It must have taken considerable grace to accede to her new daughter-in-law's redecoration of a home she had presided over for thirty years. "Down on our knees, we rubbed laundry bluing in the orange color of a fine Oriental rug, making it right for the canary brocaded furniture. That furniture was perfect and our parlor became a delightful room." Now it was "our" parlor.

Already, the seeds of discontent and disappointment were drifting into fertile soil. The anticipated joyous coupling of art and marriage was not taking place. Buffalo, then a busy port metropolis on the Erie Canal, was a prosperous city with a population that supported the arts with commendable vigor. Yet Buffalo society seemed to care little for Eulabee's accomplishments as an artist. She began to wonder if they all felt as did one New York acquaintance who had firmly stated, "A lady would never be an artist!"

> Women in my new life strove so actively in relation to house-keeping, children, luncheons, bridge—all the obvious world around and outside themselves. I felt displaced. My quiet, lonely creative world had conditioned me to react more to inner impulses and reasonings. Would I change?

On the surface, at least, she attempted to take her expected position in Buffalo's young married set. But did she really want to change? Almost immediately she took advantage of Alfred's New York Central Railroad pass to make short trips back to New York City. Before six weeks were out, Robert Henri had painted her a second time in his studio while his red-haired wife, Marjorie, plied them with tomato sandwiches. This portrait was the famous *Lady in Black Velvet.*

Alfred asked the artist for a photograph of the painting, which Eulabee could have (and probably should have) bought for fifteen hundred dollars when it was completed. On February 14, 1911, Henri wrote to Alfred:

> I should have been glad to have Mrs. Becker's portrait photographed, had intended to do so but neglected on acc[ount] of many other things making more immediate demands. The picture is now on its way to Rome, Italy, where it with two others are to represent me in the International Exposition of Art and History. . . . It will not be home until the end of the year. . . . I gave as title "Portrait of Mrs. Eulabee Dix Becker" in order to get both names in. Ask Mrs. Becker if that is as she would have it.

Three years later, Henri sent a mounted photo of the portrait inscribed "To Mrs. Alfred LeRoy Becker, Merry Christmas and Happy New Year! December, 1914, Marjorie and Robert Henri."

Lady in Black Velvet, by Robert Henri, ca. 1911
Oil on canvas, 77 x 37 in.
Gift in memory of Dr. Thomas P. Hinman
through exchange and museum purchase funds.
High Museum of Art, Atlanta, Georgia (73.55)

If she couldn't get to New York, Eulabee decided, she would bring New York to her. She lost no time in inviting her friend John Butler Yeats to lecture in Buffalo; for what organization is revealed neither in the memoirs nor Yeats's letters. Yeats turned down the first invitation in April, 1911, as too "adventurous" because travel tired him, although a postscript informs her, "Yesterday I was lecturing in Philadelphia." Finally, in December, he made the arduous nine-hour train trip to Buffalo to deliver a lecture on Irish art and literature. As the Beckers' houseguest he was taken sight-seeing. To Eulabee's amazement, he eschewed Niagara Falls in favor of a look at a still fairly pristine Lake Erie. Yeats started a drawing of Minnie Becker, with whom he seemed quite taken, but as with a self-portrait John Quinn had commissioned, he never finished it. They went to an exhibition of French art at Buffalo's Albright Art Gallery, where Yeats signed the guest book directly below the signature of Lady Augusta Gregory. She was his son Willie's colleague in the Irish National Theatre, and was in the United States preparing for the company's American tour.[9]

So much did he enjoy his stay at the Becker home that between December 16 and the end of the year Yeats wrote four times to thank Eulabee for their hospitality. Perhaps his attitude about her difficult character had softened. He had written to his daughter Lily that he told Eulabee "I would not envy the man that she married, for she would be sure to devour him. She has a clinging way like ivy which we know always kills the tree to which it attaches itself."[10]

Even as he endured with grandfatherly patience the challenges of her friendship, it was John Butler Yeats who ultimately shed the most uncompromising light on Eulabee Dix. A prodigious correspondent with everybody he knew, between 1908 and 1922 Yeats wrote seventy-five letters to the artist. They complimented, gossiped, scolded, sympathized, encouraged, diagnosed, and cajoled. Yet the letters were seldom devoid of affection.

Those written in December 1911, kept Eulabee vicariously in

touch with the Petitpas table and its colorful guests. On December 16 he wrote of the United States tour of the Irish Players. The company, co-founded by Willie and Lady Gregory as the Irish National Theatre Society, later became the Abbey Theatre. "I went last night to the Irish Players. They don't know whether they are going to Buffalo or not. Lady Gregory says the Buffalo millionaires were the nicest she ever met. I fancy I notice a change in her mental attitude towards the people."[11] The company, Yeats said, thought Irish-Americans far too materialistic.

Yeats made another observation in that connection:

> I learned a lot when with you, even though it was only in the last few days that I was in possession of my faculties. I have discovered one thing which I am anxious to impart to the world—that the American standard of happiness is very high, much higher than it is in England. Out of that solitary fact comes the American charm, which so many of us have discovered, and which the Englishman would fain deny altogether. It is also a cause of the American restlessness. You won't stand what the English woman will, or what I will.[12]

On December 20, he wrote to ask Eulabee if she would look for the book of Vera Johnston's poetry he had left behind. Because Willie was a lifelong believer, Yeats had then a passing interest in the occult, and naturally was drawn to Theosophist Madame Blavatzky's niece, who, it will be remembered, figured in Sloan's *Yeats at Petitpas.* He wistfully adds "I constantly think about you. All my journey back I kept thinking about what was happening in your house—now they are doing so and so, having lunch, or telephoning, etc. I felt quite lonely, and the country that seemed to me so uninteresting when going to Buffalo now seemed to me beautiful and full of interest. I wish so much I had stayed a few days longer."[13]

On December 24, Yeats thanked "My dear Mrs. Becker" for a set of studs, apparently sent as a Christmas gift. "They will save me a world of trouble, and it has much flattered me to know that you should have remembered me in this way." There is another nostalgic note about his Buffalo sojourn. "The day I came away, I nearly changed my mind and remained. I wish I had, and it was all because you and your husband were so kind to me."[14]

On December 27, Yeats wrote to thank Alfred for returning his book.

> I have not yet written to your mother. Had she been staying with you [Minnie Becker was away], I should have written long ago. I used to wonder which was mistress of the house, she or Madame votre femme and wondered to which I should pay chief court. I felt as if I stood in the relation of father to one and grandfather to the other. I often think of you, and wish myself again in Buffalo. . . . Wishing you all the happiness of the season and a fine litigious new year—peace inside your house and war everywhere else, I remain. . . . J. B. Yeats.[15]

During his visit, Yeats had spied Eulabee looking at her waistline in a mirror. He guessed, although she didn't tell him, that she was pregnant. Taking it in stride with a practical attitude in accordance with her frequently declared detachment from the body, she said, "All the young women told me what to do and what not to do—but I decided this was God's job and I let Him take care of it."

By this time she had cultivated the friendship of Cornelia Sage, director of the Albright Art Gallery in Buffalo, and was trying to promote an exhibition for Robert Henri. On December 11, Henri wrote to Eulabee from Ten Gramercy Park,

> Yes, I would like right well to have the show go to Buffalo with some figure or small head additions. . . . In case the ex[hibit] sh[oul]d be asked for in Buffalo the black velvet lady could go. As to the yellow lady—well, I think when we have another inspiration it will be a fancy free one and will not date back. I have not written Miss Sage because, as the catalog was sent her,

Mrs. Graves, 1911, 2 x 1½ in. oval
The National Museum of Women in the Arts
Gift of Mrs. Philip Dix Becker and Family

> I thought she would ask for the show if the idea had interested her. . . . The McD[owell] Club exhibitions are fine.

The "black velvet lady" had been shown in November at the exclusive MacDowell Club, a fine arts forum established in honor of composer Edward MacDowell. Henri initiated non-juried exhibitions there to give artists an opportunity to show in small groups without having to compete for space or prizes.[16] Both *Vogue* and *The Globe* gave good notices about the portrait of Eulabee, the latter announcing "By Mr. Henri there is one of his best achievements—a lady in black velvet wearing a large picture hat. It is full of character, and a quite remarkable rendering of flesh and blacks, so subtle and so refined as to rank with the good portraiture of modern times." Henri's reference to "the yellow lady" surely concerned the portrait of Eulabee in her wedding dress, although the artist himself apparently failed to recognize the potential for its later celebrity. Eulabee's comment about the portrait: "How thin and tired I looked."

Throughout all of 1911, Eulabee was too involved in co-opting the household, promoting a Yeats visit, engaging in social activities, and dealing with impending motherhood, to paint miniatures. Only one, *Mrs. Graves*, of Buffalo, is recorded for that year. Yeats's chatty correspondence continued. In January 1912, he is sorry Eulabee is having trouble with an old servant. "I fancy you are difficult yourself. I used to think you exacting and selfish. I now know you are exacting but not selfish."[17] The next day: "I hope I did not express myself too crudely in my impertinent attempt to describe your personality."[18] Other news from the Petitpas front was that John Sloan had returned from completing a portrait commission in Omaha, Nebraska, with two thousand dollars in his pocket. "Sloan and the little wife prosperous—just think of it!"[19]

In March, after a miserable bout with assorted ailments, he amused himself by composing an obituary for Eulabee's approval.

> The death is announced of Mr. J. B. Yeats, father of the distinguished poet, W.B. Yeats. He was a man between seventy and eighty years of age, and as is often the case with the fathers of men of genius, was a man entirely without any pretensions intellectual or otherwise. He had been what is called "a ruined Irish landlord." He had many amiable qualities and some strange personal dislikes. Altho' of cheerful and indeed optimistic nature, his doctors could find no other explanation of his death, except that it was caused by low spirits.

The essay concluded with an assessment of Eulabee's impossible handwriting, which was as bad as his own indecipherable scrawl. A postscript reveals that Eulabee had at last informed him of the coming blessed event. "Tell Mr. Becker how for his sake I ardently hope it is a daughter—a daughter is the father's friend and ally."[20]

Yeats knew whereof he spoke. His daughter Lily loved him dearly, and according to Yeats biographer William M. Murphy, she frequently but unsuccessfully entreated him to return to Ireland to live.

That he didn't was due in part to an unwillingness to return to his other daughter, Lollie. She had been medically diagnosed as neurasthenic, just as Yeats would later diagnose Eulabee. The two women, in Yeats's view, were much alike in their neurotic behavior.[21]

Eulabee tried to persuade Yeats to return to Buffalo in March. "Your letter gave me the greatest pleasure," he responded. "It would be a real pleasure to stay in your house, where I should enjoy everything and everybody, especially would I like talking about artistic theory and psychological theories, and I have an affection for that room upstairs, and I would enjoy Mrs. Becker senior." He declined, however, because "I am deep in debt and must stay on here and work it off."[22]

Often, the letters revealed Yeats's gifts as the freelance critic he had become:

> At Knoedler's there is a wonderful collection of watercolours by [John Singer] Sargent, extraordinarily effective tho' rather obvious in feeling. . . . At Macbeth's [there was] a collection of pictures by Arthur Davies [one of "The Eight"], very remarkable and very characteristic of the present time, in that while extremely poetical they are also quite vague—just figures moving about in twilight and looking extremely significant, but significant of what?. . . I still remain of the opinion that Sloan is the most interesting of them all. I resent Davies' vagueness. . . . I acknowledge that my remarks on Davies are too grudging, but then everybody is lauding him—Henri and Sloan and that solemn ass Chapman.[23]

Chapman, a New York art dealer, had joined the Yeats table without ever gaining popularity among the anointed.[24]

In another two months, Yeats would report again on the jolly atmosphere and distinguished visitors at the Petitpas table.

> We are now dining out in "the garden" except when it is raining or very cold—but no matter what happens we always dance,

> and our tables are always full. . . . Lately there has been shown at the Berkeley Theatre *The Fathers* by Strindberg, the Swedish poet and dramatist. It is as plain-spoken as the Bible and a great play. I wrote a long letter about it to the [New York] *Sun* and the actors have been here several evenings and are very popular with us. . . . I often think of my time in Buffalo, and those memorably pleasant conversations with Mrs. Becker. Please give her my respects and my love. . . . I hope all the Buffalo people are quarreling a great deal and bringing their troubles to your husband's firm.[25]

The next letter from John Butler Yeats to *chez* Becker was a congratulatory message to "My dear Becker," new father of Philip Dix Becker, born on June 4, 1912. While his first name derived from the middle names of Eulabee's father and brother, the little boy henceforth would be called "Dix." About her prize-winning, "so grand" portrait-subject-to-be Eulabee exulted, "I was as naturally natural as a cow and my baby soon looked as if he knew something the day he was born. I nursed him and all was fine, and I wanted ten children."

Eulabee didn't really want ten children. What she wanted was a storybook marriage, a beautiful child, a staff of servants to take care of them all, social position, and the resumption of a successful career.

CHAPTER 10

The Darkening Palette

1912–1918

Would I become the eternal feminine—protected and cared for? Some things I had hoped for are mine.

EULABEE CARRIED and delivered her baby with ease; the hoped-for joy of motherhood was hers. Mamie Dix came from Grand Rapids to "help out," and with the two grandmothers and family retainers in attendance there was little to do but enjoy her beautiful new son. Eulabee always would boast that she never had to perform the more onerous tasks of parenthood when her children were small.

Three months after Dix was born, she again invited Yeats to come to Buffalo. He declined, kept in New York by the impending arrival of a wealthy young woman who would pay him well to paint her portrait. Denied the pleasant distraction of a visit from her old friend, Eulabee hired a Mennonite nurse and retreated across state, without Alfred, to "a quiet spot down the Hudson." From there, they went to New York City to show off her new "so handsome and wise looking!" child.

> Alfred met us on our return, baby in lavish white, Olive in Mennonite bonnet and shawl, me in jaunty hat and sweeping black broadcloth. Why, why didn't a musical comedy show

> pick you up?" my husband remarked. . . . How amusing! Life seemed full and happy.

And why not? She was doing exactly as she pleased. Even Alfred's sarcasm seemed to amused her. And she was the most devoted mother on the face of the earth.

Yeats thought Eulabee's devotion excessive. After her visit to New York, he wrote, "I hope you got home all right and not too much fatigued. . . . If you stay too much and too long with that baby, it may be serious. . . . Nervous exhaustion is easily cured and forgotten, but it is a very serious thing indeed. . . . I think you are threatened with it. . . . In my mind you ought to wean your baby. I feel I am taking a great liberty, and I would not do so, only that I am haunted by what I know. So please don't think me a busybody trying to make himself important. I hope I am wrong. If so forgive me."[1]

That same week in October 1912, Robert Henri made a diplomatic attempt to clear up a misunderstanding about the *Lady in Black Velvet*.

> I am sorry you have made the mistake of thinking that I intended giving you the portrait. Perhaps the director of the St. Louis Museum thought from the title that it was yours and so wrote you for its loan. I hope there has been no confusion as I had already promised Mr. French (Chicago Art Institute) the picture and sent him an order on the Buffalo Gallery for it. . . . It is nice of you to want to own the portrait and if it were not that I depend on the sale of my pictures for my living I would be glad to give it. As it is I hope you will hope with me that it will be purchased by some gallery or first rate collector. . . . I really believe that should please you more than to have it yourself.

The portrait did get to Buffalo, after all. According to the Chapellier Galleries records, it was shown there in 1913. Apparently Eulabee either hoped or assumed that Henri eventually would give it to her. That minor incident, however, was nothing compared to the defining contretemps between Eulabee and her mother-in-law that occurred in the fall of 1912.

> After this trip [to New York with the baby] I went to a closet looking for bedding and found an old quilt with brilliant colors, one my grandmother made [and] had received several first prizes for. . . . I threw it open on the bed and saw at once that the well-remembered colors and beauty were gone. Stepping to my mother-in-law's door, terribly positive, though not angry, I said "Please, please dear do leave my things alone." "What is the matter, dearie?" Why discuss colors! I began to fold the quilt. But she had followed me and now my silence enraged her. Was it hatred, pride, envy, WHAT? Colors! The room filled with brown, purple, green, an ugly mix. Wild words flew from her. She grabbed my throat; as quickly as I could get one hand away, the other would be at me. She said mad things. Baby's nurse appeared at the door. Instantly, like a black cloud lifted, my mother-in-law came to herself and walked away. Prostrated, scratched and bruised I fell on the bed—then consulted our physician.

Exactly as Yeats had done, her doctor found an easy answer in the medical wisdom of the day: "Stop nursing the baby and all will be well." Alfred had been away; when he came home a week later, Eulabee poured out her story. "Quietly he said 'Let's finish reading the play'. So we read." After two years of marriage, Alfred was still retreating to a neutral corner while the strange familial *ménage à trois* played itself out.

It would seem unlikely that the patrician Minnie Becker was given to physical violence; more compelling evidence exists that Eulabee was the attacker, and perhaps more than once. Dix's grown daughter related that in a rare discussion about his childhood, her father casually—and with no feeling at all—told of witnessing his mother and grandmother "engaging in fisticuffs in the dining room."[2] Dix was only a few months old when the blanket incident occurred, so the question remains unanswered. Eulabee, however, was known to fly into blind rages over less consequential trespasses upon her aesthetic sensibilities.

She was capable at least of acknowledging her responsibility in prolonging the impasse.

> Mother and son held their own, while for months I was too emotionally disturbed to see beyond my nose. We had, in some limited, ignorant, selfish way, brought this about, a wicked and sad thing. No one moved to mend the situation. I knew that I was not perfect, that I could offend, be mistaken, or be wrong. . . . Silence was hinged to misery, imagination and sense of giving gone. My social interests ended, I sewed and read alone in my rooms—the three of us at dinner, night after night, in light pleasant conversation. The baby held me there.

How effortlessly did Eulabee slip into the role of victim! She longed for a friend to talk to. "One wonderful person, Mrs. William B. Hoyt, a social leader, was lovely to me. But I could not take the tragedy to her."

But she could take it to John Butler Yeats, whose knowledge of the affair was, of course, confined to what Eulabee told him. Nevertheless he diagnosed the problem and presented its solution with blunt, affectionate insight.

> You will never be really well and happy until you are at your work going to your studio every day and painting. . . . Its grandmother will be only too pleased to look after the Baby. . . . In this case it is only an artist that can advise. We understand each other, and besides I am old enough to be your grandfather.

To this he thoughtfully appends a graceful compliment. "I saw Quinn some time ago. He and his sister were expressing great appreciation of your miniatures."[3]

Philip Dix Becker as a Baby of Six Months, 1912, 3 in. dia.
The Metropolitan Museum of Art
Gift of Mrs. Philip Dix Becker and family,
in memory of Dale T. Johnson, 1994 (1994.317)

In late January 1913, he tried to make Eulabee face the reality of Alfred's and his mother's frustrating lack of interest in art. "Now it seems to worry you that your mother-in-law and husband don't 'understand' . . . that you are an artist, with pictures in your head. . . . You want Mr. Becker and his mother to *push* you on to do it, and are resentful that they don't seem to care. Of course neither of them knows and cares anything about it, and why should they?"[4]

The nicest people he knows, Yeats reminds her, regard art as some kind of unrewarding trade, and Alfred and his mother are indeed among the nicest people he knows.

She finally did get at her work. The mother who adored her baby was also the artist who considered him very paintable. The first of several miniature portraits of Dix was painted in 1912 when he was six-months old. Still considered one of her most important works, the miniature of the rosy-cheeked cherub won for Eulabee four prizes, including the prestigious silver medal from the Salon des Artistes Francaises in 1927.

The disintegration of the unhappy Dix-Becker extended household reached its climax one day at the luncheon table when Eulabee's mother-in-law "remarked casually that I had attacked her." That night, Eulabee left the house, took the train to New York, and by nine o'clock the next morning was sitting in the office of a physician friend. He told her that she was "going crazy" and should not return to Buffalo, whereupon Eulabee pleaded with him to tell Alfred what he had told her. Then she informed Alfred that the bedroom door would be locked until his mother was out of their lives.

It was Eulabee, not Alfred, who undertook the obvious step of looking for another place to live. She located a house a few miles south of Buffalo in the old Quaker village of Orchard Park, and the tone of the memoirs changes dramatically.

> Two stores and a few houses; its air filled with flying apple blossom petals. A pretty cottage, rolling hills, the country—a

> new horizon on the world! Here we soon came, my good husband and beautiful baby son.

There is no way of knowing how Alfred felt about the move. He was not being forced to meet Eulabee's third condition: if she was unhappy, they would return to New York. Wise old Yeats was "tremendously glad to hear that you are happy and by yourselves in the country. But do tell me have you given up for good the solitude of three for the solitude of two. . . . Never were people surer of happiness and affection than you and your husband—only impossible conditions must not be attached."[5]

Following their removal to Orchard Park, Alfred and Eulabee regained, or perhaps found for the first time, a measure of marital felicity. Eulabee unlocked the bedroom door, and by October 1913, friends in Buffalo knew that another baby was on the way.

In September, the director of the Albright Art Gallery, her old friend Cornelia Sage, asked Eulabee to participate in an important exhibition of the best works of artists who had lived in Buffalo. Eulabee's peckish response was a gushing note of thanks but she detested exhibiting with large paintings and had never been introduced or associated as an artist in Buffalo. Sage's reply was at best obsequious. "Yes, you were one of the first of whom I thought as a Buffalo artist, for the fact that you are living with us dear Mrs. Becker, and we had hoped to claim you as we need all the good art and artists that we can possibly bring to Buffalo. . . . I had so hoped for your assistance and approval of the coming local exhibition. . . . Trusting that you will change your mind and help art in Buffalo by allowing us to have a collection of your superb miniatures for February, I remain with dear greetings, Devotedly your friend, Cornelia B. Sage."

Eulabee was adamant. "I am grateful for your interest. . . . Your exhibitions are always attractive and distinguished and well hung. You are a woman doing such good works in what has hitherto been a man's

Philip Dix Becker, 1914, set in lid of ivory box, 2⅜ in. dia.
The National Museum of Women in the Arts
Gift of Mrs. Philip Dix Becker and Family

field. I feel obliged to decline your very cordial invitation. . . . I am sure you will understand." Cornelia did not understand. "I fully realize that your miniature work is much beyond that of anyone we have at present in Buffalo, but . . . it would not harm it or you to exhibit with those whose work cannot rank with yours and I think that it would be a very courteous and nice thing for you to do to exhibit with the Buffalonians, at least that is the way I look at it."[6]

Eulabee had an excuse besides pique for not participating in a February exhibit. Their second child was born on February 13, 1914 and christened Joan Lillian Antoinette, Joan after Mark Twain's *Joan d'Arc.* Eulabee wrote simply "a year later our daughter was born. How I loved the country." That is virtually all she says of her daughter's arrival.

The little girl did not at first possess Dix's full-blown beauty, and Eulabee never painted her as a baby, waiting until she was four years

Antoinette Bassett, 1914, 4⅞ x 3⅞ in. oval
Worcester Art Museum, Worcester, Massachusetts
Gift of Joan Becker Gaines

old to execute a miniature of the two children together. As Joan grew to beautiful girlhood, however, Eulabee often used her as a model.

Estrangement from her mother-in-law imposed no constraints on Eulabee's social and cultural life in Buffalo. Nevertheless, she made

K. Bliss, ca. 1914, 3 in. dia.
The National Museum of Women in the Arts
Gift of Joan Becker Gaines

a point of staying at the Hotel Touraine on Delaware Avenue whenever she came into town. The play-going and play-reading with Alfred had sustained her interest in the theater, and she became an activist on behalf of "good drama" in Buffalo. In April of 1914, she was elected president of the Buffalo branch of the Drama League of America, and was credited with organizing the local group almost singlehandedly. The *Buffalo Courier* stated the League's avowed goal in one succinct headline: "Mrs. Alfred L. Becker, Leader in Movement Here to Crowd Out Vicious Plays and Boost Good Ones."

Well provided for by Alfred, who denied her nothing, Eulabee painted now only for pleasure, and not often. She painted Dix again in 1914, a miniature which she set into the lid of an ivory box. Another miniature of that year was a portrait of her Orchard Park neighbor, Antoinette Bassett. "A rare woman," Eulabee wrote of her, "a cousin of Louisa May Alcott and could reminisce about the family." Alcott had died forty-six years previously, which casts some doubt on their cousinship. Bassett, who ran a nursing home and wrote modest poetry, does not appear in the Alcott family genealogy.[7] Eulabee was fond enough of her friend to name her daughter after her, and typically took pride in what she believed to be the connection to a famous personage.

About this time, Eulabee painted a miniature of a new acquaintance designated *K. Bliss*. The portrait is dated 1910 in the records. Katharine (Mrs. Lyman) Bliss, née Park-Lewis, of New York wrote a letter of condolence to Joan after Eulabee's death. She told of meeting the artist in Buffalo and sitting for her at the hotel on Delaware Avenue, "which I did most willingly, for she was an impressive, exciting person." There were, according to the subject, frequent interruptions while the artist gave the children their supper. That being the case, this miniature actually would have been painted after 1914. There is occasional difficulty in properly dating some of Eulabee's work.

Meanwhile, Alfred's appearances in appellate court were attracting favorable attention. Early in 1915 he was appointed a Deputy Attorney General for the state of New York. Yeats wrote "I am very glad of your husband's new office especially as it seems to promise that you and he may finally reach New York. . . . When I told Quinn of your husband's post, he gave a good-natured laugh and said 'She will yet get to New York.'"[8]

They moved to Albany, and with nanny and cook settled into a fourth-floor apartment at 346 State Street. It was indeed much closer to New York City, and while Alfred climbed the legal ladder, Eulabee found her way into Hudson Valley society. The old aristocracy still held sway in the state capital. Eulabee located two of their number in Mr. and Mrs. William Gorham Rice, who lived and entertained in a magnificent house designed by Stanford White. The Beckers and their children always were welcome at Mrs. Rice's five o'clock tea table.

But Europe seldom was far from her thoughts, Eulabee having

Boy with Red Hair, 1915, 2⅜ x 1⅞ in. oval
The National Museum of Women in the Arts
Gift of Joan Becker Gaines

long ago determined that any other milieu was provincial by comparison. It would not do to let friendships there cool, although dear Flora Baker had died, and World War I was taking its toll among her London acquaintances.

Lady Paget had established a 300-bed hospital for American soldiers at the French front. A thank-you letter acknowledging a contribution from Eulabee revealed grave changes the war had wrought at 35 Belgrave Square. "I am so touched by your sending me fifty dollars for the American Hospital and cannot tell you how I appreciate it and how very kind I think it of you. . . . Money is terribly needed to add more beds and every penny of your kind, generous present will be welcome and well used. I have been working very hard; it is the only thing that distracts my mind from its perpetual anxiety for my sons at the front and my daughter [a nurse] in Serbia. . . . This terrible war

Alfred LeRoy Becker, 1915, 2⅛ x 1¾ in. oval
The National Museum of Women in the Arts
Gift of Mrs. Philip Dix Becker and Family

absorbs every thought here and alas! seems to get more dreadful and more deadly. With every kind remembrance and renewed thanks from my heart with gratitude, Yours affectionately, Minnie Paget. . . . Do you paint now; don't lose your talent."

Eulabee did paint in Albany. She painted her children and completed portraits of the Rices. There were also a miniature of an anonymous red-haired boy and one of socialite Helen Miller Hasbrouck and her three sons. And, at last, she painted Alfred. His near-albino coloring and solemn mien behind spectacles are reproduced on a two-inch oval ivory, which Eulabee sent to Dix many years later almost as an afterthought. "Dix Dear—At least this is the coloring of A.L.B. He sat once or twice on a Sunday morning. I thought little of it till I found it the other day. It could be set in a frame, or case 8 x 10 inches." This was long after Alfred's death in 1948. If she knew how close Dix had remained to his father, Eulabee ignored it, yet the gesture indicated some awareness of their warm relationship.

Also in 1915, a showing of paintings by Robert Henri was headed for Grand Rapids, where Eulabee's mother and brother still lived. Eulabee wrote to Henri to suggest that the *Lady in Black Velvet* should be part of the exhibition. Henri let her know on November 18 that the painting was in San Francisco and could not go to Grand Rapids. He expressed interest in coming to see Eulabee and "look over those babies you write about so enthusiastically—or have you settled permanently in Albany?" At the end he, too, admonishes the artist to "Keep on painting—you are too fine a painter not to keep at it."

Eulabee did write enthusiastically about Dix and Joan. "Our children were lovely and admired—how proud we were of them." As an adult, Joan would write about her mother's tendency to "rearrange reality." This was a prime example. The children certainly were lovely and admired, but they were admired mostly by others. In fact, Alfred seemed constitutionally unable to express love for them, let alone pride. Eulabee's possessive love was constrained by constant fear that the children would appear to be, or do, something short of the standard of perfection she applied to everything and everybody.

Whether the growing tension in the household arose from Eulabee's unhappiness with Alfred or was developing without his help, there seemed no room for acceptance and appreciation. Gradually but inexorably, Eulabee was darkening the palette of her own life. Alfred escaped the storms by disappearing until they subsided, and the marriage limped along while Eulabee rearranged reality to convince herself that all was well.

Alfred must have been grateful that his work took him often to New York City. Although the United States was not officially in World War I until 1917, it was peripherally involved in it from the outset. Only thirty-five, Alfred was assigned to ferret out evidence of the German propaganda network in New York. One of his inquiries culminated in the execution of the French traitor, Bolo Pasha, and thrust the young lawyer into the public eye. In the course of another investigation, Eulabee encouraged him to undertake a dangerous wartime

Paper silhouette of character from a D'Oyley Carte opera company's shipboard performance of *H. M. S. Pinafore*, cut by Eulabee on voyage to Buenos Aires, 1918.
Author's collection

ocean voyage to Buenos Aires to apprehend the culprit in a New York graft scandal. She insisted on going with him. During the trip, she cut silhouettes of the ship's passengers, including England's renowned D'Oyly Carte light opera company and an American wrestling team. She sold the silhouettes to passengers and raised two hundred dollars for Lady Paget's hospital. Alfred got his man and raised his career prospects to new heights.

Minnie Becker died in June of 1915, unmourned in her daughter-in-law's memoirs but deeply mourned by her son, who gratefully acknowledged a letter of condolence from Eulabee's mother. Minnie's body, Alfred wrote enigmatically to Mamie, was unable to withstand the "battering of spirit."[9]

The year 1916 began auspiciously with Eulabee's participation in an important exhibit at the John Herron Art Institute in Indianapolis.

Not confined to miniatures, the show featured oil paintings by George Bellows, William Merritt Chase, Childe Hassam, Robert Henri, Mary Cassatt, and Charles Hawthorne. And in the company of outstanding miniaturists such as her old teacher William J. Whittemore, Lucia Fairchild Fuller, and Laura Coombs Hills, she maintained her position among the leaders of the revival period.

In March, amusing correspondence from Robert Henri included a delightful cartoon of himself and Marjorie in a frantic state after the "third hour of trying to read a Dix-Becker letter." The accompanying note cleverly imitated Eulabee's illegible scrawl without becoming illegible itself. That Eulabee kept in touch with the artist for reasons not entirely selfless may be indicated in his last letter to her during what he terms a "bad winter" in February 1917. It regarded some "proposition" on her part which he obviously had no intention of accepting.

Not yet forty and unhappily married, Eulabee seemed unable to find contentment in Albany. Since they lived not far from the state library, she took to reading "dreary" Russian novels that she said suited her mood. Yeats recommended Dostoevsky's *The Insulted and Dishonoured* and *The Dispossesed*, but told her to "leave *Crime and Punishment* till you feel your nerves to be very strong. I am in the middle of it and there I mean to stay."[10]

Yeats's letters also chronicled Eulabee's constant trips from Albany to old haunts in New York, usually without the children. Whenever possible she used the Petitpas boarding house for a home base if a room was available. If Alfred ever wondered what his wife was up to, he found out from one particularly telling account from Yeats of a chaotic visit in April of 1916.

> She being in a temper went off to bed at 7 o'clock then or thereabouts. Next morning woke at 10 o'clock, still in a temper, called for an egg to be boiled three minutes—everybody precipitated themselves, and she had that egg in 5 minutes. . . . When she entered my room, I said I will sit to you all day that you may paint. Like the first streak of dawn there came a smile

> upon her cloudy brow, yet she said no. . . . No, she said, I must go home. Why I said, myself now in a temper. She started to give reasons, thousands of them, all mutually contradictory and destructive. Under this rush of absurdity I sat back—a man of reason overwhelmed by a woman of no reason. . . . She did not heed. They never do. . . . She said I am going—goodbye, and as she left she called out that I was to bring her bag to meet the 4 o'clock train. . . . Mrs. Becker wished me to write a true and impartial account of her doings when here. I have done so and hereby send it.[11]

For the first time, now, Anne Squire, "the other woman" in John Sloan's *Yeats at Petitpas* appears in the Yeats letters, six years after the period erroneously implied by the Sloans. As Dolly Sloan's friend, she was attentive to their dear Yeats. Anne Squire was "enraptured," Yeats said, by Eulabee's new cloak and hat; obviously the two women knew each other, and Eulabee seems not to have disliked her.

Yeats constantly urged Eulabee to get out of herself and back into art, particularly after John Sloan began his long teaching career at the Art Students League in 1916. Yeats lost no time in writing to her.

> I . . . beg you not to lose this opportunity of becoming Sloan's pupil. He is a great painter. There is no doubt of it. I have just been looking most carefully at his pictures—and he will suit you. There are affinities strikingly to me manifest between his work and yours. Merely to be close to him for awhile and to see his work, even if you yourself do no work, will have great results. Believe me—I am in deadly earnest.[12]

It was all in vain. Here was the golden opportunity to fulfill her early dream of studying oil painting. She had the time and the money. But no, Eulabee was too busy scurrying about New York galleries and attending the theater. Yeats complained that she was wearing him out. "The fonder you are of anybody the more you will torment them. That's why I love you and resist you. That's why I do nothing while you are here and miss you as soon as you are gone."[13]

Notwithstanding, Yeats always found reasons to turn down invitations to Albany. The ascending decibels of Eulabee's disaffection are reflected in the 1917 correspondence. Until now, Yeats has couched his admonitory concerns in the gentlest of terms. On February 7, he took off the gloves and made his diagnosis.

> You have a touch of neurasthenia. Otherwise a clever and sensible and warm-hearted woman as you are would not be so much interested in yourself, complaining of all sorts of things, and finding it impossible to sit quiet, driven hither and thither by the demons of neurasthenia. I know all about it. We all know all about it. The seeds of it are in everyone. Only they are kept down by hard necessity. Having mentioned the disease let me refer to the remedy. It is in your own hands. Return to the discipline of hard necessity—have a studio and paint pictures.[14]

The ailment was described at the time as an emotional disorder, said to produce impaired functioning in interpersonal relations and accompanied by fatigue and depression. Since then, it has been dismissed by modern psychiatry as a label Victorian men attached to trouble-making women.

Almost as serious as Eulabee's neurasthenia, Yeats reported, the Petitpas table had gone dry with state Prohibition. Celestine Petitpas drowned her French horror of the unspeakable development in privately brewed "hot wine", which made everyone "hilarious." A hilarious Celestine opined to Yeats that in France Eulabee's neurasthenia would not be allowed. "They call it egotism and consider it a felony, employing against it the domestic cat o'nine tails," which Celestine's sister Marie told Yeats is in every French house "for to scourge the children."[15]

Modern psychiatry might take issue with Yeats's Victorian label of "neurasthenia" but Eulabee clearly was exhibiting neurotic behavior. On March 8, Yeats had to tell her, "I think you are one of the kindest and most affectionate women I ever met, and besides that with intellect and energy—but you are impossible. You have spoiled yourself and are determined to go on spoiling yourself. That afternoon in the Restaurant I was ashamed of you—your voice was so laden with hysteria and consequently so shrill that it must have been audible almost in the street."

He would not blame Alfred. "I think your husband one of the kindest and best men I know." He was sorry for her. Yeats finished in the frankest letter yet. "I have a real affection for the same Mrs. Becker who says such pungent things about men and women, and can look so handsome and distinguished."[16]

As Yeats hints, even at her worst Eulabee could be intuitive and generous, more so than her memoirs reveal. When Sarah Bernhardt, who had announced that she would not die until France was victorious, appeared in a wartime program of four acts from her famous plays at Albany's grand old Harmanus-Bleecker Hall near the Becker's apartment, Eulabee bought tickets and took a young friend so that she, too, could say she had seen the "divine Sarah." Her review of the performance may be as good as anything written about the legendary actress's final years on stage. Bernhardt was well into her sixties, and had lost one leg.

> The curtain rose on the fourth [act], the last scene of "Camille." Ugly colorless backdrops and furnishings, a brass bed center, with Bernhardt sitting up in it—looking old and weary. Could it have been worse? Then came the golden voice like music, and the magic of her art compelled attention. Each instant the woman in the bed held my gaze. Camille was there, dying, the brass bed forgotten. Camille, her cry for Armand: the mirror drops, is broken, sadness, superstition, the voice, *"Cassé!"* The curtain lowered. I had not understood her flowing French, but I had died with her and was dumb amidst the applause.

Eulabee went backstage and talked her way past Bernhardt's

fierce French guardian into a "hideously bare" dressing room, where the renowned actress sat alone.

> There was no one else to see her. She eagerly wished to know which play I liked best. "Camille." Disappointed, she preferred me to say "L' Aiglon"—so French, so near to her heart. . . . We stayed but a short time. I could not forget the dismal bare dressing room, its tiny mirror on the wall. When Bernhardt returned the next year, Mrs. Rice helped me fill the room with flowers, and a mirror.

Despite unmistakable signals that Alfred's notable execution of duties as a Deputy Attorney General was pointing him toward an important political career in Albany, which he wanted, Eulabee was waging a relentless campaign to get him to enter private practice in New York City. She wouldn't let him forget the promise of their marriage "conditions." To quiet her, Alfred lunched with John Quinn, who as a lawyer himself advised against such a move. According to Yeats, Alfred told Quinn he had not the slightest intention of leaving Albany, that he was only dodging his wife's importunities. Apparently Alfred did not take seriously the fact that Eulabee was beginning to use the word "divorce" during her tirades.

Eulabee's memoirs marked the formal United States declaration of war on Germany in 1917 only with a complaint that she had to start making her own bread because the cook refused to do it. By November of 1918 it was all over in Europe, but not in the Becker household, which had become a battleground strewn with the wounded spirits of unhappy adults and children.

Finally, Eulabee got her way. After a summer vacation on a Connecticut farm, they came back to New York City to stay, taking temporary lodging at a fashionable boarding house. Ironically, it was on Armistice Day, 1918.

CHAPTER 11

New York, At Last

1918–1925

Things were wrong; I could not seem to right them.

ALFRED WAS STILL Deputy Attorney General when the family removed from Albany to New York City. Eulabee's account of the next eight years is mostly anecdotal.

It was not uncommon then for professional families to live in a boarding house while looking for a permanent residence. The Beckers or, more likely, Eulabee, had chosen one run by an English woman who "collected famous people." But it was not contacts with the likes of such theatrical personalities as Eva Gautier and Isabell Hapgood that would forever haunt the artist's memory of Mrs. Cornish's boarding house.

Toward the end of her life, Eulabee, in great anguish, confessed to Joan that she had been pregnant when they arrived in New York in 1918. She didn't want the baby. Abortion was a statutory crime in the United States, but there were other ways to terminate a pregnancy. Eulabee obtained some kind of potion, not difficult to do if one knew where to look, and swallowed it in Alfred's presence. He watched in stony silence and did nothing when, in agony, she pleaded with him to fetch a doctor. It was the worst thing she had ever done, Eulabee told Joan.[1] Alfred never forgave her.

Alfred's career was soaring. Earlier in 1918 he had been encouraged to run for the attorney generalship. Teddy Roosevelt himself, after lunching with the candidate at Sagamore Hill, declared Alfred more than fit for the post. Along with New York and Albany newspaper columnists, the former President praised the young politician for exposing the German propaganda machinery and its nefarious principals who, they said, included even William Randolph Hearst.

Eulabee must have been pleased when Alfred lost the election and resigned his post to enter private practice. They had moved into the LaSalle Apartments in a good neighborhood one block from Central Park at 57 West Seventy-fifth Street. "Settling down for some years of metropolitan home life, convenient schools for the children."

In their nine rooms above the Columbus Avenue "El," Eulabee set up another of her English-style households that always included a cook, a French governess, and yellow brocade furniture. Six-year-old Dix was enrolled at Collegiate School, and in time Joan entered first the Veltin School and then the prestigious all-girls Dalton School. Both children could walk home for lunch. Their playground was Central Park, where afternoons under the none-too-watchful eye of a French governess gave them a few hours respite from the turmoil at home. Matters of minor importance often would trigger outbursts from their mother, directed at the household help as well as her husband and children. Governesses and cooks came and went with regularity.

Joan's recollections are painfully clear.

> There were no signs of affection between Alfred and Eulabee. Father was pale, blond, uncommunicative, not at all demonstrative. I don't remember him holding me on his lap, playing with me or even touching me. Between his silence and Mother's uncontrollable raging hung a violent hatred. In the middle of one of her tirades, he would silently walk down the hall, go out the door and head for the Harvard Club, where he would stay for several days.[2]

Dix simply retreated into his own world in the shared nursery, which usually was littered with erector sets and contraptions the precocious youngster designed and constructed out of materials at hand. His little sister tagged along, admiring his abilities, which Eulabee often reminded her she could never match, and passively submitted to her mother's well-meaning tutelage. Joan saw Pavlova and Isadora Duncan dance at Carnegie Hall, took piano lessons, went to dancing school, and with Dix ate healthy food, attended Sunday School, and learned good French. "As a child I tried to become something for her, an extension of herself that would fulfill her ambitions."[3]

Their lives were not without occasional excitement. When Alfred introduced William Johnson, a young employee of the Attorney General's office, into their home as a friend of the family, the ever-intuitive Eulabee disapproved both of him and the expensive gifts he brought to Dix and Joan. Alfred evidently did not share his wife's insight. The man's real name was Philip Musica, and he was earning parole on a grand larceny charge by serving as an undercover investigator for Alfred. Many years later Johnson was revealed to be the swindler "F. Donald Coster," president of McKesson and Robbins, who had extracted millions from the financial community. Until then, Alfred held fast to his belief that despite the criminal record he was a trusted friend.

John Butler Yeats continued to send the scrawled newscasts from his Petitpas headquarters. A letter of his had sold in London for ten dollars "and some cents." (In 1950, needing money, Eulabee sold Yeats's letters to the Princeton University Libraries for two hundred dollars.) "I should so much like to see you, you not the children," he wrote, and emphasized the sentiment with a sketch of two bawling youngsters. "Children spoil conversation, and spoiling that spoil the pleasure of meeting our friends."[4] Yeats did not like children, not even his own, until they were old enough to converse with him intelligently.[5] Later he observed that Alfred seemed to be doing well. "He is just the man for that troublesome position. He makes always with every-

Joan and Dix, 1918, 7¾ x 5¾ in. oval
Courtesy of Joan Becker Gaines

one a fine personal impression. Quinn, who is a good judge of men—however it be with women—has told me emphatically how much he likes him. Do come and see me and cheer one of my afternoons. I am enjoying a convalescence. I have had a very distinguished illness. . . ."[6]

The 1918 miniature portrait of Dix and Joan at six and four seems to be Eulabee's only work until about 1920, when she was commissioned to paint Mrs. Harriet Cowles, mother of the Park Avenue

Mrs. Harriet Cowles, ca. 1920–1925, 3⅛ in. dia.
The Metropolitan Museum of Art
Gift of Joan B. Gaines, 1989 (1989.98)

psychiatrist, Dr. Edward Spencer Cowles. Meanwhile, in 1919 she discovered the Provincetown art colony.

> Provincetown came in a letter from Richard Miller, the artist, [who wrote of it], "the only place in America like Europe." I journeyed in early April to look at it and was enchanted. . . . Here I must come: little white houses with green shutters and small-paned windows, snug gardens bordered by white picket fences, great old willow trees breaking the vistas. The decrepit wharves and sail houses along the shore, the sea tumbling in and out of the bay; winding streets—here and there an old woman, a rugged youth, or a girl in bright casual attire. Picturesque Portuguese religious street festivals and parades; the

town crier ringing his bell on the King's Highway, crying the news each afternoon.

Eulabee's friendship with the St. Louis-born artist, Richard Miller, probably originated in 1893 when both were attending the St. Louis School of Fine Arts. He had spent nearly twenty years as an expatriate in Giverny, France, securing a fine reputation as a teacher and second-wave Impressionist. The outbreak of World War I sent him back to the United States and Provincetown.

Aside from the connection with the Millers, the major attraction for Eulabee in Provincetown was the artists' colony founded in 1899 by Charles Hawthorne, another famous American artist who became her friend and colleague. Later, he painted two portraits of Eulabee and one of young Joan. The two of Eulabee are owned by the Grand Rapids Art Museum and the Indianapolis Museum of Art.

> Our shack by the sea was full of sand, had an old square grand piano, fireplace, and piazza on pilings; water coming under the porch at high tide, waves shaking the house in storm time. . . . The children well and happy, Alfred there on weekends. All made doughnuts for guests on the breezy porch—great fun.

Part of Eulabee's "fun" (although Joan remembers her in an almost constant state of depression) involved the celebrities that seemed to float in and out of her life. An extra cottage in the yard was used to house visiting relatives and assorted guests.

> A lady called one day and asked if she could rent it. She had come to Provincetown to see a veteran who had been in her hospital in France. . . . I loaned her the cottage and she came in several times for tea. . . . Her name was Lady Mackenzie-King, Scotch-English, her sweetheart Lord Kitchener, who had not married her because of his false teeth—being too shy. Then she said "If, at present, the Stuarts were the ruling house, I would be the Queen of England!" How shabby the

Portrait of Eulabee Dix, by Charles Hawthorne, ca. 1920
Oil on canvas on composition board, 36 1/16 x 29 7/8 in.
The Grand Rapids Art Museum
Gift of Horace Philip Dix, III, 1981.1.1

> cottage looked! . . . Lotta Crabtree, the renowned actress whom my father and mother saw and adored in St. Louis, came to call. Lotta lived in Boston where she owned moving-picture houses and was in Provincetown, at more than eighty years of age, to study painting with Hawthorne. Calling, I found her seated on the bed in white silk pajamas, gazing in half-approval at an unfinished landscape.

Dix and Joan were happy on Cape Cod. Joan's reminiscences reveal that these two beleaguered children at last had something pleasant to remember about growing up. "Provincetown meant freedom from shoes and socks, from school and apartment living . . . and rows be-

Family in a cart, Provincetown, 1920, on an annual pilgrimage across the dunes for a picnic.
Rear, Joan and Dix (left); Front: Sam Dix, Sally Dix, unidentified woman, horse and buggy driver, Eulabee with parasol, and Mary E. Dix.
Courtesy of Joan Becker Gaines

tween Mother and Father. . . . Those were the happiest days of my life."[7]

But Dix missed his father. A postcard from the 11-year-old to Alfred on June 25, 1923, reported on the pleasures of seaside life, but three times urged him to "come along up quick."[8]

Were they happy days for Eulabee? Perhaps. With her penchant for theatricality, she cut a dramatic figure during those seaside summers. Writes Joan:

> Every year there was a costume ball in Provincetown and I can see Eulabee as she looked before she started out one evening. She had made a costume that transformed her into a butterfly. She must have brought the stuff from New York, masses and

> masses of pleated light purple voile. It was unbelievably beautiful. I don't know whether she had any fun, or whether she won a prize, or whether she danced with anyone. She never told us. . . . Every summer she would go up and down Provincetown in the marvelous, artistic clothes she made, with a large Japanese umbrella over her head.[9]

Eulabee always took along to Provincetown her cook, a caged bird, and her preoccupation with the necessities of the good life. Entertaining at tea on their seaside deck, she served nasturtium-petal sandwiches, which Joan remembers as one of the delights of their Provincetown summers. Alfred would appear for a week or so and then return to his "bachelor apartment" in New York. In the summer of 1922, the children's cousin, Sam Dix, came from Grand Rapids for a visit. He fought with Dix, who was four years older, and remembered Alfred only as an austere presence whose departure signalled a relief from household tension.[10]

"Here was Eulabee in this ideal artist colony, so why wasn't she happy there?" Joan asks. "She was away from a husband who was difficult for her, free to paint, to do all the things she supposedly craved to do. . . . She did paint an excellent miniature, now in the Metropolitan Museum of Art, of a woman lying in bed. And one summer she did silhouettes of all the artists."[11]

Fourteen silhouettes, cut into sheets of white paper and mounted on black cardboard, make up the collection now at the Grand Rapids Art Museum. Each artist is listed in *Mantle-Fielding's Dictionary of American Painters, Sculptors, and Engravers*, among them: Miller, Max Bohm, Eugene P. Ullman, and Eulabee's old friends, Sidney Starr and Frederick S. Church. A silhouette executed with accuracy and a knowledge of drawing and a sense of graceful line, can transcend mere novelty to reflect the personality of each subject. An essay on silhouettes found among Eulabee's papers states that "although the outline of the silhouette is all-important, the space within the outline is not an emptiness, but the same *solid* which a bronze bust would present if

Woman on Bed, 1924, 2½ in. dia.
The Metropolitan Museum of Art
Gift of the Family of Philip Dix Becker, 1989 (1989.97.2)
Photograph ©1994 The Metropolitan Museum of Art

viewed against a light wall." Eulabee's silhouettes do, in fact, transcend mere novelty.

Provincetown was Eulabee's exclusive summer domain, but she deigned to share her winters with Alfred.

> Winters in New York, Alfred absorbed himself in legal work. We had some social life and old friends. I created clothes, designed for myself and daughter; or bought from Tappe. Radio came and my son, with his father's help, put one together. We listened as the first sounds came through, like a chick breaking its shell.

Her husband indeed was absorbed in his work. In fact an early 1919 issue of *Vanity Fair* nominated Alfred Becker for the Hall of

Fame: "Because he is an able lawyer and an author of distinction [Alfred had written a book on forgery]; because he is a wonderfully skilful [sic] bridge player; because he is a Deputy Attorney General of New York; because he was of great assistance to the French Government in obtaining evidence to convict Bolo Pasha; but chiefly because he has done more to stamp out German propaganda and conspiracies in this country than any other state or federal official." Alfred's troubles with Musica had not yet surfaced.

Eulabee, too, was absorbed in work to the extent of participating occasionally in exhibitions of miniatures, if not actually painting them. Having refused five years earlier to contribute anything to a general exhibition at the Albright Gallery in Buffalo, in 1919 she did enter a show there more to her liking, mounted by the American Society of Miniature Painters.

In April of 1920, she exhibited three miniatures at the Second Spring Exhibition of the Pennsylvania Society of Miniature Painters at the Art Alliance Gallery in Philadelphia, but nothing of recent execution. The catalogue listed her as a member of the society. She showed at the Grand Central Art Galleries in 1921, and lists another lecture and showing in 1923 at the Civic Art Center on East Fifty-sixth Street. By 1924, she had two new works, including a miniature of Mrs. Edward T. Stotesbury of Philadelphia and Palm Beach. They were shown at an exhibition sponsored by The Society of The Four Arts in Palm Beach.

Public acknowledgment of their respective successes should have brought satisfaction to both Alfred and Eulabee. It didn't seem to. Her "health was not as usual" Eulabee reminds us, forgetful of the bodiless spirituality she affected. It worsened when she was hit by a taxi skidding in the snow as she was rushing to the florist to buy flowers for a dinner party. The permanent injury to her ankle required the use of a cane from that time forward. She also had periodic bouts with eczema that covered her entire body; little Joan promptly echoed the affliction on the palms of her own hands. Eulabee wrapped herself in foul-

Mrs. Edward T. Stotesbury, 1928, 7⅜ x 5¼ in. oval
The National Museum of Women in the Arts
Gift of Joan Becker Gaines

smelling salves and gauze dressings and lay in a dark room until it passed.

The "ill health" had not gone unnoticed by her friend Yeats, who in June of 1919 expressed approval that she was painting again, and unfavorably compared the Eulabee Dix of his long-ago Buffalo visit to "the other day, [when] you claimed to be so ill, ill with nerves, etc. etc. etc.—by Jove I was quite glad when at last you took yourself off."[12] Eulabee had sent Yeats ten dollars for a portrait of himself, which he kept threatening to complete and finally got to Knoedler's for framing. There is no indication that she ever received it. Yeats had earned the right to tell her how good he was, writing, "By the way you have never seen any of my painting. In writing I am a professed amateur. In the galleries in Dublin are lots of my paintings, pronounced by R. Henri to be ten times better than Orpen's [Sir William Orpen, a prominent Irish painter], as they are."[13] Museum politics, no less in Dublin than elsewhere, the overriding fame of his two sons, and his own shocking lack of business acumen all had conspired to keep the senior Yeats from achieving the recognition he deserved. Henri's flattering appraisal was a voice in the wilderness on behalf of those who knew his work.

In December, Eulabee bullied Yeats into coming to the apartment for tea with the Irish poet and dramatist, Lord Dunsany, apparently having baited Dunsany with the presence of William Butler Yeats's father. Neither stayed in the awkward situation longer than was barely courteous, but Eulabee announced that Lord Dunsany had been "most brilliant," whereas Yeats claimed he scarcely uttered a word. After Christmas, Yeats replied to Eulabee, "Your invitation to tea this afternoon seemed to me like an invitation to come and be scolded—so with thanks I am staying here and doing my work."[14] Eulabee persisted. Three days later Yeats reiterated "In your last note just received I can make out three words—'Capt. Freeman,' 'January 1st', 'scolding.' I am engaged Jan[ua]ry 1st and Captain Freeman and I do not enjoy each other. . . . His conversation is all facts, and facts bore me. And to him my conversation is all ideas and ideas bore him. So don't bring us together."[15] Alfred, the crusty octogenarian suggested, probably would find Captain Freeman interesting because he has not heard all his facts.

Early in their friendship, Yeats had decided not to be a party to Eulabee's social aspirations. When she asked to be introduced to his son Willie's colleague, Lady Gregory, he replied, "I am quite ready to face ordinary dangers such as stopping a runaway horse, etc., but won't try to bring about your and Lady Gregory's meeting."[16]

To the end of his days, John Butler Yeats addressed his letters to "My Dear Miss Dix" or "My Dear Mrs. Becker," and never by her first name. A full year elapsed before he wrote again, unwilling to admit, or succumb, to mounting physical problems associated with his advancing age. On December 24, 1920, he declines an invitation for Christmas dinner, and implying little if any recent contact, ends, "I hope you are quite well, and that your husband is up to his ears in other people's quarrels and in other people's worries."[17] By April, however, the atmosphere had warmed and he accepted an invitation to afternoon tea.

We are indebted, once more, to William M. Murphy for details of the events surrounding John Butler Yeats's last letter to Eulabee on January 20, 1922, less than two weeks before he died at the age of eighty-three. "A touch of the irrational was distorting his perceptions. . . . Now he embarked on a series of exhausting activities that were to hasten the end. Late in the week of January 15, he went at Mrs. Becker's suggestion to see an exhibition of [Philip] Laszlo's works at Knoedler's. Though he returned home exhausted he had not lost his sense of humor."[18] Yeats wrote to Eulabee:

> I am grateful to you for having reminded me to go and see Laszlo's paintings. I had quite forgotten what horrors they are—bad in drawing, worse in modelling, and worst of all in spirit and intention—in fact a magnificent skill in vulgarity and pretense, so as to hide from the simple-minded the fact that he can neither paint or draw. But that I always express myself with great mod-

> eration and reserve I could write more strongly. The engravings and mezzotints after Reynolds are well worth a visit. Lazlo's successful incompetence makes a good foil. I was very glad to see you again the other night. I am afraid I did not show how welcome you were. I would sometimes call on you, but God knows when you are at home. Miss Squire has just been here. She is in very good spirits.[19]

Assuming that Eulabee valued her friendship with Yeats, it seems strange that his death on February 3, 1922, is not noted in the memoirs. But neither are the passings of other friends or, for that matter, family. It would not have been difficult for her to attend the Episcopal service at the Church of the Holy Apostle in New York where 250 mourners gathered in tribute to a truly grand old man. Perhaps she did.

By 1925, she was regularly using Joan as a model. *Joan in Costume* at the age of eleven was the last miniature she ever painted at 57 West Seventy-fifth Street.

> Life was getting sadder and sadder. Where had my joy gone and why? Europe would be a change, perhaps a solution. Our children were now old enough to benefit from a trip abroad; it would help all of us; enrich our interests. The children and I sailed, in June, 1925, my husband to join us in August for a long vacation and we to remain for the winter.

In a rare, and in retrospect suspiciously festive mood, Alfred took them all to a performance of the Broadway musical, *Ramona,* the night before Eulabee and the children sailed for Europe aboard the Cunard liner, *Carmania*. They went first to England for some sightseeing, then crossed the Channel to France and found quarters with a family in Equien, a picturesque village near Boulogne-sur-Mer, not far from Calais. To reinforce the educational significance of their travels along the way, Eulabee insisted that Dix and Joan read the same books about Europe and royalty that she had read as a child.

Joan in Costume, 1928, 6 x 4½ in.
Courtesy of Joan Becker Gaines

> We peeped at Paris then went to Tours to visit the chateaux of the Loire—their history, picturebook charm, and elegance so delightful; led to more chateaux in Brittany. As summer passed, each letter from my husband brought an excuse for his not coming. We were disappointed but still hopeful.

Since they were to spend the year in Europe, Eulabee was looking for schools for the children. Meanwhile, Lili Tolstoy, whose titled husband was a cousin of Leo Tolstoy, invited them to visit her at the resort town of Trois Épis near Colmar in Alsace. Typically, Eulabee does not account for her acquaintance with Lili, daughter of the Alsatian senator who negotiated the return of the Grünewald pictures stolen from Colmar by the Germans. Alfred's wartime contacts in Europe seem to explain the friendship, which lasted for many years.

When Eulabee and the two children returned to Paris in early autumn, a cable from Alfred was waiting for them. He would not be joining them, after all. The message was cruelly simple: "IN LOVE WITH A WONDERFUL WOMAN STOP CUTTING ALL FAMILY TIES STOP DON'T EXPECT TO SEE ME AGAIN STOP ALFRED."

Hatred, Eulabee's uncontrolled and Alfred's harbored unexpressed, at last had extracted its terrible price. While his uncomprehending wife wept and raged in a Paris pension, Alfred took a knife to the Charles Hawthorne portrait of Eulabee that hung in their New York apartment and slashed it across the face. So ended, in September of 1925, a fifteen-year marriage that never really had a beginning.

Peggy Froelich, ca. 1927, 5⅛ x 4 in. oval
The National Museum of Women in the Arts
Gift of Mrs. Philip Dix Becker and Family

CHAPTER 12

Let The Ship Sail On

1925–1928

How unreal my world had become; the wings of hope seemed motionless—perhaps they had been for years.

"OF ALL THE POSSIBILITIES of the outcome of our marriage, another woman had not entered my mind." Regardless of how Alfred chose to convey the news, Eulabee's incredulity at learning there was another woman in her husband's life seems inconceivable, almost as inconceivable as the naiveté of one brief flash of insight: "I thought I was a good wife. But had I been?"

Alfred and Eulabee made each other miserable: He couldn't communicate, she communicated in ugly outbursts of rage. Alfred coped by walking away from it. Eulabee didn't cope. There is no cause for wonder that Alfred waited to make the break when his wife was abroad and unable to retaliate in his presence.

If Eulabee never thought about what her tantrums were doing to the relationship, she might well have wondered about Alfred's frequent business trips to New York City when they lived in Albany. It was all right for her to go to New York alone to see friends; the idea that Alfred might seek other female company didn't occur to her. Would she have cared? Had the two of them, both avid theater-goers, ever met in New York City to attend a play together? There is no record, nor memory, that they did. Alfred had been in love with the "wonderful woman" for two years.

Although both were at fault, Eulabee more so than Alfred, the circumstances of such a precipitate change in her life were frightening. Only three months earlier, she had taken her children abroad, a woman of means married to a prominent New York lawyer and herself a recognized artist with visible means of support. Warning signals there may have been, but as far as Eulabee was concerned Alfred had unceremoniously dumped her and the children in a Paris pension without a dime. "Was this a lady or sex?" she asked, and in belated self-examination added "Had I really accepted God as stage manager? What a bad actor I was. Something was very wrong with me."

The effect on two pre-adolescent children who between them possessed few resources to comfort each other was devastating. Joan wrote, "Mother went into days of weeping. The big question was, what now? How in the world were we going to live?"[1]

Eulabee didn't know. "I wrote long letters, tore them up, began again. I had been stupid; we had made mistakes; the children must be considered. Then—what was the use? I hoped he'd be happy." Of course she didn't hope he would be happy. Men were hateful, she told the children. They couldn't be trusted. Alfred would be made to pay. "I had never faced so much."

But there was an unplumbed reservoir of courage in Eulabee, and somehow she managed to find it. It was the same courage that in 1899 took a 20-year-old small-town girl to New York to seek an independent career as an artist. Courage had propelled her into a life far less conventional, and far more interesting, than the one into which she had been born. Now she must rediscover its source.

The artful dismissal "Let the ship sail on" was written long after the fact, but it was what she did. While no stranger to self-sufficiency, she had accepted without question the perquisites that Alfred's law practice and his political position had made possible. Now it was over;

no more nine-room Manhattan apartments, no more French governesses, no more cooks, no more summers in Provincetown.

Facing at last the terrible finality of their predicament, she groped through her agony to discover that the favorable exchange of thirty francs to the dollar made it possible to put Joan and Dix in French boarding schools as planned. Then she would be free to return to New York and haul Alfred into court.

"Eulabee was dependent on her own earnings from the day my father said 'goodby'," Joan writes. "Always in a highly emotional state, [she was] determined to force him to come through with alimony and child support the judge ordered him to pay. She put him in alimony jail several times. But Alfred would go into court and claim he had no money. . . . He never gave her a cent."[2]

Sullen and homesick, but glad to escape his mother's rampaging self-pity, Dix went off to École des Roches at Verneuil in Normandy. Joan was sent to a school in Tours reputed to teach "the best French in France." Two weeks later, the unhappy 11-year-old was back on Eulabee's doorstep on the rue Notre Dame des Champs in Paris.

It was one more unexpected calamity, but it would not interfere with Eulabee's intention to inflict his just desserts on Alfred. She installed Joan in a school run by unfrocked nuns in the Bois du Bologne. It, too, was a disaster. Fortunately, an attack of appendicitis brought her home again, and when she recovered, Joan persuaded her mother not to send her back. She attended a day school within walking distance of the pension until the dread specter of sex, a not unnatural consequence of her being the only girl among thirty prepubescent boys, ended it. On a dare, the handsomest boy in class had walked up and planted a kiss on her innocent mouth.

"I immediately went home and reported this to my mother. Typical of her and her puritanical notions, she marched in to see the principal, who threw up his hands and said in French, 'Boys will be boys,' and thought it was all very funny. Eulabee decided that I must get out of that school. 'God knows what was going to happen to me next.'" [3]

Despite this distraction, however inconvenient, nothing could deflect Eulabee's struggle to return to Art. Regrettably, Eulabee failed to record the name of the man who encouraged her to start painting again.

> Could I recapture the success of years ago? With several miniatures in hand I called on a celebrated artist and his wife, asking them to tell me if they were worth going on with. "By all means—splendid! Go on!" They were convincing, and how easily I could be convinced, when my art was near my aching heart—and in Paris, where art has roots and vital interest.

Eulabee found another boarding school for Joan in a nearby village. The school appealed to her because it was in an old chateau with beautiful leftover statuary, and one of the headmistresses claimed descent from the court painter of Louis XVIII. Satisfied that her daughter would settle in, Eulabee scoured her Paris connections for portrait commissions, and got to work.

Alas, her dread of sex produced yet another crisis when Eulabee told the headmistresses that Joan reported the older girls were sneaking out at night to meet the village boys. It was casually mentioned in an innocent letter written home by a desperately lonely child, but the retaliations inflicted on the outsider *jeune Américaine* by those two worthy harpies and their French charges, who turned out to be relatives, were of Dickensian proportions. Cruelly goaded or icily ignored, Joan spent her imprisonment at Chateau d'Heudicourt drenched in tears, befriended only by the school chickens she was assigned to feed. Dutiful letters to her mother continued, but with troubles of her own, Eulabee had no inclination to read between the sad lines nor to remove Joan from her tormenters until the school year ended.

By then, Eulabee's income had improved enough to take the children to spend the summer in the Basque village of Ascain, five miles by trolley from Saint-Jean-de-Luz, which in turn was convenient to nearby Biarritz and prospective patrons.

Here in 1926, several months after Alfred's desertion, Eulabee's fortunes began to rise. An exhibition at the Taylor Gallery in Saint-Jean produced a commission to paint Elizabeth Park, the daughter of Vice-Consul and Mrs. Samuel Park of Biarritz. Mrs. Park was so pleased with the miniature that she ordered a gold frame for it from Cartier.

Additional portrait orders encouraged Eulabee to remain in the resort town and put Joan in school in Saint-Jean. Nevertheless, when one of her clients went off to Paris, Eulabee followed, and once more took up residence in the Montparnasse pension. She probably didn't consult God, but for once she'd made a good decision. An American woman invited her to tea one afternoon and suggested that she bring along some miniatures.

> There I met a man, Francois Monod, who looked at my work and began to exclaim, continuing with such praise as I had never heard. "This," he said "is the finest example of French eighteenth-century technique in miniature painting."

There was more than mere Gallic gallantry here. M. Monod was a member of the French Ministry of Art and deputy *conservateur* at the museum of the Luxembourg Palace. His quasi-official support helped to bring Eulabee's reviving career into prominence. When *Philip Dix Becker as a Baby of Six Months (My Son)* was awarded a top prize at the 1927 Salon des Artistes Francaises, Francois Monod paid high tribute to the artist.

Eulabee had his monograph reproduced in French and English, and extracted three paragraphs for inclusion in her memoirs. Monad wrote:

> The real tradition of miniatures is not that of the "mignard" portrait, treated as the work of ants—so reduced as to be only a

> curious trifle. The real tradition is that of the artistic miniature—a small picture which is valuable as showing the talent and originality of the artist—a tradition founded by the great French miniaturists of the eighteenth and early nineteenth centuries.
>
> It is in drawing inspiration from this tradition that the art of miniature painting, which has today become a poor and commonplace thing, can be raised to its old level. Eulabee Dix-Becker, an American miniature painter, has realized this. She has pondered on her art; and from attitude, gesture, stuffs, dress—everything that her subject can offer of character and color, she draws, as a true portraitist should, an expressive composition and a picturesque method.
>
> On the other hand, she frees and varies her work. Her faces and flesh stand out, as they should do in a miniature, which must never be uniform and dull. This explains the success of Madame Dix's portraits, which are so living and full of charm. She has, among miniature portraitists, an international reputation. She is a great artist and painter.

The prize-winning portrait was reproduced in color in the Salon issue of *L'Illustration*.

Monod's patronage gave Eulabee great heart, but it didn't deter her relentless pursuit of Alfred, who so far had failed to pay any of the alimony stipulated in a separation agreement reached the previous December. She hired another lawyer and took him back to court. The *New York Times* of October 21, 1927, reported with ill-concealed glee the domestic troubles of Ex-Deputy Attorney General Becker, whose personal and professional reputations were fast sliding downhill. Court papers revealed two letters from Alfred written at the time of the agreement: "I want you to understand that I love her. That cannot be changed. We may as well face it. When a love like this comes to a human being it controls his life and is bigger than anything else in his life. All I can say to you is, goodbye."

Even more revealing, in light of his refusal to pay alimony, a second letter claimed "I am absolutely devoted to the other woman. If I can be married to her it will bring me the greatest happiness. I realize I have no right to a divorce until I can take the best care of the children and you."

Alfred was being less than forthright. He had told the judge that he was penniless, had been sleeping in his office, and that because of his wife's attitude he had permanently severed his relationship with the other woman. It was patently untrue. They lived together until Alfred finally obtained a Mexican divorce and married his "Daisy" in 1933. Eulabee had refused to divorce him unless he paid for a trip to Reno, which he would not do.

Meanwhile, "How truly grateful for France!" Eulabee wrote. She was a professional artist again, working hard, supporting her family, meeting people, being recognized. Her miniatures fetched from five hundred to a thousand dollars each. One of her pencil landscape sketches illustrated a story in the Paris edition of the *New York Herald.* The writer pointed out, for no particular reason, that most miniature painters live to be eighty and that Eulabee had been inducted into the Paris Society of Miniature Painters.

While there were real gains in her life, Eulabee continued to pay an awful price for the corrosive years of domestic conflict. It finally cost her the promising, "so grand" first-born child. In 1927, the gifted 15-year-old insisted on going home. Dix knew exactly what he was going to do with his life, and neither France nor his mother figured in his plans. For a time, he lived in Grand Rapids with Eulabee's brother, Philip Dix, whose grimly avuncular duty toward his sister's children provided them sanctuary when it was needed. Dix finished high school on a scholarship at Exeter, the New Hampshire prep school, and went on to the Webb Academy of Naval Architecture in New York.

Philip Dix Becker, 1927, 5 x 4 in. oval
The National Museum of Women in the Arts
Gift of Mrs. Philip Dix Becker and Family

My Children, 1927, 7½ x 5½ in. oval
Courtesy of Joan Becker Gaines

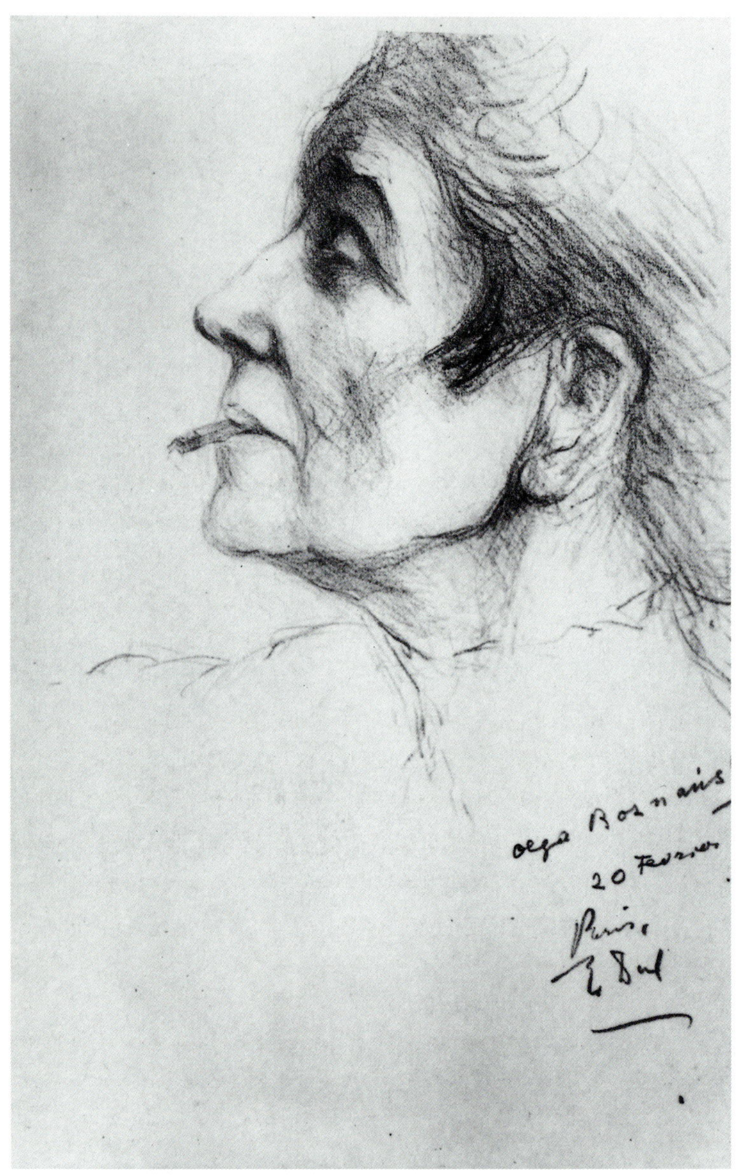

Sketch of Polish artist Olga Boznanska, 1927
Pencil on paper. Photograph of original.
LRC Archives of The National Museum of Women in the Arts

He worked his way through MIT and became a successful engineer, but the hatred he felt for his mother deeply affected his ability to achieve wholeness as a brother, a husband, or a father.

Before Dix left France, Eulabee painted both of the children separately. She also portrayed the two of them together. Never again did she paint Dix.

Portrait commissions brought them to Cannes in the fall of 1927, where Joan was enrolled in École Cours Maintenon, the sixth and, mercifully, last French school she would have to attend. In "delightful Cannes with the blue Mediterranean, clear and crisp sunlight, hills, villas, nightingales, flowers" Eulabee painted Lily Wickersham, stepsister of the United States Attorney General, George W. Wickersham. She was also called to a "rambling old chateau near Cannes" to paint Honor Paget, the daughter of Admiral Sir Alfred Paget and niece of Lady Paget's niece, Amy. Another miniature, *Peggy Froelich*, also dated 1927, was of the daughter of an American friend. Eulabee liked it so much that she copied it for her own collection.

Although the emotional and financial consequences of Alfred's abandonment never ceased their assaults on Eulabee's consciousness, her pilgrimage gradually became less bleak. Joan, for a change, was reasonably happy in Cannes. Seeing old friends and making new ones played a pleasant counterpoint to the pressures of earning a living, and the artist's substantial fees helped preserve the lifestyle to which she was accustomed. Besides, if the need arose she was clever enough to fabricate its material aspects.

Among Eulabee's Paris friends was Olga Boznanska, a noted Polish expatriate working in a neighboring studio at 49 Boulevard Montparnasse. Boznanska was three years older than Eulabee and was half French. After art studies in Munich, she had moved to Paris, where she had lived since 1898. Her work, predominantly in portraiture, skirted the edges of French impressionism. Prior to World War I she had exhibited annually and with great acclaim at the Salon de la Société National des Beaux-Arts. But the war's profound effect on her fragile spirit had made her a virtual recluse. She worked in a dusty studio, dressing as she had at the turn of the century, and offered refuge to titled Polish exiles who flocked to Paris. She taught at the Académie de la Grande Chaumière and knew all the important French critics, but apparently was not interested in the fame that should have been hers. Today in Poland, Boznanska still ranks as one of her country's most notable painters; in France, where she died in 1940, she remains virtually unrecognized.[4]

There is scant reference material available about Olga Boznanska, but what there is describes her exactly as Joan does in a moving account of the indelible impression Boznanska made on both mother and daughter:

> She lived up several flights of very dark stairs. We would rap on her door and she would open it a crack and say, "Who eez eet?" We would go into the dusty, gray place where Olga lived and painted. She seemed to be dressed in rags. There would be a painter's stand with someone posing while Olga stood at her easel. She took sixty sittings to paint a portrait. She would stand there, a cigarette hanging from her mouth, and put one little dab on the canvas. Then, there would be nothing for a while, until she was ready for the next dab. Eulabee did two pencil sketches of her painting. . . . Around the room sat women who were bundled up, Polish refugees . . . exiled aristocrats who had no money and came to Olga's studio to keep warm. Amongst all this were dozens of mice, running in and out and over everything, including the teacups from which we drank tea. It was all taken for granted that Olga Boznanska loved the mice more than anything. The sad part was that Boznanska finally made a trip to Poland after many years of being away, and by the time she got back, the tenants in the building had the mice exterminated. I think she died of a broken heart.[5]

Eulabee's Salon prize had done its good work. In 1927, she showed at the Knoedler Gallery in Paris, and in December lectured at the American Woman's Club with great success. The reporter assigned to cover the event, clearly out of her depth and never having heard of Richard Cosway, insisted on referring to the great English miniaturist, "Richard Causeway."

But while life in France was pleasant, even improving, they could not remain there forever. By early summer 1928, "The time . . . had come when my children needed to return to the United States schools." Never mind that Dix already had flown the nest. She booked passage from Marseilles on an old French ship that meandered to Palermo, Lisbon, and the Azores, before docking in New York harbor three weeks later.

Eulabee walked down the gangplank that sultry July day to face an unknown future in the very city that shaped her past. She had sentenced herself to carry the bitter baggage of Alfred's desertion. Yet among its consequences was the reaffirmation of her unique creative forces. Art, and only Art, would direct her path now. She did not know where that path would take her, only that she was resuming a journey that had come to a halt eighteen years ago.

"I should have looked poverty stricken, but never could."

Publicity photo of Eulabee on return to New York from France, 1928
LRC Archives of The National Museum of Women in the Arts
Photographed by Florence Van Damm, New York

CHAPTER 13

Beginning Anew

1928–1931

Fifty years of age, in good health, full of energy, my art revived in France, I was ready to re-establish my professional life in the United States.

THE EXPECTATIONS that brightened a hopeful young artist's arrival in New York in 1899 were the same expectations that supported the wounded divorcee's return in 1928. Only one thing had not changed: Her commitment to Art was as strong as ever.

In a somber publicity photo taken after her return, a beautiful, affluent-appearing woman stares from beneath a velvet cloche. She is wearing furs, four strands of pearls, and a large diamond ring. Just as she did almost thirty years before, Eulabee looked in the mirror and appraised herself. She wrote on the back of the photo, "After three years in France, 1928, with a hat $5, a cheap Paris dress, a $50 fur piece. Two children to support on art. I should have looked poverty stricken but never could."

> Now I look at [the photo] with wonder. In France, prices were low, but I had $500 to $1000 for miniatures, some ten or twelve, and paid our expenses, for no money came from ex-husband. Now I faced NY and we were very poor, and [I] expected my lawyers would get money for us. If my ex-husband saw this photo he may have thought we needed no help. The gorgeous ring on my finger was made in Paris with old stones,

> and cost only $35 after my design. It pleased me so that it was my joy and comfort.

If her great-aunt's diamonds comforted her, it was the brilliance and vitality of New York City that once again excited Eulabee. Obsessed with prosperity and confidence, the city was spinning in the eye of the Roaring Twenties. Surely it was the right place for her, but it would have to wait.

On August 26, she was in Newport, Rhode Island, listing in a letter to another famous miniaturist, Margaretta Archambault of Philadelphia, some of her titled sitters. Archambault was planning the 1929 annual exhibition for the Pennsylvania Society of Miniature Painters. Expecting to participate, Eulabee optimistically suggested, "There is a splendid new picture of myself. Do you wish one for papers?"[1] She also went to Buffalo and foraged the familiar establishment enclaves for portrait commissions, living briefly, as Joan recalls, in a studio belonging to an old friend.

The 14-year-old was still reeling from the first meeting with her father in three years. The day after her return to New York, they lunched together. "I was excited. Finally, I could confide in him all my pent-up rage about the awful schools in France and his treatment of the family. There is no question that I took my mother's side."[2]

Still, she had retained "warm feelings" for Alfred and had written to him regularly. Even as an observer, she was too young to comprehend fully what had happened between her parents. Alfred telephoned Eulabee afterward and told her, "I never want to see Joan again. She talked to me like my grandmother." Eulabee triumphantly reported this to her daughter. It was the ultimate personal rejection that threw Joan into the pit of her mother's anger, making her Eulabee's unquestioning ally. Learning later that Alfred resented her lack of effort to become "close," Joan wondered how she could have done it. Alfred married a comfortable, ordinary lady whom Joan never met, adopted her young son, and lived in the Bronx. Joan didn't see him again until 1936.

Dix, though, saw his father frequently. The relationship included the affectionate Daisy, who often appended a greeting to Alfred's letters to his son. Joan, however, was deprived of a father. As far as Alfred was concerned, Joan was an extension of Eulabee, and he hated Eulabee. In later years, Dix angrily refused ever to discuss this part of their lives, even their childhood, with his sister.

Now that they were back in New York, Eulabee needed a good address, and it seemed logical to return to the familiar Sherwood Studios where Robert Henri and John Sloan had lived years ago. Her apartment soon acquired the ambiance deemed essential to gracious living in a Dix-Becker domicile. There must be birds, of course! Eulabee thought it would be pleasant to have some doves, who would fly gracefully about the neighborhood and return to roost in a cage at her window sill. Dix built the cage, and Eulabee located a bird seller underneath the Manhattan end of the Brooklyn Bridge. She brought two white doves to the apartment, only to watch the wretched creatures refuse to fly and finally flop to the street below. Their wings had been clipped. Her ensuing altercation with the bird seller resulted in her being taken to court and cited for assault and battery.[3] She did not bother to mention the incident in her memoirs.

Eulabee persuaded the Dalton School to re-admit Joan on a full scholarship. She was a prize example of what Dalton could turn out: fluent in French, an excellent student, and unspoiled. Naturally, the wealthy girls who attended Dalton with her daughter were high on a list of connections for potential clients, but it wasn't to be. Joan could visit their Park Avenue apartments and suburban estates countless times and never once encounter a parent, paintable or not, let alone one interested in a miniature of a son or daughter. Eulabee was somewhat inured to rejection by this time, her latest failure having been a miniature, from a photo, of Queen Alexandra which Her

Highness politely turned down. She saved the formal rejection letter from a palace equerry. It bore the royal crest, an echo of happier times among Warwicks and Pagets.

Titles still were important to Eulabee, and a titled husband for Joan was more to be desired than money. She never failed to put her daughter in a situation where a proposal might come about. Joan's first date, arranged by her mother when she was sixteen, was with Prince Alexis Droutzkoy, editor of *Universe* magazine in New York. He was "a wizened little man with a cracked voice. I wore a red velvet dress and sat most uncomfortably listening to balalaikas in a Russian restaurant. Droutzkoy must have been 50 or 60 years old, but I think Eulabee would have favored a match. It was a title."[4]

Eulabee was nevertheless practical enough to sublimate her delusions of grandeur while she threw herself back into the quasi-Bohemian life in which she had matured as an artist. Her reputation still was known and rampant prosperity bode well for commissions. She dropped "Becker" from her name and divided her inexhaustible energies between the promotion and production of miniature portraits.

That year she painted a miniature of Isaac Josephi, the miniaturist who was her first New York suitor and mentor in 1900, and who had remained a good friend. She went to Grand Rapids and painted her brother's youngest son, 5-year-old Horace Philip Dix III ("Bud"). Presumably, she visited her mother, who inexplicably remained absent from the memoirs but who lived to ninety-five.

Eulabee's brother, Horace Philip Dix, Jr., had married well and held a managerial position at the American Boxboard Company; later he became a trusted investment advisor to wealthy Grand Rapids families. He tried to help his sister by buying her paintings and taking in her children when the necessity arose. Eulabee's visits, however, are remembered mostly for confrontations over wrongly hung pictures, ending in Uncle Phil's absenting himself from the house until she

Horace Philip Dix III ("Bud"), 1928, 3¾ in. dia.
Courtesy of Samuel M. Dix

went back to New York. It seems that Eulabee's sibling had his own set of family neuroses to battle.

Regardless of her obsessive personality, Eulabee was an attractive, gifted woman and an amusing companion. It was not difficult to re-establish her artist's credentials. In January 1929, a portrait of Mrs. Henry Strater of New York won the Levantia White Boardman prize at the American Society of Miniature Painters annual exhibition at the Grand Central Galleries. It was her second medal in as many years. The following October she won the Medal of Honor at the Pennsylvania Society of Miniature Painters in Philadelphia with her miniature of Joan at the age of twelve. The next year, 1930, Joan, now sixteen, was the model for *Youth in an Old Gown*, which brought the artist further favorable reviews.

The catalogue for her first solo exhibition in New York, however, has disappeared, possibly discarded by the artist because the entire episode was a financial and artistic disaster despite the prestigious names Eulabee had provided as patrons—her friends and clients the Otis Skinners, the Rices of Albany, the Tolstoys, the Wickershams, and the Cuban sugar baron, Manuel Rionda, among them.

> September 1929, an exhibition at the Milch Gallery was offered free of charge, in a room hung with brown velvet. "Very expensive invitations—they must be expensive," said the lady in charge. "We will send them out for an exhibition of 'table portraits!'" Gracious, everything was expensive! From Paris I had brought new settings and frames. The price put on the large 6 x 8 was $2000. In fine settings, these could be accommodated in apartments where life-size portraits were no longer suitable. . . . No sales or commissions resulted. . . . The invitations were lovely outside, but inside they had a list of "patrons" not sufficiently important to swing me. The prices were too high, especially for this gallery and on October 29, 1929, in the midst of the show came the terrible day all living then will remember.

Joan Becker, 1926, 4⅞ x 3⅞ in. oval
The National Museum of Women in the Arts
Gift of Mrs. Philip Dix Becker and Family

Youth in an Old Gown, 1930, 7½ x 5½ in.
Courtesy of Joan Becker Gaines

Eulabee ignores the social prominence of her own patrons and typically places blame for failure elsewhere, although the stock market crash surely had something to do with it. She described the awful consequences of "Black Tuesday" as she watched them unfold in New York City. "A strange hush fell over the losses and tragedies, everyone stunned . . . but shortly after the first shock, people picked up hope." "Dear blind Hope," she called it. But with stockbrokers plunging out of Wall Street office windows, there was little hope for a painter of miniature portraits, luxuries no longer fashionable or affordable. She adjusted. Lowered her fees. Friends were loyal, she said, and from here and there came clients. And when she was painting, she could forget. "I was in a world apart, all the sad and perplexing problems of my domestic life seemed to fade away."

One month after the crash, Eulabee gave an illustrated talk on "The Masters of Miniature Painting" at Contemporary Arts on East Tenth Street and showed the "table portraits" she and other miniaturists were beginning to paint. They were in a larger format that could be displayed on a parlor table. Tickets cost fifty cents, and tea was served. Art was surviving.

Nor did the Depression dash her plans for Joan's college education. "She fought and succeeded in getting me a full four-year scholarship at Vassar from funds raised by the New York Vassar Alumnae Association. It paid for everything. Eulabee never said, 'We're poor. Of course you must go to public school.' It had to be the best and she went out and argued for it. . . . I don't remember ever being consulted."[5]

Eulabee would miss Joan when she went away to school. Not only as a model but as her "best critic," the fresh eye that could detect a drooping eyelid or a too-small ear after hours of long, close work on a subject where perspective might be lost.[6]

By 1931, "dear blind Hope" had sunk into the country's economic depression and Eulabee's growing despair over a dwindling art market. A New York friend offered a solution to her problems.

Maud Skinner was the wife of the famous actor, Otis Skinner, and the mother of Cornelia Otis Skinner, who would follow her father into the theater and eclipse even his fame. She "gave me friendly and sound advice. 'Surely you'll get no orders now. Go to Paris, live in a garret, and study. . . . When spring comes, the Depression will be over. Come back and I will give you a party, set you up again.'"

Why not? Dix was in training as a marine engineer aboard the South America-bound freighter, *S. S. Leviathan;* Joan would be a sophomore at Vassar. Here, at long last, was an opportunity to study oil painting. It was to earn money for this very training that she had taken up miniature painting in the first place, never dreaming that three decades would pass before it would come about.

Eulabee vacated the Sherwood studio and put her possessions in storage. She was about to sail for France when her lawyer called to say that Alfred had offered a cash settlement instead of the alimony he had never paid. She should stay around for a week and see what happened. Joan went off to France to spend the summer as a paying guest of the Tolstoys in Trois Épis. Titles abounded in that household. Eulabee went to a hotel and waited.

> It occurred to me that it was just the moment to look over old letters from my husband. For years, every letter, when found here or there had been saved; the turning of a phrase or some sweet memory kept them. The entire accumulated lot now in two gunnysacks were in storage and were sent for. In my room, after an early dinner, I drew the fat, filled sacks to me, sat down on the bed . . . and opened the nearest sack. Letter after letter passed. Some must be saved. . . . Letters, links of time over space. All I had read and known. Some written in tenderness, some with concern, others with the business facts of living. Eighteen years of letters: the lover, the lawyer, the husband, the father. . . . Here were the vibrant remnants of hopes and plans and dreams. . . . At last the task was done. Out of the past, and now suddenly I was conscious of the

> room filled with light. A clock struck eight a.m.

If she saved any of Alfred's letters, they have yet to be found.

Word came from her lawyer. Nothing had been accomplished, after all, so she sailed. Once in Paris, she went straight to a *pension* in the rue Grande Chaumière near the Boulevard Montparnasse and Raspail.

> A beautiful young housemaid came to the door, with such a heavenly expression. Surely I must live here; she would compensate for starving and freezing. Only one room was unoccupied. Up we climbed by a winding stairway to the very top floor, a tiny place with light through square panes of glass set in the sloping ceiling; a garret room with pretty striped white and yellow paper. In it were a commode of fine dark walnut, a ten-inch-across fireplace, a clean-looking comfortable bed, ancient wash bowl and pitcher on stand—complete invitation. . . This room had an air of arrested time and ghosts; I took it.

The picturesque pension appealed to her sense of drama, but even better, it was next door to the Académie de la Grande Chaumière! At the age of fifty-three, when the less determined might retire to contemplate their laurels, Eulabee plunged into the Paris art school's rich curriculum with the breathless enthusiasm of her youth.

> Each day paints and canvases back and forth up and down the winding stairs; each morning a portrait class in oils. At two I would go and draw from costume models, in odd poses, just seeming to sit around, but especially thrilling was the five to seven period, in a big room filled with old and young from all over Paris, a hundred and fifty more or less. Student artists packed together on low benches around the model stand and big hot stove, others on high stools at the back of the room. This was the *croquis,* the pencil sketching class; exciting, peculiar to France, where the sketches of the old masters are appre-

> ciated, valued, treasured. Nude professional models, men and women, taking five minute poses; five of them, then resting five minutes; falling into beautiful positions quickly and with ease, keeping us in a frenzy of effort to get all we could out of the pose and on paper; working for accuracy, action, and facility. Such a scratching and scrawling of pencils and pens. Joy in working. It was wonderful!

Facile as always, Eulabee learned to draw large portraits in an hour or less. "Why use pencil unless quickly and well?" She was less excited about modern art. The miniature tradition was lodged firmly in the eighteenth century and there the miniature artist stayed. She saw nothing to admire in abstraction or impressionism.

> Many ultra-modern studies seemingly made with unrelated attention to the model. The model, if standing, was painted on the canvas as seated; if a red background, it would be green. Why did these artists and magicians bother to come and labor along with those who seemed to be digging for another kind of solution?

She tramped about Paris and sketched buildings and the landscape. When winter came and days were gloomy and bitterly cold, she repaired with fellow expatriates to the Dôme Café to warm up on "Grog Américain," a concoction of rum with hot water, lemon, and sugar. Maud Skinner wrote, hoping to shake Eulabee out of her bitterness at Alfred's desertion.

> Otis is playing Shylock again and Cornelia is doing "Wives of Henry VIII" and I come in on the edge of their achievements. I had a birthday recently that made me quite philosophical. I realize that my real job in life is done. I've shared my husband's years of labor and he can rest and retire—my child is beyond needing me any more. You must come to this, too, in a short time. Your children do you credit and soon they will be

Pencil sketch from Paris studies, 1932. Peter Juley photograph of unlocated original.
Peter A. Juley and Son Collection,
National Museum of American Art, Smithsonian Institution

> on their own. You have prepared them for life and done a good job of it. Never feel sorry for yourself. It is your very genius that makes you feel intolerant of present day conditions. Turn your bitterness into triumph.

Dear Maud was so generous, so perceptive, so wise! She died before Eulabee could see her again. One of Eulabee's scrapbooks contains a photograph of Maud Skinner with Cornelia as a child. A notation on the back reveals the artist's inclination to use her friends to her own gain, especially if she were to write an autobiography: "This would make the book!"

She now was living on the few miniature commissions that came along in Paris. When rum and brioche at the Dôme no longer took the chill off her *La Bohéme* garret, she moved to the rue Ponthieu. It wasn't as romantic, but it was warm, atmospheric enough, and the food was good. A *nouveau*-poor Irish aristocrat who had raced horses in Spain told Eulabee to go out to Fontainebleau, where the king of Spain, Alfonso XIII, and his family had fled their country's Civil War to live in exile. She might get a commission to paint one of the infantas. "Be sure to ask for the Duke of Miranda." It was a tantalizing prospect.

> On a balmy winter's day I gathered my courage and with two examples of my work, went by train to Fontainebleau. A bus completed the journey, leaving me at the massive iron gateway of a rambling building, the Hotel de Ville . . . set in a park, which had been opened for the accommodation of the escaped royal family. . . . I asked for the Duke of Miranda and was told to be seated. Soon a handsome tall man, about fifty years of age, appeared, impressing me with his attractive elegance. He would show my paintings to the queen and hoped she would grant my request. In a few days he would know, would I come back.

When Eulabee returned, the duke regretted that the royal family remained in strict seclusion, and that there would be no portraits commissioned. He nevertheless expressed approval of her art, and after "further regrets and a gracious farewell," she walked light-heartedly (her words!) down the long way to the gate to take her bus.

> There were footsteps behind me. . . . I crossed the little road at the gateway and stopped, stood facing the old highway to the great palace of Fontainebleau and then turned to see who had followed me. Standing quietly at the road was the King—Alfonso of Spain. He was gazing at me, and all the gladness that had been mine now vanished. I, who had stood in a

> crowded London street, watching Alfonso and British royalty drive by, now had my private view. But why had he come? Why was he waiting? Here the very ground on which we stood had held the courts and kings of France. . . . The banished king still looked at me. Had he too seen the past pass by! We neither moved nor spoke. . . . Was I dreaming of kings whose slightest glance prompted women to risk their lives? The bus stopped. In I went and on back to Paris. Days later a friend said "My dear, I lived in Spain for years. Alfonso XIII is not complex. You should have SMILED at him. Then EVERYTHING could have happened!" But what? It was the elegant Duke of Miranda who intrigued me.

With a paid-for return ticket safely in hand, Eulabee wanted to remain in France for as long as her money held out. Paris was full of American expatriates, so she called one of them, a woman who wanted to be painted but who had always complained that she couldn't afford it.

> She offered to sit, if I cared to do it for two thousand francs, which had just come in the mail. Someone had borrowed two thousand francs, here it was back, along with a pile of unpaid after-Christmas bills. Forty dollars was like crumbs, but something, and she was good looking. It would be fun to do her. We began the next day. . . . What a lovely thing I made of her. More and more I realized how spiritual portrait painting is. Just let the likeness come through. She had a pretty face, her chief interests men and food. Lanvin made her clothes.

A friend was incensed when he saw the beautiful finished miniature. "She thinks nothing of spending a hundred dollars a night in Montmartre clubs!" he fumed. Eulabee was philosophical about it, but when the forty dollars were gone she knew it was time to go home.

CHAPTER 14

Roses

1932–1941

Immigrants had more in pocket than I, when stepping ashore that spring of 1932. The Depression had not lifted; it had settled.

SHE MAY NOT have had any money, but Eulabee had plenty of something else, and a good word for it is *chutzpah*.

> Surely there would be a place to live in Greenwich Village, so I called on a French friend at her hotel in Tenth Street. Dropping off my luggage at the door, holding a bunch of anemones still fresh from Paris, I was pleased to find her at home. "Here to search for a roof!" I said gaily. "With hardly a penny to pay." She emptied her purse. Goodness and kindness. What a help! We visited—laughed and talked of Paris and I departed to find and enjoy a time with my son, then left for a peep at my daughter at Vassar.

That is how she tells it, anyway. Perhaps the friend emptied her purse in order to get rid of the importunate artist who appeared so blithely on her doorstep.

Her son Dix would have greeted her return with even less enthusiasm, but noted in his diary on March 22, "mother back about the

(left) Detail of image on page 225.

9th." He was having a difficult time, trying to stay in school and looking for some help from Alfred. A February diary entry reports, "Father more broke than I thought."[1] To the regret of the faculty, he resigned from Webb and shipped out again to earn tuition for enrollment at MIT.

On the other hand, Joan had little choice in the matter of seeing her mother. Eulabee turned up in Poughkeepsie two weeks before Vassar graduation ceremonies with a scheme to make some money. To Joan's mortification, she fingered a classmate to round up the twenty-four juniors who had been selected to carry the traditional daisy chain. "It was arranged for me to make pencil portraits of these for an exhibition in Taylor Hall Gallery." She planted a story in the society section of the *Grand Rapids Herald* that made the Vassar "exhibition" sound like the triumph of a native daughter. The campus newspaper announcement touted the drawings as Daisy Chain girls immortalized in black and white, "This is probably the first time that a college has exhibited portraits of its own students."

In 1932, few of the girls or their parents could afford to buy the pencil portraits for the twenty dollars asking price. The only good thing that came out of two weeks on the Vassar campus was an invitation to give the lecture she had given the American Woman's Club in Paris on the art and history of miniatures. The fee paid for her room and board and a visit to the dentist. She bought a train ticket to New York and gave the rest of the money to Joan, who was still smarting from her mother's behavior and the landlady's blunt "That mother of yours is no lady!"

Eulabee boarded the train, stacked her luggage in the entrance of the coach car, and settled into a double seat facing the door. In her purse was $2.40. She hadn't the vaguest idea about what she would do next, but the Eulabee Dix brand of faith was tied to her brashness. No matter how badly people treated her (her version), no matter how foolishly she might behave (the truth), God was out there watching over her.

A few stops past Poughkeepsie, a drunk boarded the car and sat down in a vacant seat opposite her.

> The train started, my eyes looked past him, but soon he leaned over with a polite hiccup. "You're a nice-looking lady. What's your name?" "Smith." He was not objectionable, so I decided to be patient; possibly he would soon be sober. He had to talk to someone. . . ."I am going to Philadelphia," the drunk said. "Will you come with me?" From his side pockets into my lap came bills and bills, a flow of fives and tens—two hundred dollars or more—and a return trip ticket to Philadelphia. . . . I gathered and returned the bills, but back they came. "You can have them." Again I picked them up, suggesting that he put them in an inside pocket. . . . Again all the bills came back to me. . . . I decided finally that all that money would never get to Philadelphia. God had remembered me, so I took ten dollars and somehow I did not feel like a thief at all.

Evidently God hadn't finished with her yet. Housing came from a New York City friend who offered the use of her Fifth Avenue apartment for the summer. Eulabee spent June and July getting Joan ready for her junior year at Vassar's foreign program in Munich. Joan remembers it well:

> Eulabee had a wonderful time making clothes for me. Nothing else was quite like them—hats, suits, everything. She used no patterns. She would get an idea, and buy material, often at the street stalls on the lower East Side. Then she would take out her scissors and start to cut. No matter what the cloth, velvet, tweed, taffeta, she would sit down on the floor and cut. There would be a lot of pinning and basting, no careful, finished sewing. Everything was put together quickly, but the effect was stunning."[2]

After her mother painted one more miniature of her, *Joan at Eighteen*, Joan sailed for Europe, well-dressed but trying to forget the

Joan at Eighteen, 1932, 7½ x 5⅜ in. oval
Courtesy of Joan Becker Gaines

litanies of complaint that accompanied the sewing sessions. "Why am I doing this? You're not a grateful daughter. You don't appreciate this. I'm a great painter. You're not proud of me." The parting shot was "Make sure you come back from Europe engaged to a man with a title!" Having dispatched her daughter to school, the artist, rejuvenated and inspired by her Paris studies, was anxious to get back to work. She searched for a studio in New York's less fashionable, less expensive, parts and found an apartment in a shabby house on East Fifty-seventh Street next to the elegant French and Company antique galleries. The Third Avenue address was good, but the house had been tied up in an estate for twenty years and was badly neglected. Whether or not it fit the technical definition of a "tenement", the place looked and smelled like one. Even the rental agent tried to discourage her.

> "You can't live in this." I assured him, nevertheless, that it might be possible and he took me into an unkempt entrance, smelly hall, untidy stairs, two flights up to a four-room apartment in bad condition. No heat, no hot water, wash tubs with wooden rims in an old kitchen off the hall. There was a large front room, however, with unobstructed north light and a fireplace. Back of this were two smaller rooms. "What will you do for me?" "Paint. Give you a bath tub." "Rent?" "Twenty-one dollars." I gave him ten. He looked aghast at the deposit, and well he might, for it was almost all my money.

Excited because the north light was perfect for painting, she rushed off to tell a friend about it. The friend—Eulabee's memoirs seldom identify friends or clients, now—ordered a drawing of her child "and we were rich again!" She hired a painter to cover the "tenement tan" walls with her own perfect shade of French gray tinted with raw umber to show off the little marble fireplace and mantel. She drew squares on the kitchen floor and painted them brick-red and battleship-gray. A wooden top covered the kitchen bathtub, which she draped with a floor-length pleated skirt.

Out from storage came the antique furniture and Oriental rugs acquired from auction houses for next to nothing over the years. Paintings were hung everywhere, even in the tiny toilet room, where guests always found an excuse to visit its floor-to-ceiling display of art. She weather-stripped the windows, installed a pot-bellied stove, and in winter kept warmer than her wealthy friends in their uptown apartments. "All was cozy and elegant as if renting on Park Avenue!"

Eulabee lived at 206 East Fifty-seventh Street for the next seven years. Her neighbors mostly were poor, working-class people. After seeing what Eulabee had accomplished, however, couples whose fortunes had been wiped out by the Depression began to move in, and out again when their circumstances improved. The building's dilapidated ambience attracted Gypsy Rose Lee as a tenant, and is said to have turned up in one of author Mary McCarthy's novels. As she could do so well, Eulabee took her downsized situation in stride.

> The Depression brooded over us like heavy clouds after a storm; blackened, clouded, tangled finances. Everyone talked poverty—could not afford this and that, clothes fixed over by the maid—groaning, moaning about money and the things it could buy. Few called on me, as no one wished to find a dead artist on the floor of a tenement! For me, "hard times" were old friends.

The irony somewhat obscured the reality. People did call on her. To promote work, she held tea parties and invited old friends and potential clients. And they came, those sable-draped ladies, emerging from their limousines to climb the sagging stairs for an admiring look at Eulabee's "miracle." There was some justification for poking fun at the wealthy who were not coping with reduced circumstances. Eulabee knew how to make do.

> My shabby clothes did not seem to matter; it was enough to be presentable. Rummaging through a property trunk I found an old Tappe dress of ten years back, a thinnish black wool, tight bodice, long tight sleeves, full, long skirt yards around. I wore it one afternoon. "What a lovely gown," everyone said. "The style suits you." I liked it too, and adopted its long-sleeved tight top and full skirts. I was stared at but this made little difference, for I was well dressed, in a classic and comfortable

mode which I have never changed.

Joan recalls her mother setting forth in those unfashionable but somehow becoming outfits, always wearing a hat and carrying her cane. She also remembers the embarrassment of overhearing a man in Central Park comment "Why did they let a tart like that come in here?" Even if Eulabee had heard the remark, she'd have said she didn't care what other people thought. Joan believed that indeed she did care. "To her dying day, Eulabee felt that clothes were important and I don't think she ever lost her sense of being beautiful. She had created her own looks. She prided herself on the fact that she seemed younger than her age and kept her figure, which was tiny."[4]

Eulabee might recreate a past in her "poet's pocket" studio, but she must bend to the present to survive. Occasional commissions to paint a miniature from life came along, but more and more clients were bringing photographs for her to reproduce on ivory. "The art I had created, labored over, starved for, in a devotion like love for one's beloved, was dying." Department store "artists" were fobbing off little colored photographs, sold at Bloomingdale's for $4.95, as true miniatures. Worse, hardly anyone grieved over the demeaning attenuation of an age-old art form. Few people knew any more that the word "miniature" came from the Latin *minium*, the red paint used by Benedictine monks, who were the *miniatori,* to decorate illuminated missals. These days it simply meant "little."

In one of her rare confrontations with reality, Eulabee accommodated to the dilemma.

> Few miniatures would be commissioned so I painted flowers in oil, especially white roses. It seemed to me I could paint white roses the rest of my life.

And so she did. But not to the exclusion of miniatures, which she would never abandon. But now she put her Paris teaching to work and began to paint large oils. Some time later she recalled that old Bishop Gillespie, as he was dying in Grand Rapids, said to her mother, "I dreamed of your daughter last night—surrounded by white roses, white roses."

She always had loved roses, but Eulabee was a city dweller whose gardening had been confined to tossing a handful of fecund nasturtium seeds at a fence on Cape Cod. Now, the flowers came from Goldfarb Brothers, a Third Avenue florist across the street from the apartment. Eulabee bartered a portrait of one of the owners for a continuing supply of fresh roses and lost herself in committing them to canvas. This was how Joan found her upon returning from Munich in the spring of 1933:

> The canvas propped up somehow on a few chairs, its back to the stove. Beyond, our long Italian refectory table with its glossy, light-reflecting surface. Behind the table a drape of creamy satin hung along the wall, creating a rhythm of light and shadows. And on the table there was a luxuriant arrangement of white flowers. . . . The work must proceed rapidly before the taller flowers droop and the rose petals fall off. Eulabee would start before breakfast, sitting in her nightgown after she'd put an egg on to boil on the three-burner gas stove. With a palette of whites and umbers and bits of vermillion she'd lay on her paint, sometimes with a brush, sometimes in thicker globs with a palette knife. The egg and pan sometimes burned up. Eulabee was happy, absorbed in working her magic. Nothing else mattered. At five in the afternoon she might still be wearing her nightgown, oblivious to time or hunger; adding a few last brush strokes before daylight faded."[5]

Loosed from the tyranny of laying watercolors on unstable ivory with fine sable brushes, Eulabee was delighting in the freedom of applying oil paint to forgiving canvas with a palette knife and large brushes. Her strong color sense and broad brushwork resulted in extravagant compositions of pliant, uncomplaining subjects. Eulabee had

Delphiniums and Roses, 1933. Oil on canvas, 47 x 54 in.
Courtesy of Samuel M. Dix
Photographed by ©1997 Charles Heiney

difficulty dealing with people; flowers were different. They didn't dictate the terms of a sitting, nor complain if a leaf or a petal were not perfect.

> With the first white flower compositions I at fifty-five entered a new phase, a serene consciousness; released an unknown battery within me, a current of harmony and rhythm came into use. I painted white roses, small and large canvases; some four by six foot, new arrangements, veritable gardens of flowers in glass containers, six or seven reflected on a highly polished table . . . working madly.

The dramatic florals were not successful at first. At one point, down to her last dollar, Eulabee dragged two canvases downstairs and hired a husky vagrant to carry them to an art dealer. "Yes, very good," said the dealer. "These stand up well with any of the pictures on my wall. But can I sell them?" He thought not.

French and Company, however, finally agreed to hang the paintings, and they began to sell, if not always for the posted price. She asked $750 for the first one, but desperate for money, accepted $250 in cash a few weeks later "with a lump in my heart." As personal evocations of the artist's intense love for beauty, the floral paintings are exuberant in their use of colors ranging from bright, riotous hues to skillfully manipulated whites.

Although she was painting few miniatures now, as one of a handful of leading miniaturists trying to keep the art before the public, Eulabee continued to lecture about them. Early in 1933, she spoke at the Society of Fine Arts in Washington, D.C., which produced not only a fee of sixty-five dollars, but an invitation to exhibit at the Corcoran Gallery of Art. Critic Leila Mechlin's review in the Sunday *Star* of April 9 was full of praise. Of *Youth in an Old Gown* she wrote, "Rarely has an artist achieved greater success than this—technically, spiritually." Among the thirty miniatures on display was the portrait of Mark Twain.

Eulabee hadn't yet painted the great man's granddaughter, Nina Gabrilowitsch, the only child of Clara Langdon Clemens and her first husband, the pianist Ossip Gabrilowitsch. The sitting took place in 1934 and is not referred to in the memoirs. But the portrait of 24-year-old Nina never was claimed by her parents. Possibly because Eulabee posed her in a beautiful formal gown, they said it didn't look like her. Clara and Ossip Gabrilowitsch were said to be so obsessed with each other that they paid scant attention to their daughter, who never married and lived what appeared to be a troubled life on the proceeds of her grandfather's estate. She died in a Los Angeles motel room at the age of fifty-five, clad in blue leotards and a jumper.[6]

Nina Gabrilowitsch, 1934, 7¼ x 5¼ in. oval
The National Museum of Women in the Arts
Gift of Joan Becker Gaines

Eulabee's success on the lecture platform inspired the development of a more structured presentation of the history and art of miniature painting, which she entitled *Red Paint and Butterflies* after the *minium* used by Medieval miniaturists and the "butterflies" of society she so enjoyed depicting. The lecture was illustrated by her own paintings and by slides of other miniatures from various museums. She extracted endorsements from friends, critics, clients, and other artists, printed a brochure, and signed with Shearwood Smith, Incorporated, a New York booking agent. In Washington, D.C., she lectured for the Society of Fine Arts, the Mount Vernon Seminary, National Cathedral School, and the Congressional Club. Often in conjunction with exhibits, she appeared in Philadelphia for the Art Alliance, in Grand Rapids for the Art Association, and in Buffalo and Albany. In New York she lectured for the Junior League, the School of Design for Women, on radio station WOR, and the Brooklyn Museum, where she had exhibited in four annual shows sponsored by the Brooklyn Society of Miniature Painters.

When she showed two flower paintings in a group exhibition at the Grand Central Galleries in March of 1934, the critics began to take note of the new *oeuvre*. "These canvases, carried out in opaque whites, really carry off the honors," wrote the *New York Evening Post*'s Margaret Breuning.

Characteristically indulging a restless nature, Eulabee went to England in the spring of 1934, sure that her London connections would lead to commissions for large portraits. There wasn't much left of the familiar social scene to smooth the path. Minnie Paget had died in 1919, as had most of her other old friends. Only the Countess of Warwick was around, now living at Easton Lodge in Essex. How times had changed! For one thing, the countess had learned to type her own letters. The once-notorious beauty and still ardent Socialist was seventy-three years old and sounded world-weary.

> I have your letter and am so truly sorry that you should have

> come over to England in these very pagan times. I mean, that there is hardly an artist of renown even, who is able to sell a picture and miniatures seem to have quite gone out of fashion. . . . Everyone alas is very poor, I mean the sort of people you used to know. The moneyed people seem to care nothing for Art and no one would sit still to have a portrait done.
>
> My grandchildren at Warwick are so poor that it is as much as they can do to live in a few rooms of the Castle with great economy. The big places of England are being rapidly absorbed into public institutions or schools and I fear Warwick will have to go.

Warwick Castle did go, bought lock, stock, and contents by Madame Tussaud's Wax Works and turned into a tourist attraction. According to Paul Barker, curator of the castle's house department, Eulabee's miniature of the countess was not among the contents. He suspects the generous "darling Daisy" gave it to a friend.[7]

She would like to help, of course, but the London Season "such as it is" was over and everyone gone. Then, "Comrade Warwick," as the press enjoyed calling her in the Socialist salad days, goes on to explain the profound changes in English life:

> It is true that socialism is coming in our time, if not already here, and the transition stage is always a most difficult one, and we are experiencing now a change from the old order to the new. . . . We have no Court now and most of the people immediately round it are quite ugly and rather old. Then please get out of your head that I am any use at all socially, any more. I don't know any of the younger people; I have not been in London for years, and have lost touch with so many people, except my old friends who are of no use to you. When you think of the time when dear old Minnie Paget used to run London Society, we indeed remember a past age.

How the Countess of Warwick so comfortably conjoined the

Alphonse and Josette, Mouvement de Jazz, 1929, 5 x 3⅝ in.
The National Museum of Women in the Arts
Gift of Mrs. Philip Dix Becker and Family

philosophies of Socialism and London society is beyond conjecture.

She wished Eulabee had come to London under the auspices of "some big people like Knoedler's," but the countess underestimated the artist, who already had lined up a two-week show of miniatures and flower paintings at Knoedler's Bond Street gallery. The *Morning*

Post called her an able American artist whose "series of vivacious miniatures . . . typify the characteristics of her fellow countrywomen, quite at home in daringly sumptuous wearing apparel." Singled out for special praise again was *Youth in an Old Gown* and *Nina Gabrilowitsch*. Noted, too, was the debut in England of the *Alphonse and Josette* series, Eulabee's experiment with articulated figures in various poses. "Mrs. Dix's skill is best displayed in the exceedingly humorous movements of two supple-jointed lay figures."

The Knoedler show brought good notices throughout England and produced three portrait commissions. Eulabee also claimed she was invited to spend Christmas in Ireland with Lord and Lady Dunsany. Lord Dunsany had fled her contrived tea party with John Butler Yeats fifteen years ago, so why the invitation was issued remains a mystery. "Lady Dunsany was beautiful, a member of the Villiers family; and Lord Dunsany extremely interesting—he painted well." She was still impressed by titles, but didn't go, remembering how uncomfortable ancient castles could be in winter.

When Eulabee returned to New York, the rose paintings and miniatures were shown together at the Grand Central Galleries. The exhibit garnered enough publicity and reviews to keep her name before the public. And Joan was back home, a Vassar graduate, class of 1934, and lucky to find a job selling jewelry at Bloomingdale's. Contrary to her mother's instructions to bring back a title, she had fallen in love with an English student during her junior year in Munich. She went to Alfred's office and asked for some financial help so they could marry. He coldly refused. It would be giving money to Eulabee. She didn't see her father again, nor did the romance survive her inability to raise the dowry her class-conscious fiancé required. They could not have lived without help in the house, and he could not afford it.

By now the split loyalties of brother and sister were fixed. Dix had graduated from MIT and, unable to find work, once more had gone to sea. Even several impressive letters of introduction from his prominent California lawyer grandfather, Tracy Becker, could not penetrate the Depression-ridden job market. This was the side of the family Eulabee would have nothing to do with, but letters signed "Gramp" indicate that Dix kept in touch not only with Alfred, but with the grandfather who had "disappeared" before he was born.

Joan, embarrassed by their "reduced circumstances" but still unable to cut the umbilical cord, moved into an apartment immediately above her mother's. Her roommate was a Vassar friend and, in 1935, the subject of one of Eulabee's best "table portrait" miniatures. Joan always insisted that because Eulabee was fearful of sexuality, she often depicted her female subjects somewhat flat-chested. Nevertheless, *Betty Sadler* appears as a sullenly flirtatious young woman of the Thirties, languid with sexual overtones the artist probably never intended.

Joan may have been embarrassed, but her mother refused to be circumscribed by the rude surroundings.

> After an evening with wealthy friends on Park Avenue, my daughter and I came home to our tenement, and walking up the sagging stairs she said "I suppose they think we are very poor." Poor? I never thought I was poor! I could create beauty out of nothing. Rich people said they wanted my pictures, but could not afford them. We had them to enjoy. . . . We could cook very well, make a home attractive, had our health? Poor? Living on a shoestring? No—a golden thread.

They always had a cleaning lady. They ate in the French style. No matter how modest the meal, the effect was always perfect. She could not compromise, once spending several weeks shopping Manhattan for a kitchen spoon that she could live with. It had to be beautiful.[8]

Roses took Eulabee, now a recognized "rose painter," back to England in 1936. Through Marion Cran, author of widely read books about flowers, she met the Cant family, whose famous rose gardens in Essex supplied the royal gardens. She rented a room at the King's Head in Lexden, near Colchester, and painted roses for four months. Not only did she paint them, she studied their culture, learned to

Betty Sadler, 1935, 5⅜ x 4 in.
The National Museum of Women in the Arts
Gift of Joan Becker Gaines

identify each specimen by name, and acquired enough expertise to lecture about them.

It was almost like old times. Daisy Warwick invited her to paint her own celebrated roses at Dunmow, where Eulabee and a London friend were served tea in the garden by the countess's liveried footmen. In August, along with four hundred Essex neighbors, she attended the coming out party for Lady Warwick's granddaughter, Felice Greville. The formal engraved invitations directed guests to "dress as you please" for the "merry party" in the floodlighted gardens at Easton Lodge. There would be tea and cocktails, a garden theater, dancing on the lawns, and supper, all to the accompaniment of music played by those royal favorites, the Coldstream Guards.

This was the Coronation Year. It seems fitting that Eulabee Dix, an American painter of London's celebrated beauties, should be present at a last rite for remnants of the old Edwardian court just as the new, and short-lived, Edwardian court was about to sound the death knell for it all.

In September, the Garden Club of London showed twenty of her new rose paintings in Mayfair, and gave a dinner at which Peter Cresswell of the BBC spoke on "The Rose in Art." Eulabee returned to New York with fifty-two canvases and a small profit.

The years-old connections with New York City galleries still worked for her. Immediately, she mounted a show called "Roses of England and Roses of France" at the Marie Sterner gallery. From the beginning of the "rose period," critics had noted her capacity to move between miniatures and large floral paintings without sacrifice. One of the paintings fetched $350. When she exhibited again, at the Grand Central Art Galleries in March of 1937, visitors were treated to a lavish display of horticultural art. Eulabee's joyful palette had produced dozens of specimen and prize-winning roses, many titled according to their famous namesakes—such as Queen Alexandra, Elizabeth Arden, and Earl Kitchener—as well as splashy portraits of anemones, pansies, daisies, and peonies.

There were other exhibits, at the Arts Club in Washington, D.C.; the Telfair Gallery in Savannah, Georgia; the Mint Museum in Charlotte, North Carolina; and the Delphic Studios in upstate New York. Usually she placed a few miniatures among the flower paintings in effective juxtaposition. Knowing her fine reputation as a miniaturist, one critic looked at the flowers and decided that "Remarkable as it may seem, [she] has so handled this somewhat hackneyed subject that she has given it new character and meaning."

The year 1939 produced an interesting "table portrait" in which a languorously slouching model dangles a slipper from one foot seductively extended from under her long gown. Some viewers speculate that *Idle Hours* depicted repressed sexuality on the part of the artist. Late that year, Eulabee entered *My Children*, the portrait of Dix and Joan painted in Cannes, in the Pennsylvania Society of Miniature Painters exhibition, where it won the Howard Tracy Fisher Memorial Prize. Much as it meant to her, the award was overshadowed by an unthinkable development at home. Joan finally had found the courage to sever the umbilical cord.

For several months she had been dating David Gaines, a young CBS sound effects specialist who was fascinated by the theater. Visiting Joan, he was bound to meet Eulabee, and Eulabee was theater. "The way she dressed—tight bodice, collar, hair swept up, long skirts. The apartment so wonderful, Bohemian. Just a fascinating world. So elegant. I knew all about East Fifty-seventh but here was something different."[9]

As he saw more of Joan, David came to the conclusion that everything about her, even her beautiful clothes, was her mother, and that it was suffocating a talented, warm-hearted, and frightened young woman. He urged her to get an apartment of her own. The decision to do it came only after the morning mantra, "You'll never be able to get through a day without me," at last sparked Joan's sublimated anger into a frightful explosion. A grim silence between them lasted for three months. Joan rented an apartment on Sixty-second Street and

Idle Hours, 1939, 6¾ x 4¾ in.
The National Museum of Women in the Arts
Gift of Mrs. Philip Dix Becker and Family

Madison, and at the age of twenty-five tried to move out of her mother's life.

Eulabee raged, but she couldn't prevent the move. So she did the next best thing and ordered a truckload of auction house furniture delivered to Joan, quickly following it in to decorate the apartment. "I think she couldn't bear the idea of my living in a place that wasn't beautiful," Joan wrote. "So she took over and I sat there and let it happen. I felt empty and she was going to fill me up, which she always had."[10] Nevertheless, Joan had taken the important first step toward controlling her own life, albeit at the price of an inevitable estrangement.

Eulabee never fully accepted Joan's declaration of independence. She already had lost her son. In 1937, Dix had married a Charleston, South Carolina, girl and was raising a family in Hingham, Massachusetts. When his mother came to visit, Dix usually ignored her. His wife, Mildred, played the gracious hostess even as her mother-in-law reminded her that Dix had not married well.

Now Eulabee's daughter was moving out of the maternal orbit, too. Nothing was left for her but art. She was sixty-two years old, still attractive, her faculties undiminished. But she had been working hard and felt ill, her system poisoned by fumes from the gas-fired steam radiator that had replaced the old pot-bellied stove in the apartment. When Florence Dickey, a Southern California acquaintance through Garden Club of America connections, invited Eulabee to spend a month at her ranch in the Ojai Valley, she accepted. A change of scenery was just what she needed. Eulabee sublet the apartment and left for the West Coast and a nice vacation in an exotic place she had never seen. "A new world!" she predicted, little knowing that five years would pass before she was to set foot in New York again.

CHAPTER 15

California

1941–1945

Beautiful, enchanting California! Could I leave its flowers, its sunshine, desert, snow-capped mountains and climate, to look at the East, then return and possibly remain?

FROM THE MOMENT she stepped through the stuccoed Spanish archways of the Los Angeles railway station, Eulabee was enchanted by California. It seemed indeed a new world, the perfect *mise-en-scène*, the way things ought to be everywhere.

> My hostess met me at eight, and we breakfasted under blooming trees on the landscaped sixth floor terrace of her club, then drove far down the shore of the Pacific, past the forest of oil well structures, to purchase water lilies for her Japanese garden. Then we were off for miles and miles of driving to her mountainside ranch in the Ojai Valley. Here sophistication—roses, lilies, pots of flowers, great and small trees, shrubs, all in profusion. Swimming pool with guest house. Orange blossom-scented sunshine. Paradise after New York!

She well may have thought she had come to Paradise. Twin Peaks Ranch, built in the 1920s by geologist Donald Dickey and his wife, was a famous estate in Ventura County's Ojai Valley east of Santa Bar-

(left) Detail of image on page 252.

bara. Dickey had attended the nearby Thacher School and went on to work for the U. S. Geological Survey. He returned to Ojai, where he acquired a citrus grove and built an elegant complex surrounding a historic Spanish Colonial Revival house at the edge of Los Padres National Forest.

Thus amid trappings of wealth, where she was never destined to linger for very long, began one of the more curious interludes in Eulabee's life. Her aimless five years on the West Coast appear in the memoirs as selective and disjointed recollections. Yet they convey her unique resilience and resourcefulness, as well as her constancy to art, despite all. An implicit consent to the benign lunacy sometimes encountered in those Southern California environs also informs the memoirs.

That she may have taken on some of that coloration herself is indicated in a page-long discussion of an encounter with a friendly housefly, probably recorded in a lonely moment. Consider, too, her undertaking to immortalize on canvas the doorway gardens of famous motion picture stars' homes. Clearly, though, the palette is fading into a pale wash of color laid on courage.

Eulabee most likely detrained in Los Angeles sometime in the spring of 1941. She must have remained at Twin Peaks Ranch for several weeks, content to stay there alone when her hosts went off to attend to the family gold mines. That was the circumstance in which Sally Dix, the only daughter of Eulabee's brother, and her new husband, L. William Lisle, found her in April. On their wedding trip from Grand Rapids to Pasadena, they stopped for lunch at Thacher, Bill Lisle's prep school alma mater. Twin Peaks Ranch, it turned out, was practically next door, and Eulabee invited them to spend the night in the guest house. The Lisles could hardly forget their noisy departure next morning, when an unexpected clatter arose from empty tin cans tied to the rear bumper of the newlyweds' car.[1] This was Bill Lisle's introduction to his bride's famously eccentric aunt.

Eulabee "sang" for her suppers in Ojai. On April 28, she gave her illustrated *Red Paint and Butterflies* lecture as a benefit for the Ojai Art Center. The occasion rated no fewer than three successive news stories in *The Ojai,* noting her prominence in the art world as well as her presence as the Dickey's houseguest at Twin Peaks Ranch.[2] As far as Eulabee was concerned, that kind of publicity was as good as a lecture fee.

The salubrious combination of sunshine and admiring new friends impelled her to find some way to extend the visit under more fixed circumstances. "A month of rest, drives and parties brought the longing to paint flowers and not be a guest." Florence Dickey thought an exhibition would be in order, and to that end she dispatched Eulabee to Pasadena with the family chauffeur and an introduction to the Grace Nicholson Galleries.

Miss Nicholson immediately reserved two galleries for a May showing and Eulabee sent to New York for a group of floral paintings to hang with the miniatures she had brought with her.

Arthur Millier, the art critic at the *Los Angeles Times,* urged his substantial following to see the show; they did, although neither sales nor portrait commissions came of it. However, an invitation to exhibit at the Ebell Club in Los Angeles the following November followed the initial exposure. Her work was being seen.

Eulabee always was susceptible to advice, and she got a lot of it as she sought footing in the Los Angeles art community. Her friends said she would need at least three exhibitions to get known. If she had her own studio, people would flock to it, her friends said. And they all seemed eager to help. She had charmed them.

> We whirled through Los Angeles looking for studios. Through endless streets; thousands of houses; glare of sunlight. A dazzling confusion, while I thought of dingy squeezed-in cubbyholes in Paris where one could create.

As much as the social climber in Eulabee Dix enjoyed moving in the best circles, California's "dazzling confusion" was taking its toll on the artist in her. She was feeling a growing sense of dislocation. When at last she asked to be taken somewhere to be quiet for awhile, a well-connected friend knew just the place. In the hills above La Crescenta, north of Los Angeles, Eulabee found her refuge as a guest at the Ananda Ashrama.

The community was founded in 1923 by Swami Paramananda, a Ramakrishna monk who brought the East Indian teachings of Vedanta to the United States. After establishing an East Coast center in Boston, he moved West and gained a substantial following among Southern Californians. After the Swami died in 1940, his disciples, struggling to retain the ashram's identity with its founder, withdrew from the parent order over matters of his successor. Ananda Ashrama still functions as an independent religious community, where workers and worshippers live monastic or family lives according to the Swami's teachings.

It was that ancient teaching from India with its tolerance for all religions, that captured Eulabee's imagination as she read for the first time the writings of Vedanta:

"May He who is Jehovah of the Jews, Father in Heaven of the Christians, Allah of the Mohammedans, Buddha of the Buddhists, Ahura Mazda of the Zoroastrians, and Divine Mother and Brahman of the Hindus, grant unto all peace and blessing. Peace! Peace! Peace be unto us and to all living beings!"[3]

> Here was something of which I had never dreamed. The ashram was set in groves of orange, grapefruit, and lemon trees, through which a dirt road wound past small houses to a library, and on a rocky platform, a beautiful chapel. Beyond the chapel a spacious building with assembly room, dining room, kitchen, and cloisters enclosing a rose garden, a beautiful retreat from the world. Chapel twice a day and books such as I had never read. . . . The simple, faithful life of the ashram

> with its inspiring books and cultivated people was ideal. I longed to remain there to the end of my days and wondered why I had arrived at a mountainside in California to discover ideas older than Christianity by thousands of years, which should have been part of my knowledge long before.

Never firmly grounded in any philosophical or religious conviction (although she thought she was), Eulabee was an undiscriminating intellectual sponge. Vedanta seemed familiar to her, with its superficial resemblance to the oneness of God and man she knew from other religious readings undertaken over the years. What was vastly unlike former experiences was the overt mysticism, the chanting, the symbolism, the unworldliness; it appealed to her sense of theater. Nor in the past had she ever given herself time for uninterrupted quiet, to read and to meditate.

As it turned out, even the possibilities of acquiring the gifts of karma were unable to keep her there. If she entertained any appetite of the flesh, it was a liking for good food, which she had learned abroad and was quite capable of preparing, however simply. To her dismay, the ashram's transitional problems took their toll on the cuisine, which in turn took its toll on Eulabee's spiritual resolve.

> It was a rare period. Unfortunately, at that time, the sister in charge of the guest house, where we were only three, was old and not interested in food. My lofty desires to remain were discouraged by hunger. Soon all I could think of was a lamb chop, or a ham sandwich, and I began to wonder how I could get back to the world.

She was rescued by a visiting luncheon guest, an artist's widow, who invited her to stay at her home until she could find her way back to the world.

> I regretted that I was such a mundane creature, with little

spiritual training. That dear old sister could probably live on ten grains of rice a day. There, I learned of humility, a humility of grace and dignity and service, of God who knew no evil.

This experience in the ashram, although apparently brief, was a major element in the gentling process that Eulabee, now in her sixties, underwent in California. The new discipline shortly was to be reinforced by the onset of World War II.

Suddenly now, just as Eulabee is telling us that she has departed the ashram and her new friend is helping her search for a studio, the trail simply vanishes. It reappears only because Sally and Bill Lisle remember that they were with her on December 7, 1941, listening to radio reports of the bombing at Pearl Harbor.[4] Joan was on a train en route to California to visit her mother and would arrive the next day. Eulabee doesn't tell us about it, but they do; all three agree that she was living in a bungalow "somewhere in Los Angeles."[5]

Joan's visit just as the war was beginning offers some insight into the order of Eulabee's California sojourn.

Their relationship had not been improved by Joan's hard-won emancipation, and Eulabee was still seeing to her daughter's education. Joan, between jobs at the time, dutifully traipsed around Los Angeles to look at what her mother considered important attractions. There was a revival meeting led by the colorful and popular evangelist, Amy Semple McPherson, and a short trip to San Francisco. Best of all, Joan met a famous movie star.

Margaret Sullavan, then married to the prominent Hollywood agent Leland Hayward, was the first motion picture actress Eulabee met in Los Angeles, although she doesn't say how that came about. In any case, Miss Sullavan commissioned the artist to paint miniature portraits of her three young children, Brooke, Bridget, and Bill, at their home in the Hollywood hills. Joan's own upbringing, which was nearly as chaotic as the movie capital's highly public family, made her an observant guest as they lunched poolside with the Haywards.

Bridget, Bill, and Brooke Hayward, 1941
Photograph of original miniatures presumed lost in Bel Air fire.
LRC Archives at The National Museum of Women in the Arts

> On my one trip to L.A. I was invited to lunch to be introduced to this splendid movie actress at her home. She was from the South, loved miniatures, and said she would keep Eulabee busy for years painting the family. I was impressed by the fact that the children and their nurse lived in a separate house where almost everything was child-size. "What a superb idea!" I thought. "The perfect way to make for a successful marriage!" Soon after, Margaret Sullavan and Leland Hayward were divorced, and he married a series of other women. . . . One of the daughters committed suicide. The other, Brooke Hayward, wrote a book called *Haywire* about her life and her mother. . . . It appears that Margaret Sullavan, also, was torn between domesticity and her artistic career.[6]

The original portraits of the Hayward children have disappeared, which is unfortunate because they were Eulabee's only commissioned work in California. Brooke Hayward, who married the music impresario, Peter Duchin, was too young to remember much about the sessions except that her mother cherished the miniatures. Nor does she know what happened to them. They may have been lost in the Bel Air fire that burned the actress's home in 1961.[7] Aside from one set of black and white photographs of the miniatures, the only other confirming memento of the commission is a small sterling silver frame that holds photographs of the three Hayward children. The actress had it engraved with an inscription thanking Eulabee for her work.

On her way back to New York early in February, Joan stopped off in St. Louis to see David Gaines, who had enlisted in the Army Air Corps after Pearl Harbor but was on hold in a military hospital recovering from pneumonia. In June, he proposed to Joan. They were married on July 29, 1942, in an Army chapel at Belleville, Illinois. Neither of them remembered if they told Eulabee of their plans.

The war separated the family for nearly four years. Dix, whose bad eyesight kept him out of the military, but whose naval architectural skills were important to the government, spent the war years working for Bethlehem Steel at the Fore River Shipyard in Quincy, Massachusetts.

World War II literally trapped Eulabee in Los Angeles. This exigency she took in stride with the pragmatism that had cushioned past vicissitudes. After Joan left, she had to decide what to do.

> Back to New York? But why worry the railroads with a lot of pictures? Better to stay and get a war job. I applied at the United States Employment Bureau, stood in line there and heard the man sending people away who were over forty-five. I was sixty-three. Soon I was told of a place that needed help badly, the Jean Le Seueux Company, manufacturers of modern apparel ornaments. I had never in my life gone out to work so it seemed a good idea to try the eight-hour day. Possibly I could make something out of it.

She gamely tried, but one month of making frivolous ornaments for ladies apparel was enough. As soon as Eulabee learned that the government employment bureau had relaxed its age restrictions, she went back and registered. "Artist, miniature painter. Writing it down thinking I might as well have put 'Fool.'" The application led to a call from the Plas-Tex Corporation to paint radium on small airplane parts.

This was *real* war work. But before long her mouth began to feel "puckery"; she and the other employees, all of whom showed glowing radium specks on their fingers under purple light, were let go. "You're allergic," they said. Although no apparent lasting effects resulted, her brush with radioactive material was serious enough to provide a small Social Security disability pension. It was almost the only regular income Eulabee received in her last years.

She applied for a job at every war plant within reach of the sprawling Los Angeles bus system. Tired of hearing that she was too old for war work, she sent to Illinois for her birth certificate and hoped that perhaps she wasn't sixty-three, after all. It was discouraging business. One employment office deemed her too refined. Lockheed needed women to work inside airplanes, but the personnel office told Eulabee she couldn't climb ladders. "They should have *seen* me climb ladders!" she fumed. "'My country 'tis of Thee, be mine; I want to be thine' I sang and searched for a job."

When patriotism gave way to hunger, Eulabee swallowed whatever pride she had left and asked for a job ironing in a commercial laundry. The proprietor, so desperate for help he was thinking of closing the business, gladly took her on.

> I went at nine and was given an ironing board and an iron. There were two other women and a man. I ironed and ironed; hot work, hot weather. The man relieved me by letting me shake out damp clean clothes from big bags. Again I would iron, doing forty-two napkins an hour; I could never be slow. The laundryman was grateful, but by the third day was sure that soon I'd be nothing but a glistening drop of moisture.

When the birth certificate arrived verifying that she was sixty-three, Eulabee, the forever elegant, clothes-conscious sexagenarian painter of miniatures, climbed into a pair of blue jeans and presented herself at the Beverly-Holly Machine Works a block away from where she was living. She had been there once before; this time, without even asking to see the birth certificate, they hired her. Eulabee joined the International Association of Machinists and stood at an electric lathe to drill holes in large aluminum airplane parts. Intrigued by her unlikely new role in the blue-collar world, she attended union meetings, and at work fell into "rhythm with the sound and movement of the machine, so quick, so dangerous. It was wonderful, but I was sure there must be more delicate work for my experienced fingers and eyes."

There was. The nearby Mitchell Camera Company had government orders for small cameras and airplane parts, and they could use her special skills.

> I began with tripods, then advanced to magazines, the part outside the camera in which the film is wound. These had ball-bearing pulleys, on which there was much careful work. Several hundred were completed and did not operate properly. Three of us were given the job of doing them over. Again they did not buzz and whirl as they should. "Let me take them to the window," I said. "I will work out the difficulty." I completed a box of fifty and took them to the boss. He picked one up and twirled it. "Perfect." I insisted that he try each one. "Perfect. Perfect."

Later she was transferred to a job better suited to her skills at miniaturization. The fine inner parts of the cameras had to be fitted, taken out, adjusted, cleaned, packed, and repacked for final delivery. When she wasn't doing that, there were screw tops to polish, which she found to be a hugely amusing challenge.

> A box looked like a million. Surely it would take a year, but by patiently keeping on they were done and I took the box to my boss. "Here they are—nine thousand nine hundred and nine-ty-nine. One dropped down a crack." Of course I had not counted them. He took the box and did not smile. For the first time in my life I was working as just another person amongst others, not someone apart as an artist, but "pin-up grandma" to old men and young girls and everyone seemed so nice. Little conversation went on during work, but I was thrilled with a new world of pictures and sounds.

Eulabee took the "pin-up" appellation seriously enough to have herself photographed in a swim suit, a small conceit this particular grandmother might be forgiven under the circumstances.

Going out to work alongside others for the first time in her life, Eulabee had good reason to be proud of her contribution to the country at war. Yet, she offers not a single clue as to how long she worked for the Mitchell Camera Company. Several references to her age indicate that she began to work before her sixty-fourth birthday in October of 1942.

And what of art? When and what or whom did she paint? What was the circumference of her being during five years in exile from the only life she had known for six decades? In 1941 and early 1942, she was working on the three commissioned miniatures of the Hayward children. She tells us, too, that Mr. and Mrs. Frederick Walter of the Southern California Rose Society supplied her with flowers from their garden and that, "It was painting time again. Roses . . . roses." In all likelihood this was just before Pearl Harbor upended the lives of most Americans. It was difficult enough for well-settled households to get along, and it must have been an even greater challenge for a newcomer who was alone, older, and had practically no income. Fortunately, the oil paintings sold well and Eulabee was invited to lecture for the society.[8]

Eulabee's artistic path re-emerges briefly in December 1942, with an announcement that appeared alongside a feature story about a Sunset Boulevard exhibition of paintings, prints, and sculpture by employees of the six Los Angeles area aircraft plants. She might have participated had Lockheed deemed her able to climb in and out of airplanes. In any event, she had her own show, which was reviewed by Arthur Millier under the headline "Filmland Home Doors Pictured." The exhibition at the Allotria was one of the artist's most venturesome, certainly innovative, attempts to promote her work.

> I had an idea, through a tea party at Mrs. Jesse Lasky's house, of painting doorways of homes of the movie stars, their style, flowers, and landscaping most attractive. Completing a series of these, which never sold and are some of my best work, I had some pleasant adventures.

Eulabee painted at the homes of eighteen motion picture stars. Carrying a portable stool and her paintbox, she would find the house, knock on the door to obtain permission, and sit down to work in oil on board. In these paintings, the entrances seem to reflect their famous owners' personalities.[9]

The list is impressive even by Hollywood's outsized standards: Joan Bennett; William Powell; Claudette Colbert; Jack Carson; Ann Sothern; Gracie Allen and George Burns; Michelle Morgan; Jesse Lasky; Caesar Romero; Bob Hope; Shirley Temple; Hedda Hopper; Barbara Stanwyck and Robert Taylor; George Cukor; Basil Rathbone; Irene Dunn; Joan Fontaine; Brian Ahearn; Joan Crawford.

Millier wrote that the twelve pictures shown were "small and intimate, and each is strikingly individual. While there is much architectural variety, it is Miss Dix's choice of the right lighting and her perception of the important part that planting plays in these typically Southern California entryways, plus her lively and tasteful painting, that give these pictures charm and distinction."

In light of the complimentary review by the well-regarded critic for the *Los Angeles Times,* it is surprising that none of the paintings sold. Few of the occupants even bothered to meet the artist. One exception was Brian Ahearn, who came down from a balcony to talk theater with Eulabee while she worked.

The review stated that the project occupied most of the summer of 1942. Eulabee's remaining three years in California are virtually non-existent in her chronology. An undated printed brochure indicates that at some point she moved into a storefront studio at 511 North Robertson Boulevard in Hollywood. To judge by a packet of exterior and interior photographs, it was a tiny space fronting the street behind store windows framed by a white brick facade, another one of her trademark "poet's pocket" studio-homes. The brochure copy is quintessential Dix promotion:

EULABEE DIX

Internationally Known Painter

HER ARTS and GALLERY

511 North Robertson Blvd. Hollywood

INVITES YOU

Admission With Tea

25 Cents

Each Afternoon Mornings by Appointment

MINIATURES

PORTRAIT DRAWINGS

FLOWER PICTURES

DOORWAYS to the MOVIE STARS

Telephone: CR 6-3083

It would be comfortable, if not necessarily accurate, to conclude that Eulabee had saved enough money from working in the camera factory to return to art for her living. One of the pictures in the studio

Shirley Temple's Doorway, ca. 1941
Oil on canvas 16 x 20 in.
Courtesy of Peter Becker

Brian Ahearn's Doorway, ca. 1941
Oil on canvas, 16 x 20 in.
Courtesy of Peter Becker

folio shows Eulabee wearing a raincoat with an identification badge that hints of war work. We know only that she kept painting. In 1943, she took first prize in the miniature division of an exhibition sponsored by the California Art Club at Exposition Park in Los Angeles. The celebrity doorway paintings remain in the Dix family; otherwise only three funny little mementos of Hollywood are to be found in the Dix collection at the National Museum of Women in the Arts. One of them is a portrait of evangelist Amy Semple McPherson, which Eulabee probably painted from memory after attending a revival meeting. The others are two miniatures of Edgar Bergen's famous dummy, Charlie McCarthy; one is about the size of a dime. Did Eulabee actually hope to gain the patronage of Edgar Bergen, who was among the most popular entertainers of the early forties? We shall never know. So, with no other guide to the years between 1942 and 1945, and with

Eulabee in studio-gallery, Hollywood. Celebrity door paintings in background.
On her raincoat is a war worker's identification badge.
LRC Archives at The National Museum of Women in the Arts

Eulabee's studio-gallery home at 511 North Robertson
Hollywood, California, 1942
LRC Archives at The National Museum of Women in the Arts

Charlie McCarthy, ca. 1943
½ x ½ in.
The National Museum of Women in the Arts
Gift of Joan Becker Gaines

family recollections equally vague, Eulabee's trail finally scatters into a rough mosaic of unrelated anecdotes. "Going about Hollywood and Los Angeles one meets people and life stories; anything can happen in Southern California and everything does." The examples she provided border on the bizarre and certainly confirm the truth of that unoriginal observation.

She had a gentleman friend, a retired actor with ambitions of becoming a painter, who sold his piano for money to take Eulabee to dinner. At a meeting of the California Miniature Society she talked to a woman who had walked across the United States with her widowed sister and 12-year-old nephew, armed only with a pistol and a letter of introduction from the mayor of New York City. While shopping in downtown Los Angeles, she spotted elderly twin sisters identically dressed like baby dolls in blue and white checked bouffant dresses with matching hats perched on their gray curls. She wanted to paint them, but they were horrified at the notion and refused. They would have to meet their Saviour some day, and being painted, or going into the wicked movies as they had once had a chance to do, was not permitted. They fled, trotting up the hill, she said, "toward heaven."

The last of these "people" anecdotes is about the dancer Ruth St. Denis, who may have connected with Eulabee through the Ananda Ashrama where St. Denis had been a "celebrity guest."[10]

> Often I walked up the hill to Ruth St. Denis's studio on the Sunset Strip, five long blocks, all up hill and not a stop to take a breathing spell. But I could not lie on the floor, like Miss Ruth, or do the graceful stunts she could, although I tried several times. . . . The studio was in front of her house, with a black linoleum floor, mirrored walls, grand piano. One day I arrived when she was giving a private lesson, her head wound in a towel and over her pink panties a piece of old batik. In her hand was a broom, broom up, directing her pupil, lovely as ever, grace and beauty in every movement. I must paint her, so she sat for me as Radha, a Burmese temple goddess, elaborate headgear, gold jeweled bodice, voluminous skirt.

Radha was the subject of one of her important dances. St. Denis was in her sixties, exactly Eulabee's age. She was waiting for Hollywood to acknowledge her place in the dance world after her separation from husband and dance partner, Ted Shawn, and hoped there would be a part for her in the movies. The miniature, not one of Eulabee's better efforts, is an unwitting reflection of the unfulfilled hopes of two talented but aging artists.

It may seem silly to read into her recorded encounter with *Musca domestica* more than an eccentric discursive ramble, and in fact it was excised from the family-edited memoirs along with the other episodes perceived as déclassé. Without apology, however, it is offered here as a clue to her elusive character.

> Weekends, after the noisy whiz of the factory, silence hushed about me. . . . On a Saturday morning, breakfasting in silence, a fly buzzed over my head. "Company?" and I considered it. "Buzz," it said, flew on and came back to my saucer. . . . The day was hot, lazy in suggestion, but the fly was full of action and inspection. As I moved about it buzzed a cheerful song, and followed me while putting order, lighting on a long-

> neglected spot. Cleaning! A good idea, and I was pleased and busy. While I was sewing, the fly buzzed over and about me. It rested on my hand, its legs touched and retouched with seeming consideration. The head, pivoted on the smallest possible neck, moved rapidly in contemplation of my flesh, then off it flew. All about nothing, it seemed, yet with apparent intention. Was it seeking food or seeking facts about man. Constant action! Not an instant was it still. Its legs, head, its wings of thinnest film and iridescent design. What was the purpose of this busy creature? I looked for my fly on Sunday morning. It was with me again at breakfast and seemed to say with cheerful buzz, "Good morning!" While I was reading, it traversed the pages of my book. When I was primping before the looking-glass, the fly promenaded over the surface of the mirror. I saw the perfection of its body from beneath, legs moving, moving as if watchful of light and shade. It rested on some flowers. Could it know their scent and color? Carefully it touched their tender surface. A polite fly. It did not "stick" or annoy me. At my door, the screen open, my fly was gone. A little fly. I thought of God.

V-E Day, spring, 1945, the door opened and Eulabee, too, was gone. She had loved California, and even thought about coming back. But she didn't. New York was home.

CHAPTER 16

Under the "El"

1945–1956

The enchantment of California faded after being in New York a few days. At every turn I seem to be invited back by pleasant memories. I had seen fifty years of the city's growth, and belonged here.

NOBODY WAS THERE to welcome Eulabee Dix back to New York City in that spring of 1945. Joan, already seeing her first psychiatrist, had begun to worry about her mother's return as early as February, and was dreading it.[1] Dix was busy in Massachusetts. Old friends could expect further impositions on their forbearance. Three times, now, she had left, and three times returned to beseech help in re-establishing herself. The pattern, people drifting away as relationships soured, her intriguing personality attracting new ones, was bound to be repeated.

Perhaps pleasant memories alone were sufficient welcome. Eulabee always rejoiced in the evolving cityscape she loved.

> Changed from a brown city to grey, New York had grown taller and towered into the sky, now the great metropolis, port, and workshop of the world. What other city has New York's dynamic magic? It gives inspiration and a gladness to be back in its stirring activity, beauty, fashion, crowds, and towers. Those startling towering masses casting their shadows high and at dusk their lighted windows, jewels in lacy screens against the clear sapphire sky, fairyland at the end of another day.

The war may have been over, but not the housing shortage in the great metropolis. Eulabee rented a room in a friend's apartment and spent three months searching the city for a studio she could afford to rent. Finally, she found it on the East Side, under the rattling Third Avenue elevated railroad.

> Third, with all its saloons, pawnshops, second-hand stores, Chinese laundries and food shops, as far down as the Bowery. The block between 94th and 95th had still the air of old upper Third where children grew to be policemen and thrifty citizens. There a dingy little store with a For Rent sign stood before us—a curiosity. All evening, all night, I saw that sign and returned to it next morning. A young German woman unpadlocked the door, explaining that the place had been vacant some time; they were particular about who took it.

The conversation about being in the beauty business took place in that unpromising little storefront at 1690 Third Avenue. "You could live here," the young German woman told her. "There's a stove, bath tub; lots of hot water and heat." The last tenants had run a laundry.

How small it was! Only nine by eighteen feet, with a high ceiling and ornate old gas fixtures. Behind it, like a railroad flat, were two small rooms, the alcove where she would sleep, and a larger one at the back, with a window looking into a tiny concrete courtyard. That would be the kitchen, dining room, and bathroom with the traditional tenement tub. She would share the toilet with the next door delicatessen and thrift shops. "Bless me, what a place—an amazing idea—life in a store!"

She took it, thinking the situation temporary until quarters more suitable to her profession were located. Far from being discouraged by what lay ahead, Eulabee, at sixty-seven, tackled the transformation with her usual zeal for turning ugliness into beauty.

> The landlord had the walls painted light grey. The studio-

> gallery, pale sea blue, like the satin upholstery of my Louis XVI day bed. Furnishings came out of storage. It was fun to arrange them, to make a store on slummy Third look nice, even though I were to stay but a short time. I could put shelves where needed. Climbed ladders, hammered nails, hung pictures, dyed white muslin sheets grey for drapes. Then came the biggest problem: the old worn brown oilcloth left on kitchen-bathroom-dining-room floor by former tenants. Why buy new if not staying long? I marked off and painted a checked floor in white and tile red enamel, which with clean windows produced an entirely new and interesting effect. A Vermeer interior, giving light and joy to the whole place.

Gold leaf letters on the door announced her return to the art business in what she was first to admit was an unlikely venue. It is especially unlikely that her shopkeeper neighbors knew anything about miniature painting, nor about artists who did it.

Anybody with evil intent could walk in off the street by breaking the glass in the front door, and on the first night someone did. She installed a doorbell that rang as long as the door stood open, and engaged a detective service to keep watch at night. It didn't happen again.

Eulabee was quite alone now. Joan was in New York but they were virtually estranged. Whatever filial affection that Dix, in Hingham, could muster was reserved for his father. When his and Mildred's first child was born in 1940, Alfred wrote, "I wish the enclosed check many times as large. While your mother won't believe it, 'tis true that we have just barely enough to live on." A postscript from his wife expressed the same regret.[2] Other letters to Dix reveal not the cold, undemonstrative man of their childhood, but a caring father who offered gentle advice and sent "grandfather's kisses" to the three children.

Alfred was welcome in Dix's home but not often could he afford the trip to Massachusetts. He conducted a modest law practice in the Lincoln Building on East Forty-second Street, his once-brilliant reputation eroded by bad publicity during the divorce proceedings and bad judgment in the long-ago Philip Musica affair. In his last years, Alfred devoted most of his time to genealogical research and traced the Becker and LeRoy lineages back to their Colonial beginnings. For his son's sake he looked into the Virginia and Kentucky Dixes, but showed an understandable lack of interest, giving short shrift to his documentation.

David was overseas and Joan had gone to Grand Rapids in 1943 to await the birth of her first child at her uncle's home, now empty of its own young as two sons went off to war and their sister married. The prominent occupants of the fine old three-story house at 540 Cherry Street represented to Grand Rapids society a stability Joan had never known in her own family. Yet, behind its hospitable facade she felt an almost Gothic undercurrent in the household. Uncle Phil was preoccupied with dosing chronic ulcers with cream and criticizing fellow executives at the American Boxboard Company. Aunt Helen, warm and compassionate, acted as surrogate mother for Joan during her lonely pregnancy, but suffered undiagnosed blackouts that Joan guessed were reactive flights from her husband's difficult nature. Joan, brought up to be the perfect houseguest, was a compliant niece who provided welcome companionship for Helen; and she was grateful for their care during a difficult wartime situation.[3] After her daughter, Valerie, was born, she returned to New York and waited for David to come home.

Joan's husband did not possess a title, but he came of good stock and Eulabee approved of him. Nevertheless, upon learning that Joan was expecting, she had railed, "How could you want to have a baby, knowing how unhappy my life has been!" It was an irrational and hurtful thing to say, and was at variance with Eulabee's earlier thoughtfulness when David went overseas. She painted a miniature of Joan and encased it in a khaki frame to fit into the breast pocket of his uniform. Although David got on well with Eulabee and appreciated her gestures, he later conceded that he never fully realized the depth of the problems his mother-in-law had inflicted on his wife.[4]

As she merged gradually into upper Third Avenue's melting pot, Eulabee soon forgot that she didn't intend to stay for long. The struggle to keep going in California, the ashram's influence, and the war years already had buffed some of the hard edges of her temperament; now, new challenges chipped away at old snobbishness.

> Possibly the very oddity of this place gave me a sense of being removed from the world, and within my own inner security . . . the people. Weary men, and buxom women, the children. The ice man so cheerful and willing. My impersonal personal neighbors. Soon I threw my worldly pride away. . . . What does it matter where one lives. It is what one thinks. Often people ask "Aren't you afraid to live here?" Perhaps I should be. A strange abode . . . a cave . . . so dark a bulb is always lighted. Here, separated and alone, I could be murdered. Indeed my neighborhood supplies everything but an undertaker. Always a surprising delight to find all I wish to buy within a block or two. My grandson wanted a ship in a bottle. The brother of a nearby janitress, a sailor, made them at sea, sold them through her. Beautiful ones. Literature can be picked up off the street tables at the second hand store. A remarkable place with constant renewal of things. . . . It is Montmartre in New York.

Like a dislocated duchess, "the artist lady" became a neighborhood fixture, her creativity winning the affectionate respect of passers-by who stopped to look into the windows flanking her iron-grilled front door.

> For one window I picked up a beautiful old triptych: Madonna and Child protected by Saints George and Michael. In the other, a sweet madonna statue, some thirty inches high, which

> was left one day in the doorway. Soiled but sacred to a group of little children and I took her in and soon mended her hands and painted them. Then she had a wreath of flowers on her head and silver roses at her feet. Stopping to admire her, Kelly the trash man and street drunk said he found her in a rubbish can, thought that I would appreciate her. I wrapped the compliment round my heart.

In spring and summer there were tubs of red geraniums on either side of the doorway. The geraniums wintered in the back courtyard and over the years grew tall as trees, reaching for the railway overhead. "Old ladies and some men linger to wonder and inquire. I must stop painting to answer them."

At first, Eulabee wondered if friends and clients would come to such an unfashionable district. Would they still think it was fun to sit on a covered kitchen bathtub and drink tea? Joan saw that Eulabee simply had picked up where she had left off at the East 57th Street "tenement" five years earlier.

> She was satisfied to live in the storefront under the El because, now that she'd transformed her environment, it became for her a palace. She presided at tea parties in the back room, inviting the social register's "grand" people she had known in the old days. A Russian samovar heated water. "Will you have Indian or Chinese?" (With Indian tea, cream and sugar were served. Neither with Chinese tea.) There were little cakes. Eulabee would sit there "on stage" in some wonderful costume she'd made. She'd tell amusing stories, often about her frequent, outrageous adventures. She could be totally entertaining and people left with a sense of immersion in a make-believe world of magic."[5]

David returned from overseas in 1946 to greet a 2-year-old daughter he had never seen. Another daughter, Nonie, was born in 1947, and in 1949, a son, named John. Except for an unsuccessful portrait of Dix's youngest daughter, Lisa, Eulabee never painted her attractive grandchildren. She told Joan that she didn't consider them "paintable." The Gaines children retained a few indistinct memories of their grandmother, while distinct Janus-like aspects emerged from the memory of the Becker offspring, who had more opportunities to observe her mercurial temperament. Eulabee's genius, however, fell on all six of them in one way or another. Joan and David's daughter Nonie is an exhibiting artist and teacher, while their son John is a fine craftsman. Valerie is an educator. Both of Dix's daughters are involved in the arts, Ayala as an artist and teacher, and Lisa in marketing. Their brother, Peter, is an internationally recognized marine biologist.

Ayala Becker Talpai (christened Linda when she was born in 1940) was Eulabee's first grandchild. In appearance and as a gifted artist, she is most like her. But unlike Eulabee, she is sympathetic and forgiving, particularly of her grandmother's perplexing foibles.

When she was ten years old she was sent to visit Eulabee in New York. She slept on the antique blue divan in the gallery and played in the courtyard geranium forest with neighborhood children who didn't speak English. With this granddaughter there was a reenactment of the long-ago battle over hair ribbons that didn't match a pink sash.

> It was a windy, nasty biting cold and I had a navy blue coat and a straw hat with a bunch of flowers and a ribbon down the back and we were going to the zoo. She was afraid I was going to freeze to death. Grandma's solution to this was to bring out this old cloak and wind it around me. I felt like a walking mummy and objected fiercely. . . . It felt really weird. . . . It struck me later that it probably belonged to her grandfather, Benjamin B. Bartholomew. It was definitely not a garment I wished to be associated with. . . . We had a big struggle over this. I ended up not having to wear it.[6]

Although her profession as a working artist was nearing its end, Eulabee could not be idle. The New York press noted her return to the East Coast by publicizing the shows that opened the little gallery, taking special note of the Hollywood doorway paintings. She had Christmas exhibitions of "Floral Paintings and Custom Designed Dresses" and handbags. She held her "salons" and received occasional commissions to paint a miniature from a photograph. "How degrading to my art!" she complained, forgetting to be grateful. She always was ready to lecture about miniatures and exhibit when she had the opportunity. In 1952, she spoke on the history of miniature painting at the National Arts Club, and the following year showed two oils in a group exhibition there.

This is the time, and the place, where Eulabee began to write her memoirs. In their way, and for all their sallies into rearranged reality, they fashion as lustrous a record of her life as her paintings do.

> My store was like a cocoon, or was it my tomb, in which I learned to be from the inside out, to push beyond my cells . . . peepholes for my spirit. Painting with neatness and order about, daylight a precious thing. Or I write with disorder around, and midnight is good, so still, so undisturbed. New York asleep! Asleep akin to death. Who knows what happens? The world is closed. The soul hushed in consciousness. Perhaps it journeys for refreshment. Waking again, the all-about is here; the sun good, the wind fresh, the air pleasant, each day a gift.

Eulabee also had been thinking for a long time about incorporating her research and lectures on the history of miniature painting into a book. Before she went to California she wrote to Alice Beckington, a founder of the American Society of Miniature Painters, who responded with a brief history of the organization's beginnings. Now back in New York, she wrote to William J. Whittemore, her teacher at the Art Students League, and received a vigorous response.

> My dear Eulabee Dix: We were very glad to hear from you and

> know are alive and dynamic as ever. . . . We are interested in the new book and your point of attack. I am sending the best I can find in the way of prints. . . . The biographical notes are a poor thing, but my own. Reconstruct as you will. I looked it up in Who's Who anyway. The incredible age is 87, and I had it removed a dozen years ago for business reasons as I was still going strong. . . . Bless you, and let us have a word now and then.

Nothing came of the book project, although Eulabee prepared some essays on the subject, presumably for publication. Surely her book would have included Whittemore's optimistic observation, "The lovely art of the miniature will not die while prominent men have fair wives and beautiful children."

In 1948, the Gaineses moved to Minneapolis, where David was to establish a television school for post-war "GI Bill" training. The distancing, while fortuitous for Joan's battered psyche, undoubtedly gave Eulabee more to deal with than did her ex-husband's death in July of that year. "What makes you think I care?" she said when someone told her the news. She had hounded him for money almost to the end. Alfred Becker's obituary in the *New York Herald Tribune* was long enough and laudatory enough to make Dix, at least, proud of his father. Understandably, Joan reacted to his death with equal parts of sadness and guilt.

When Sam Dix moved from Grand Rapids to New York City to work for General Foods Corporation, Eulabee channeled her managerial instincts into furnishing her nephew's Brooklyn Heights apartment. Sam found her an entertaining companion who, far from dwelling on her past, expressed lively interest in what was going on in New York and the world in general. A bachelor *bon vivant* at the time, he escorted her about town and took her proprietary ways in stride. The two of them haunted antique shops and auction houses and walked away with splendid furniture and accessories, which Eulabee long ago had learned how to acquire for less than their true worth.

Thanks to her exquisite taste and his willingness to indulge it, when Sam married two years later he brought his bride to a splendidly furnished apartment. Eulabee liked Sam's wife and continued to see them both until they moved back to Grand Rapids. Why wasn't she as congenial with her own offspring?

"I never had any controversy with Eulabee," Sam said, "but always there was a shadow, battle with Joan, battle with Dix. Joan couldn't do anything right. Dix just gave up. I can't explain it."[7]

Nonetheless, living in the same town with his aunt had its challenges. One day she telephoned Sam's office and insisted that he be called out of an important meeting. "All she wanted was to tell me that I should read the *Bhagavad-Gita,*" Sam recalled with amusement. Only once did she severely try his patience. When he was out of town, Eulabee talked her way into the apartment and removed a painting he had bought from her, apparently unhappy with the way he had hung it.[8]

In 1950, Eulabee was "reminded by friends," she says, of an upcoming anniversary. She had been painting in New York for fifty years. Apparently not taking it too seriously herself, she shared a chuckle or two with Sam about the fuss, and decided to celebrate with a retrospective exhibition in the tiny studio-gallery.

> So all the little portraits came out from safe deposit, many invitations went out. Miniature Exhibition, Daily 2:00 to 6:00 P.M. The store became jewel-like; a big flower picture, pale pink, white and blue at the far end of the room; large miniatures in grey silk mats on the walls, two miniatures in handsome gold frames, some in shadow boxes, some in gold-bronze vitrine. Center fixtures lighted the art on the walls, antique lace fans shaded the table lights with miniatures behind them. My blue satin couch, rose-wood table, and good rugs helped the effect. A lot of people came and there were good press notices.

And not only in New York were there good press notices. The

Louisville Courier-Journal ran a lengthy piece in recognition of the artist's Kentucky background. Stories about her appeared as features, now, not on the art pages. Reporters were more interested in her life story than in the art and its unique setting. The miniatures did not elicit the rave reviews of her youth, she observed wryly.

As she moved into her seventies, Eulabee began to confront two dreaded demons: age and accidents. She broke her hip in a fall in a revolving door at Radio City Music Hall, which left her lame because she insisted on cutting off the cast before the bone had healed properly. Afterward she walked with a permanent list, even with the cane. A generous settlement from the insurance company eased the pain for a number of years. A second fall broke her right wrist. It was no more than an annoyance, Eulabee said, since she could paint with her left hand anyway, a fact she probably neglected to tell the insurance company when she claimed that her means of livelihood had been seriously impaired.

Worse yet, though, was the loneliness that blanketed her days. The anguished metaphysical exercises of her first Christmas away from home in 1899 echoed from the closing-in walls of the 1950s.

> I growing old, should, in my lonesome cocoon place, have grown dry and content. But no, I was active, doing, creating. A dress, a hat, some watercolor flowers . . . And then I would fly, then I would be lonesome, curse my fate here on Third in a store. Why was I not getting about more, dining, grand dinner parties with conversation, more people? I felt so young, so frisky . . . not living in Time but living in Eternity.

Loneliness and old age, however, could not staunch Eulabee's irrepressible creativity and her love of beautiful materials.

> I remembered yards of white satin bought at a sale, with a weave that made a dimply surface. I rushed to the trunk and to the near bottom of it. . . . It would make a dress for a party.

> . . . How I loved cutting into material, the more expensive the greater thrill. . . . A skirt full, six yards wide, longer in the back, trailing a bit, gathered at top, but not to be bulky . . . bodice tight, of course. . . . Around my bare shoulders a bias piece two and one half inches. I could always fit a back with my hand mirror. . . . Some lovely pearl buttons for the front . . . a bow of the satin for that tail of the basque. Oh, it was lovely! And when the last stitch was in, I folded it and put it in a big box.

For a year the dress haunted her dreams. Was it too glamorous? Was she too old for it? She called a young friend and asked her to invite her to dinner "for the sake of a dress. The friend liked the dress so much she called in others for drinks after dinner." It gave her courage to ask a "tall, dark, and handsome" man to take her to the opening of a John Singer Sargent exhibition at the Metropolitan Museum of Art.

> Sargent painted white satin so well. . . . The portraits were of my period in London and Paris. . . . We had only gotten well started in the galleries, when from behind me popped a man I knew. "Eulabee Dix! You are the most beautiful thing here!" "Eddie, how sweet of you! The bright lights are on the pictures . . . I'm pleasantly in the dark." "Just risk the light. You are beautiful!" "Thanks Eddie. Aren't the pictures wonderful?" And we parted. Of course I was thrilled, and then three other people told me I was beautiful . . . in the dark! Home again on Third Avenue. The dress in a box. Would I ever see it again?

Eulabee seemed consumed by her need for acceptance, real or illusory, wherever she found it. Her desperate loneliness was not new. Ten years earlier, one of the three Samuel brothers who owned French and Company was walking through the third-floor galleries late one afternoon and found Eulabee, dressed in an evening gown, sitting quietly among the French antiques. "I am so depressed I either have to commit suicide or get married!" she told him. He took her arm. "Come on, Eulabee, I'll take you out to dinner."[9] Why did she never record these acts of kindness? Possibly for the same reason she never recorded the time she sneaked into the same gallery to alter one of her paintings. She would have said "it never happened."

On paper, meanwhile, Eulabee once more pondered her relationship with God.

> After these periods of fluff and flurry I would drop into silent meditations and try to know the essence of my being. And the world's worldliness would fade away and the face of things would change. With all my movements, eventualities, and touching the bottom, long stretches of quiet produced the most searching, plunging moments. The most valuable . . . finding peace and understanding. "Be still and know that I am God.". . . God right here within me, and it is my business to be still, quiet, and shine Him out in manifest form, expressing harmony and beauty. This is the mission of an artist.

French and Company negotiated her last important portrait commission in 1951. Robert T. Keller, president of the Chrysler Corporation, who was active in Detroit art circles and the proud grandfather of twelve, came to Eulabee's studio to order a miniature of each grandchild to be painted from photographs. She accepted the commission, but was unable to finish it. Her eyesight was failing, her hands disobedient to the demands of delicate work. After the accident at Radio City she gave up, and delivered the seven miniatures she had completed.[10]

Eulabee held another retrospective showing in her studio in 1954, hoping to sell some of her collection. Again the newspapers paid homage, more to "Grandma Dix" at seventy-six than to her accomplishments.

Her old friend, Isaac Josephi, died that year at the age of ninety-four. Eulabee had kept in close touch until the end, often having dinner with him in the apartment where he spent his last days repainting old miniatures. Joan recalled an amusing episode in their long relationship. Josephi once telephoned and asked her to spend the night in his apartment. Eulabee had drunk too much wine at dinner and was unable to go home, but she wouldn't stay with him without a "chaperone."[11] She was in her sixties and Josephi well over seventy at the time.

When Joan came from Minneapolis for a short visit to New York, four years had passed since she had seen her mother. Unbidden, even resisted, the old magic reasserted itself when she went to have lunch with her.

> I arrived at her door around noon, rang a tinkly bell and Eulabee came to the door. . . . In the kitchen a small stove stood in the corner . . . there was a small icebox for which the iceman delivered a block of ice every few days. She rationalized that she'd lived in France long enough to know that "refrigeration spoiled the flavor of food." She was perfectly content without modern equipment of any kind. In the back room was the round rosewood table that had been in the family. As we talked, she laid out lunch. Green plates were put down, one for me and one for her. She laid a piece of celery on each plate. I'll never forget how beautiful it was. When I tell you that I had entered a world of magic, that's what it was. There was something fantastic about her arrangements, the whole wonderfully unique something.[12]

After lunch, one of Eulabee's new friends, a New York numerologist named Carla Patsuris, came to visit. Eulabee left them alone in the gallery while Patsuris pulled a crystal ball from a suede drawstring bag and proceeded to astound Joan with accurate details about her family. Patsuris's psychic powers perhaps derived in large part from what Eulabee had told her, but her talent as a poet was unquestionable. This portrayal of *malaise* prompts speculation that Patsuris might have written the poem for Eulabee.

MIRROR MIRROR ON THE WALL

How stark these mirror-mirror thoughts
Where dream worlds end in real debris
Behind the eyes of beauty's skull
With Truth the last catastrophe.

Exploring this reflection here
With more and more and more dismay
At alteration-ravagement,
Still wishing some divine delay,

Undone and faint I scrutinize
And brood with shattering appall
Then weep for every kind and kin
Who once was "fairest of them all."[13]

The tearing down of the Third Avenue El, built the year she was born (1878) and no longer useful in the city's transportation system, was a mid-Fifties paradigm for the end of Eulabee's twelve years on Third Avenue. She collected rivets from the wreckage outside her door, tied red ribbons around them, and gave them away as paper weights for Christmas presents.[14]

> I hear the voices of my neighbors rejoicing. A parade goes by, inaugurating the demolition of the elevated structure, widening the streets for motor traffic, letting the sun shine on the saloons at every corner and finding with its beams the dusty thrift and pawn shops, antique stores, denizens and passers-by, which were the charm and fame of Third. Here I came with so much of the past, furniture, pictures, love of beauty, color, which I have lived with and wrapped myself in. This, my street, the store my cocoon. Soon I will let it go, fly away, like a butterfly.

Eulabee makes no explanation for her abrupt departure from

New York in March of 1956. Logic suggests that she was terrified of running out of money. Her sole income now was interest on an eight thousand dollar legacy from her uncle George Hassett's estate, and a modest Social Security check from war work in California. There wasn't much left to keep her in New York. Certainly not family. She wasn't painting. The storefront gallery and the neighborhood no longer seemed amusing.

A friend told her about a pension in Lisbon, Portugal, where one could live well on three dollars a day. As it still does, York House attracted diplomats and well-heeled American and European expatriates, exactly the kind of people Eulabee admired. She was always happy in Europe, so why not move there? Except for the collection of miniatures, which she took with her, Eulabee dispersed other paintings and her personal treasures, which her children eventually inherited, among forebearing friends in Connecticut. Everything else, the antique furniture and *objets d'art* collected for so many years, she sold.

Frank Dobbs, a New York decorator friend, came to help her sort things out. He picked up a cup from a set of Löwenstoft china she had brought from England many years ago. It had cracked in transit. "This is so lovely, Eulabee," Dobbs commented. "What a shame that it's cracked."

"It's not cracked!" Eulabee shot back. "It's beautiful."[15]

CHAPTER 17

L'Envoi

1956–1961

My circle filled, and refilled, must become a sphere.

EULABEE SAW in Portugal's tortured past the portent of her own destiny in Lisbon.

> Here Christopher Columbus learned of ships and sea from the great navigators, Phoenicians left traces, Romans left their footprints, and Moors left their influence. The history of Portugal is as sad as the lives of artists—courage, dreams, grief, and glory.

Courage had brought her to Portugal at the age of seventy-eight, with old dreams wrapped in the remnants of old griefs. The glory—an honor she could not have foreseen—was yet to come. Though drained by the exertions of the move, she looked about as she rode from the airport to her new home at Rua das Janelas Verdes 32, and knew she had made the right decision.

> Lisbon on the hills, streets slipping up and sliding down. One longs to walk its winding ways and broad stairways, stroll in parks with storks and peacocks; past old palaces and ancient dwellings that line the pavements, shielding gardens in the rear, past tiny shops of every ware and human interest. . . . Delightful, pastel-tinted Lisbon, houses pink and blue

and yellow, with lacy balconies and fluttering wash. Facades of beautifully designed tiles. Could I but pick out just one, for me to keep.

York House delighted her. The converted sixteenth-century convent, which she insisted on calling a monastery, had been established as a residential hotel in the 1920s by a French couple named Goldstein. Eulabee immediately felt at home in its antique-filled reception rooms and cloistered gardens. From her tiny upstairs "cell" she could watch boat traffic on the broad Tagus river and admire the Renaissance style of the city's ornate Manueline architecture dating back to the fifteenth century. The daily rate included three meals a day and maid service; she wanted for nothing. Furthermore, she had a built-in audience. Once she had acquainted the permanent residents with her fascinating past, there were the transient guests to regale with tales of triumph and tragedy.

Eulabee soon found her way to Lisbon's art museums. One of the most distinguished of them, the Museu Nacional de Arte Antiga, was located close by at Rua das Janelas Verdes 73. Learning that the museum occasionally sponsored talks by foreigners, she made an appointment with the director, Dr. João Couto, and offered to lecture on the history and art of miniature painting. Dr. Couto studied the few works she had brought for him to see. Clearly impressed, he declared "Madame Dix, we will have your lecture, and we will give an exhibit of your miniatures!"

The exhibition, which the American embassy co-sponsored, originally was scheduled to open in November of 1957. Eulabee's decision to send to New York for several floral oil paintings caused endless complications and delayed the opening to January 3, 1958.

By all accounts, the handsomely mounted retrospective, said to be the first by a living artist in Portugal's prestigious national museum, was extraordinarily successful. Opening night festivities began with the hour-long illustrated lecture, followed by formal ceremonies at which United States Ambassador James C. H. Bonbright and Dr. Couto presided. Erect and elegant in her full-length velvet coat, the octogenarian artist gave her lecture and then repaired to the gallery to greet guests and accept their praise with the aplomb of an aging actress playing her last great role. She had waited a long time for this moment; now the museum had seen to its flawless execution.

> Dr. Couto spared no attention for lighting or detail. Two long light tan couches were back-to-back in the center; a fine Louis XVI commode held two handsomely framed miniatures, with greens behind. Four vitrines held fifty miniatures . . . while standing screens held each two of the twenty-four more accomplished miniatures in wide grey silk mats. Two large 6 x 5 feet oils, mauve, white and grey flower pictures seemed to hold it all together.

Lisbon never had seen anything quite like this artist's six decades of work. Mounted in gold frames, ormolu stands, and ornate triptych-like reliquaries fashioned in Italy from Eulabee's designs, or set in silver boxes and jewelry, seventy-six miniature portraits in watercolor on ivory were arranged by period against folds of rich blue velvet. She could not have asked for more nor, for once, did she.

Newspapers in Portugal and New York carried stories and Eulabee's picture. The Portuguese critic Fernando de Pamplona wrote in *Diário da Manhã*, "We are here in the presence of a miniature painter of sure and subtle technique and of refined sensitivity." Dr. João Couto's introduction in the exhibition catalogue placed Eulabee's art in historical context.

"This display has a special charm, being a product of the first decades of the 20th century, and affording us a vivid and attractive glimpse of the American society of that time, with its peculiar traits, its originalities, its types of beauty, its notorious ostentation."

Like the characters in the Edith Wharton novels she had read as a young woman, Eulabee surely had been an advocate for ostentation. But beyond that, the exhibition was the chronicle of a personal evolution. As had so many of the people in her life, some of the finest miniatures had slipped away, but the collection nevertheless held captivating reminders of the journey begun in 1899 with the supremely confident self-portrait, *Me*.

"My last exhibition!" she recorded in the memoirs, leaving unmentioned a final attempt to sell some paintings in a disastrous show, in 1959, at Livraria a Bibliófilia on the aptly named Rua da Misericórdia. Only the catalogue cover survived with her notation, "This was the most dreadful experience. Ida Turner Donnat [a York House friend] said this Baron Catier knew all the smart people in Lisbon. As I knew none, it seemed good to turn his dirty little back room into a show . . . . What a time! He said he sent out 200 invitations. Not one person came." Except, apparently, for "all of York House, the American ambassadress, and João Couto" on the first day. "I never went back."

There is no evidence other than a few desultory scenic watercolors that Eulabee ever painted seriously again. Her days seemed to pass amiably enough without it. She worked on the memoirs, explored Lisbon, and scrawled sad letters home to American acquaintances. The latter were mainly a rehash of past wrongs, little more than epistolary bids for attention.

The memoirs, now, no longer are a careful record of events, but musings. "From my room in an ancient monastery . . . I reminisce of activities, people, times, and places with gratitude for smiles and helpful hands as I grew from the me that was to be to the I that I am." Ruminant quotations from her past cast little light on the present: Mark Twain on "the constant sweep of hurrying thoughts" and a Taoist metaphor, "Of clay the walls and base of a bowl are made for our advantage, but it is the *void* of the bowl that is the usefulness of the bowl." There were thoughts of death. "The golden hearses here are beautiful, piles of roses—pink and white roses. My friend says they are expensive. Oh well, perhaps!"

Although she had chosen to live abroad, Eulabee clung to her

Three miniatures in elaborate frames designed by the artist are displayed on velvet in vitrines at her Lisbon retrospective exhibition. LRC Archives of The National Museum of Women in the Arts

Eulabee (right) at opening of the Lisbon exhibition with Dr. João Couto, director of the Museu Nacional de Arte Antiga, and U. S. Ambassador James C. H. Bonbright. LRC Archives of The National Museum of Women in the Arts

tenuous family ties as though estrangements were non-existent. She needed to put her affairs in order and asked her brother in Grand Rapids to draw up a will. Exasperated letters from Phil to "sister" pleaded for a sensible disposition of her art works, to little avail. The modest expenses at York House and checks from her brother permitted occasional trips to the United States, sometimes by air, to see Joan, who had moved to Washington, D.C., in 1952. But she did not see her son. The last of a few holiday visits with Dix's family was at Christmas in 1955.

During the summer of 1960, Joan and David came to Europe with their three children and scheduled a week-long visit with Eulabee at York House. She was overjoyed to see them. While her pleasure-bound teenage grandchildren headed for the beach, she became the couple's tireless guide around the city.

Realizing that her mother had become become very deaf, Joan took her to be fitted for hearing aids, but Eulabee refused to wear them because "Nobody says anything worth hearing." Otherwise, David recalls the visit as relatively peaceful, and Joan thought Eulabee seemed more contented than she'd ever seen her. Yet the 46-year-old mother of three, a successful public relations executive, still hadn't managed to exorcise the demons. "Eulabee's voice continued to run through my head like an audio tape, commenting on everything I did and thought."[1] At the end of their visit while Joan was packing, Eulabee flew into a rage over an awkwardly tied-up parcel and Joan left Lisbon determined never to see her mother again.

Other than one futile exchange of letters, there was no further communication until February 21, 1961. But Eulabee had not forgotten the incident.

> Joan dear, I think I should write to say that I am sailing tomorrow 22 Feb. '61 for New York on the Vulcania. . . . If it goes down you will know. I appreciate that I will get to a tired city, one snow storm after another, but for a long time I have hoped to go. Lisbon is lovely, but even the ambassadress advised me to go. I am taking all my miniatures, hoping to dispose of them in some way, and my teeth need Dr. Irving. I will be in Connecticut with Doris Leets. I hope you are well. I worry, for the last year of my "change of life" at 47 was a trying one for me. One does things differently. You surely know that I have never lost

> my temper with you as I did. For this I am deeply sorry, but also, because of this I must see you and this is the chief reason I am coming to U.S. I will be at the Allerton Hotel, 57th and Lexington (if it is still there) and mail will reach me at #1 East 57th Street c/o Dr. Irving. You may be coming to New York. Let me know, but I hope you will not undertake a heavy job until your "change" is over. . . . I love you dearly, Joan. I want to see you. . . . Mother.

Although letters indicate that Eulabee planned to return to Lisbon, her preparations betrayed a sense of finality about this trip. She gave three miniatures and nine floral paintings to the Museu Nacional de Arte Antiga with the understanding that one of the florals would go to its sister institution, the Museu Nacional de Arte Contemporânea, now known as the Museu do Chiado. Trunks were left at York House; the other art accompanied her back to the United States.

Joan refused to go to New York to meet the *Vulcania.* David went alone, arriving at the dock in time to greet the 82-year-old artist as she made her slow way down the gangplank carrying an old brown suitcase full of miniatures. Gentle and patient as he always was with Eulabee, David took the luggage and stood by while a large flat crate of carefully packed paintings was off-loaded, smoothing ruffled official feathers when she fussed at customs inspectors. After the crate was repacked and forwarded to Dix's home in Connecticut, he took her to lunch, then by cab to the Allerton Hotel. "We had a very nice visit," David poignantly recalled of the last time he saw his mother-in-law.[2] His long-time fascination with her stories about the famous people she had known, and painted, along with his inherent compassion for her, was the basis for their warm relationship. With her nephew Sam Dix, it seemed, Eulabee had been more interested in the contemporary scene, yet his relationship with the artist was equally affectionate.

Eulabee spent some time in New York City, then moved on to visit her friend in Connecticut. In May, she arrived at the Beckers. Nobody knew what she planned to do next, nor, probably, did she. In any case, Eulabee was not well. Whatever was wrong with her seemed real enough even in light of a propensity for feigning heart attacks. She needed care, and it was Mildred, not Dix, who brought her home to Woodbury.

Mildred Becker always had borne Dix's cold behavior with sweet stoicism. Now she rose just as stoically to the demands of her difficult mother-in-law, apparently conscience-stricken that her own mother recently had died alone in a sanitarium.

"Here was Eulabee and no one would take her in," their daughter Ayala remembered. "She had managed to alienate everybody. My mom's heart went out to her. My father, though, spent all his time either in the living room or away from home, totally ignoring his mother."[3]

The woman so long scorned as not good enough for Dix took care of his bedridden mother for five weeks. When Eulabee suffered one of her "heart attacks," Mildred called a doctor. The young physician looked her over and admonished, "Mrs. Dix, you're faking it!" Nevertheless, he sent her to the hospital for tests. Informed that she was to be moved to a nursing home the next day, Eulabee chose instead to die. It was June 14, 1961. Her grandson, Peter Becker, called on her at the hospital on his way home from college. He was the last of the family to see her alive.

Philip Dix in Grand Rapids made the appropriate arrangements as instructed by the will his sister had finally approved. Following cremation, the ashes were placed in a pint-sized carton and sent by air mail to the family plot at the Bellefontaine Cemetery in St. Louis. She had asked to be interred with the Hassetts, the great uncle and aunt who had seen to her first art schooling. Nobody was present except the officiating Episcopal priest and an old friend, Dr. Adrian Blyer. The obituaries that chronicled her accomplishments in the Grand Rapids and New York papers would have pleased her. Joan believed that her mother willed her own death:

> Doctors found no evidence of a heart attack. She died in her

> sleep. I last saw her in her coffin at the funeral parlor just prior to cremation. She lay there like a brightly plumed bird, ready to take flight. I said goodbye to her and wished her well. Estranged as we were, with no contact for many months, I was overcome with grief, not so much for my own loss but for the sadness of her life, for the creative artist who should have soared happily but who felt defeated and who died alone.[4]

Dix, who had not said goodbye to his mother, took his sister into his arms that day and, for the first time since they were children, tried to comfort her.

The family held a memorial service at St. Paul's Episcopal Church in Woodbury. The Reverend Earl S. Estabrook never had met the artist, but he had come to the cloth after a career in architecture and was sensitive enough to select the most fitting eulogy he could have delivered for Eulabee Dix: Rudyard Kipling's *L'Envoi.*

> When Earth's last picture is painted,
>   And the tubes are twisted and dried,
> When the oldest colours have faded, and
>   The youngest critic has died,
> We shall rest, and faith, we shall need it
>   Lie down for an aeon or two
> Til the Master of All Good Workmen
>   Shall set us to work anew!
> And only the Master shall praise us,
>   And only the Master shall blame;
> And no one shall work for money,
>   And no one shall work for fame!
> But each for the joy of working, and each,
>   In his separate star,
> Shall draw the Thing as he sees It, for
>   The God of Things as They Are!

"Shall draw the Thing as he sees It!" When the letters of condolence began to arrive, they drew Eulabee as their writers saw her, differently but invariably as a "remarkable woman."

Katharine Bliss, living in Manhattan and one of the few left who remembered sitting for her, wrote, "There are a few people so vital, so individual, so positive in their meeting of life and its responses, that one gains the feeling that they are invulnerable to old age and death. Such is the feeling I had about your remarkable mother."

"Her departure from York House in February was the occasion for a very sincere and heartwarming display of the high regard, understanding, and affection the entire staff and her many friends in this country had for her," wrote Frances Dabell, a friend in Portugal. "She seemed ageless, and we all hoped for her return. In her last letter to me of June 6, she, too, seemed anxious to resume her residence in this gentle country . . . . She was, without a doubt, a very remarkable lady."

But Ida Turner Donnat, another York House friend, wrote, "I miss your mother, but perhaps it is best God took her before she became too helpless and unhappy. In her letter to me she seemed delighted to be back in the U.S.A. and more at peace."

Carla Patsuris, the numerologist Eulabee often consulted, offered yet another kind of reassurance. "Do not be sad over Eulabee's going, as she wanted desperately to die. Even in her last letter she told me again that it is far too much effort to go on, and she wanted me to pray for her release."

For Joan, however, there was no release. "Why Eulabee's dual personality? . . . Was she afraid of her own reality? Did she ever acknowledge her own destructiveness? Or was her self-image, her self-portrayal as an innocent, perfect 'child of God' maintained until her dying day?"[5]

Horace Philip Dix, Jr., considered his sister's accomplishments important enough to edit her memoirs and have six typewritten bound copies produced for the family. The project appeared to be his own search for Eulabee, but when he encountered passages that told more about her than he thought the world should know, he excised a number of insightful realities she had *not* rearranged.

Of her own exhaustive and admittedly subjective search for her mother, Joan wrote in her autobiography, "Exhuming Eulabee has become my personal challenge. What I hope for is a rational explanation of this mother who was both a powerful force and a baffling mystery. . . . The feeling persists that Eulabee wants to be exhumed, to be understood, perhaps better than she ever understood herself. And by understanding her I may be able to see myself more clearly."

What others have seen in Joan clearly is the best of Eulabee. A petite, elegant, bright, and articulate woman, she retired from a prestigious public relations position in Washington, D.C., in 1976, and moved to the West Coast to begin an active new life in Seattle. Twenty years later, in her eighties, she gained at last some measure of peace as she worked closely with Eulabee's biographer. She and David had divorced in 1976; he moved to Santa Fe, New Mexico, and later to Honolulu. They remained always good friends.

Philip Dix Becker, of course, didn't try to find his mother. He tried to erase her but could not, for the simple reason that her genius, in spite of his ability to erect an impenetrable wall of self-containment, glowed through his own achievements.

The enigma that was Eulabee never will be resolved by stumbling about in the dark corners of her psyche. May we not dare to question its verity when darkness vanishes in the presence of light? Art was Eulabee's light. She wanted to be remembered for her art and for her love of beauty. Eulabee Dix demanded with every breath she drew that everything must be beautiful. It was how she portrayed her subjects, what she brought to every space she occupied, and how she saw herself.

Many years passed before Joan could bring herself to read her mother's memoirs. Only then did she discover the remorse buried in an obscure sentence on the last page of the manuscript.

"Could I but weep to cleanse the paths of past stupidities that blinded the LOVE that was mine to give."

In the end, it was Eulabee who found Eulabee.

Woman in White Dress, n.d., 4⅝ x 3½ in. oval
The National Museum of Women in the Arts
Gift of Samuel M. Dix

Ivory and the Art of Miniature Painting

by Carol Aiken

> Nowadays, when we talk about a miniature we have in our minds a small portrait or painting on ivory. . . . [F]or its qualities of smoothness, fine texture of grain, permanence, translucence . . . nothing seems to equal ivory as a surface on which to execute work so small and delicate.[1]

THE ENGLISH MINIATURE-PAINTING TRADITION, INITIATED DURING THE 1520s, was transformed at the beginning of the eighteenth century by the introduction of ivory as a material for support for the painted surface. Ivory slowly but completely replaced vellum, the material previously used. By the end of the American Revolution, which coincided with the beginning of the heyday of the American miniature, miniatures in England and in the United States were essentially defined as small images painted in watercolors on ivory supports. The inherent qualities of ivory that made it a desirable support for painting—smoothness, fine texture, and translucence—not only led to the use of brighter, more transparent colors, but also encouraged a change in the basic techniques of paint application. Short controlled strokes of color that had been necessitated by the more absorbent vellum supports began to yield to washes of color that could be freely applied to the less-absorbent ivory.

From the time of its introduction to miniature painting, ivory was available for purchase in pre-cut sheets called leaves. The leaves were formed from slices cut along, but never across, the length of an elephant tusk. For most of the period during which portrait miniatures were painted on ivory, the size of a leaf was limited by the width of the tusk from which it was taken. Not until interest in the miniature began to decline, after the introduction of the daguerreotype in 1839, did technological processes become available for the production of larger sheets of ivory. Due to the tremendous popularity of the upright piano (invented in 1800), a gradual increase in the demand for ivory piano keys eventually led to the creation of lathes capable of cutting continuous veneers of ivory from elephant tusks.

By rotating a section of tusk against a blade, broad ribbons of ivory could be "unrolled" by a lathe. In 1834 an ivory veneer measuring 30 by 150 inches was displayed in London. Even larger sheets of ivory were eventually produced in the United States by the Pratt factory in Connecticut, which exhibited a single sheet of ivory 14 inches wide and 52 feet long at the Great Exhibition of 1851, held in the Crystal Palace, Hyde Park, London.[2] Veneer-cut ivory was prone to shattering into thin parallel segments, so that its use for miniature supports never became especially widespread. Miniaturists, ever concerned about the permanence and stability of their materials, continued to prefer leaves cut in the traditional manner, just as they continued to use the same methods and techniques that had been initiated in the eighteenth-century for the preparation of the leaves.

The miniaturist's water-based paints would not properly adhere to an ivory support until natural fats and oils that were inherent in the material had been removed. In 1800, Archibald Robertson, a Scottish miniature painter who had emigrated to New York, wrote to his brother, Andrew, describing how to prepare an ivory leaf for painting:

> I make choice of Ivory as free from veins as I can get—and to whiten, fold it in paper and lay between two common ironing irons to extract any oiliness, which is absorbed by the paper, the irons being heated, so strongly, as not to risk scorching the paper—or what I greatly prefer, bleaching it in the sun—laying the ivory upon white paper, and when it warps or bends with the heat, turn the other side. . . . [T]he simple idea is to extract the oily moistness in the easiest way, by heat generally. . . . Next, I rub one side of the ivory clean of grease, with sanded paper, or sea-dog's skin—lay it over with gum [arabic] water, not very strong—lay it on a thick piece of imperial paper, the whitest I can get (or if the ivory is thin, on a card). . . . I then scrape the ivory, till it is perfectly free from scratches, and is quite smooth. I then rub some pumice stone with a file on the ivory—and rub the pumice with sanded paper, till the ivory is of a proper equal roughness, fit to receive the color.[3]

In the early twentieth century, artists such as Eulabee Dix were able to purchase ivory leaves fully prepared and ready for use. In unpublished notes Dix recorded that the "Ivory is prepared with a velvet-like surface, not polished, and in leaves of various sizes. The largest, about 6" x 7", are expensive and difficult to get in the United States." It has been noted that the American miniaturist Lucy Stanton generally ordered ivory "from the London or Paris market, cut very thick."[4] Percy Buckman, an English miniaturist, sounded a cautionary note about the problems inherent in using the larger sheets of ivory that were bought in England:

> Ivories are stocked by most artists' colourmen, bleached and unbleached, in sizes ranging from oo to number 12, 6 in. by 4 in., and even larger sizes may be obtained by ordering them. These large sizes could not be cut from any elephant's tusk, but are pieces steamed till soft, then subjected to hydraulic pressure to flatten them to the necessary size. Such extreme sizes are apt

> to become somewhat wavy in surface, and should therefore be firmly laid down on stiff card or panel before work is commenced.[5]

Alert to the unique characteristics of the material upon which she worked, Dix described ivory as being:

> more of the consistency of fingernails. . . . It is brittle and cracks when cold and dry. When a leaf of ivory (not too thick) is laid in water for a time it can be cut cross-grain with scissors . . . well soaked the ivory becomes larger than when dry, and it is important to have the finished ivory slightly smaller than the frame which is to hold it, as there is a spread, under certain atmospheric conditions. If the ivory is snug when first placed it is likely to spread and crack later. When properly framed, a miniature will last for hundreds of years, as they have, but they must not be left in the snow nor in the hot sun.[6]

Dix's concern with characteristics of the materials also embraced the process of producing a likeness.

> My paints were the best of water colors (it was thought they were painted in oil when I finished); brushes not small, but with a good point from putting a little gum-arabic in the water. . . . To paint a head the size of a nickel, drawing must be firm and forms delicate, character not neglected . . . a matter of accurate, minute detail and proportions.[7]

Buckman provided additional insight into the more general details concerning the watercolor paints that were preferred by miniature painters. He cautioned that some paints, prepared by colourmen especially for miniature painting, might actually "restrict one's freedom and are difficult to manage." For this reason, he offered, "in common with the majority of miniature painters, I prefer the ordinary watercolours sold in cakes, pans or tubes. Cakes, I think, are preferable, as being less liable to collect dust, or small hairs, both enemies of the miniature painter. . . . Permanence and transparency are the chief qualities to be looked for in selecting colours."[8]

Throughout the centuries the best miniaturists have been readily distinguished by their highly developed personal styles. Styles emerged partly as a reflection of the specific techniques that were chosen by an artist for the application of the paint to an ivory surface. Among Dix's contemporaries there were more than a few individuals who reveled in innovation. The manner in which they handled the paint, and even the colors they selected for their palettes, challenged long-standing traditions. For example, stippling (applying paint with the tip of a brush), hatching (applying paint in short dashes), and washing (flowing wet colors over a surface using a loaded brush) had been synonymous with miniature-painting techniques over the preceding centuries. Mastery of these techniques was not taken quite as seriously by the innovators of the revival period as it had been by their predecessors. Yet Percy Buckman was able to assert that any collection of works by "modern" miniaturists could be divided into three distinct schools. The first endeavored "to carry out their subject entirely in washes without retouching." The second covered "the ivory in every part with fine stipple or dot." The last group chose to "mingle both the above methods according to the different qualities of the various parts to be represented."[9] Buckman observed that "The best artist is he who can most successfully defy and overcome the conventions and limitations of his medium. . . . It is only deadly monotony that kills."[10]

Buckman was equally observant about the perspectives of the clients that miniaturists were expected to please.

> The public is on the whole fairly sane. Many would not understand the wash work and would call it sloppy. Others, brought up on photographs with all the character stippled out of them, might prefer the highly-stippled miniature; they like to see evidence of great labour, and to examine it through a magnifying glass, but I think that those whose education had gone further would prefer the happy medium.

In regard to stippling, in 1915 Lucy Stanton wrote that it was "a method of work I have long striven to do without as I believe face, drapery, and all should be kept fresh, charming and free from this tedious dry method of work."[11] The methods preferred by Stanton included the wet-in-wet techniques of "puddling" and "broad washes," techniques virtually without historical precursors in the preceding centuries, except perhaps, in the completely non-traditional nineteenth-century watercolor miniatures on ivory by Goya.[12]

The difficulty of painting on an ivory surface has been repeatedly over-emphasized in discussions of miniature painting. It is sufficient to note that ivory, even after careful preparation to remove its natural oils, does not absorb watercolor. But with experience and knowledge, there is far less difficulty in controlling the paint than has often been claimed. As the process was articulately described by Percy Buckman:

> The first washes are plain sailing, though it takes considerable skill in handling, and judgment in the amount of fluid necessary to ensure an even wash. It is in adding subsequent washes that the trouble begins. The first touch of the wet brush will moisten the dry colour, a second touch applied in the same place will remove it altogether. Therefore, in overpainting you must avoid touching any part of the underpainting more than once before allowing it time to dry. . . . If you can master the art of laying an even wash on ivory, half your technical difficulties will be overcome.[13]

The number of sittings required to complete a miniature has always varied considerably among artists. For Buckman, "two to five sittings of an hour to an hour and a half" were sufficient. This did not include the additional time, without the model, to blend and finish the painted surface. Dix described her own experience:

> After each sitting I would work on and on for hours from memory, and for what I wanted—intensely—lost to the work, becoming one great eye. Eight hours would sometimes pass.

> All evening resting my eyes, I would lie in the dark. The next day at it again. Then another sitting—four or five in all, over two weeks.[14]

When the artist's initial work was finished, a miniature still required the protection of a frame or case before it could be released for exhibition or to an eager client. Because the frame was the most important means of protection for a miniature, its choice and fitting was handled with care. In fact, Eulabee Dix designed many frames for her miniatures. No matter how large or small an image might be, or the style of the case or frame in which it was housed, the painted surface of a miniature was traditionally covered with a convex glass. The slight dome offered transparent protection while avoiding direct contact with the delicate painted surface. For the almost four hundred years during which miniature-painting was a continuing tradition, the cover glass, called a crystal, was attached to the miniature with a thin transparent membrane called goldbeaters' skin (originally used in the making of gold leaf). Eulabee Dix and her contemporaries continued using the traditional methods and materials for framing during the early years of the twentieth century when miniature painting enjoyed a brief and glorious revival. The goldbeater's skin was used to hold the crystal securely in position, and to seal out dirt while gently retraining the ivory in a flat position. Although larger miniatures might be covered with flat glasses, those glasses too were carefully raised above the painted surface of the miniature through the use of a fillet or a mat, before being bound to the picture with goldbeaters' skin. The type of case or frame in which the miniature was finally placed was of less importance than the fact that careful preparation before framing would help to ensure the survival of an inherently fragile work of art, as Dix herself had observed, "for hundreds of years."

NOTES

1. George C. Williamson and Percy Buckman, *The Art of the Miniature Painter* (London: Chapman and Hall, Ltd., 1926), p. 167.
2. *Ivory, A History and Collector's Guide* (London: Thames and Hudson, Ltd., 1987), p. 141.
3. Emily Robertson, ed., *Letters and Papers of Andrew Robertson. . . . Also A Treatise on the Art by His Eldest Brother, Archibald Robertson* (London: Eyre and Spottiswoode, 1895), p. 21.
4. W. Stanton Forbes, *Lucy M. Stanton, Artist* (Atlanta, Georgia: Emory University, 1975), p. 30.
5. Williamson and Buckman, p. 168.
6. Unpublished Dix papers, courtesy of Jo Ann Ridley.
7. Ridley, *Looking for Eulabee Dix*, p. 67.
8. Buckman, p. 169.
9. Williamson and Buckman, p. 179-180.
10. Williamson and Buckman, p. 182.
11. Forbes, p. 28.
12. Christies (Catalogue) *Sale of Old Master Paintings* (New York, January 31, 1997), p. 258.
13. Williamson and Buckman, p. 172.
14. Ridley, p. 67.

Museum Holdings of Works by Eulabee Dix

Miniatures

The National Museum of Women in the Arts
The Metropolitan Museum of Art
Worcester Art Museum
National Museum of American Art, Smithsonian Institution
National Portrait Gallery, Smithsonian Institution
The Albany Institute
Museu Nacional de Arte Antiga, Lisbon

Floral Paintings

The National Museum of Women in the Arts
The Grand Rapids Art Museum
Museu do Chiado, Lisbon

Above: Untitled, n.d., 1¼ x ⅝ in. oval
The National Museum of Women in the Arts
Gift of Joan Becker Gaines

NOTES

Other than the sources noted here, all biographical material about Eulabee Dix, including the original and family-edited memoirs, newspaper clippings, and correspondence, was extracted from the Eulabee Dix Papers in the archives of the National Museum of Women in the Arts, or supplied by the Dix-Becker family. The author gratefully acknowledges their cooperation and assistance.

Chapter 1. THE CIRCUMFERENCE OF MY LIFE TO BE (1878–1888)

1. Martha Owens Hume to Eulabee Dix (letter), November 13, 1946, Dix family papers.
2. Joan Becker Gaines, *Exhuming Eulabee*, unpublished.
3. Ibid.
4. Thomas J. Schlereth, *Victorian America, Transformations in Everyday Life, 1876–1915*, (New York: HarperCollins, 1991), p. 246.
5. Abby Meguire (Mrs. Neill) Roach, *A Tale of Two Sisters,* (Louisville: Filson Club History Quarterly, 1965), p. 13.

Chapter 2. BEGINNING ARIGHT (1888–1899)

1. William Innis Homer, *Robert Henri and His Circle,* (New York: Hacker Art Books, Inc., 1988), p. 7.
2. Gaines, *Exhuming Eulabee.*
3. Gaines to author (telephone interview), January 27, 1995.
4. Charlotte Streifer Rubinstein, *American Women Artists from Early Indian Times to the Present,* (New York: Avon Books, 1982), p. 91.
5. J. Gray Sweeney, *Artists of Grand Rapids 1840–1980,* (The Grand Rapids Arts Museum and the Grand Rapids Public Museum, 1981), p. 71.
6. Horst Delacrois and Richard C. Tansey, *Gardner's Art Through the Ages (Revised), 7th Edition,* (New York: Harcourt Brace, 1980), p. 71.

Chapter 3. ATTENDING TO ART (1899–1902)

1. Gaines to author (interview), March 3, 1994, Seattle, Washington.

Chapter 4. TO THE TOWER! (1902–1904)

1. Richard Covington, "The House on Goat Hill is Alive with the Sound of Music," (*Smithsonian Magazine*, February, 1991), p. 76.
2. Gino Francesconi, Museum Director and Archivist, Carnegie Hall, to author (letter), February 16, 1993.
3. Sweeney, *Artists of Grand Rapids 1840–1980,* p. 71.
4. Lewis Hoyer Rabbage to author (letter), June 29, 1993.

Chapter 5. THE LONDON LADIES (1904–1905)

1. Frances E. Hughes, "Amalia Kussner, High Priestess of the Daintiest of Arts,"

(*Traces of Indiana and Midwestern History,* Fall, 1990), p. 39–45.

2. Marian Fowler, *In a Gilded Cage—From Heiress to Duchess,* (Toronto: Random House of Canada Limited, 1993), p. 20–35.
3. Virginia Cowles, *Edward VII and His Circle,* (London: Hamish Hamilton, 1956), p. 267–268.

Chapter 6. FILLING THE CIRCLE (1905–1908)

1. Selena A. Spurgeon, *Henry E. Huntington, His Life and His Collections,* (San Marino: Huntington Library Press, 1992), p. 3.
2. Ibid. p. 26.
3. Carol Aiken, conservator, to author (letter), May 16, 1997.

Chapter 7. FIVE SITTINGS WITH MARK TWAIN (1908)

1. Rabbage to author (letter), September 26, 1994.
2. Ibid.
3. Maura Haggerty, Assistant Curator, The Mark Twain House, Hartford, Connecticut, to author (telephone interview), May 5, 1995.
4. Edited with introduction by Paul Baender, *What Is Man and Other Philosophical Writings,* (Berkeley: Published for the Iowa Center for Textual Studies by University of California Press, 1973).

Chapter 8. THE CREST OF THE WAVE (1907–1910)

1. Gaines, *Exhuming Eulabee.*
2. William M. Murphy, *Prodigal Father: The Life of John Butler Yeats (1839–1922),* (Ithaca and London: Cornell University Press, 1978), p. 234.
3. William M. Murphy to author (letter), July 17, 1995.
4. John Butler Yeats to Eulabee Dix, November 3, 1908, General Manuscripts (Misc), Box X–Z, Manuscripts Division, Department of Rare Books and Special Collections, Princeton University Libraries. Published with permission of the Princeton University Libraries. Copyright by Anne B. Yeats and Michael B. Yeats, Dublin.
5. Robert Gordon, *John Butler Yeats and John Sloan: The Records of a Friendship,* (Dublin: The Dolman Press, New Yeats Papers XIV, 1978), p. 12.
6. John Sloan, *Gist of Art,* (New York: American Artists Group, 1939), p. 227.
7. William M. Murphy, *Prodigal Father,* p. 645, n. 103.
8. Gaines to Murphy (letter), July 6, 1988.
9. Van Wyck Brooks, *John Sloan—A Painter's Life,* (New York: E. P. Dutton & Co., Inc., 1955), p. 35.
10. Murphy to Gaines (letter), September 6, 1985.
11. Conrad Aiken, "The Orange Moth," in *The Collected Short Stories of Conrad Aiken*, (Cleveland and New York: The World Publishing Company, 1960), p. 523.
12. Murphy, *Prodigal Father,* p. 614, n. 165.
13. Gaines to Murphy (letter), July 6, 1988.
14. Appraisal by Chapellier Galleries, Inc., September 11, 1982.
15. Judy L. Larson, Donelson Hoopes, and Phyllis Peet, *American Paintings at the High Museum of Art,* (New York: Hudson Hills Press in Association with the High Museum of Art, 1994), p. 138.

Chapter 9. THE MARRIAGE (1910–1912)

1. Gaines, *Exhuming Eulabee.*
2. Peter Becker to author (interview), December 20, 1995.
3. Gertrude Himmelfarb, *Marriage and Morals Among the Victorians and Other Essays,* (New York: Vintage Books, 1987), p. 5.
4. Murphy, *Prodigal Father,* p. 615, n. 171.
5. John Sloan diary, June 28 and 29, 1910, John Sloan Trust, Delaware Art Museum, Wilmington, Delaware.
6. J. B. Yeats to Eulabee Dix, October 6, 1910, Princeton University Libraries Collection.
7. Mabel Collins Donnelly, *The American Victorian Woman, The Myth and the Reality,* (New York: Greenwood Press, 1986), p. 46.
8. Ibid. p. 47.
9. Murphy, *Prodigal Father,* p. 618, n. 38.
10. Ibid. p. 615, n. 171.
11. J. B. Yeats to Eulabee Dix, December 16, 1911, Princeton University Libraries Collection.
12. Ibid.
13. J. B. Yeats to Eulabee Dix, December 20, 1911, Princeton University Libraries Collection.
14. J. B. Yeats to Eulabee Dix, December 24, 1911, Princeton University Libraries Collection.
15. J. B. Yeats to Eulabee Dix, December 27, 1911, Princeton University Libraries Collection.
16. Homer, *Robert Henri and His Circle,* p. 166.
17. J. B. Yeats to Eulabee Dix, January 11, 1912, Princeton University Libraries Collection.
18. J. B. Yeats to Eulabee Dix, January 12, 1912, Princeton University Libraries Collection.
19. Ibid.
20. J. B. Yeats to Eulabee Dix, March 13, 1912, Princeton University Libraries Collection.
21. Murphy to author (telephone interview), January 19, 1996.
22. J. B. Yeats to Eulabee Dix, March 28, 1912, Princeton University Libraries Collection.
23. Ibid.
24. Murphy, *Prodigal Father,* p. 619, n. 65.
25. J. B. Yeats to Eulabee Dix, May 17, 1912, Princeton University Libraries Collection.

Chapter 10. THE DARKENING PALETTE (1912–1918)

1. J. B. Yeats to Eulabee Dix, October 15, 1912, Princeton University Libraries Collection.
2. Ayala Becker Talpai to Gaines (tape recorded interview), 1986.
3. J. B. Yeats to Eulabee Dix, January 6, 1913, Princeton University Libraries Collection.
4. J. B. Yeats to Eulabee Dix, January 28, 1913, Princeton University Libraries Collection.
5. J. B. Yeats to Eulabee Dix, June 18, 1913, Princeton University Libraries Collection.
6. Becker-Sage correspondence, 1913, Albright-Knox Art Gallery, Buffalo, New York.
7. Susan E. Strickler and Marianne Gibson, *American Portrait Miniatures,* (Worcester: Worcester Art Museum, 1989), p. 52.
8. J. B. Yeats to Eulabee Dix, January 31, 1915, Princeton University Libraries

Collection.

9. Philip Dix Becker family papers.
10. J. B. Yeats to Eulabee Dix, March 19, 1916, Princeton University Libraries Collection.
11. J. B. Yeats to Alfred Becker, April 11, 1916, Princeton University Libraries Collection.
12. J. B. Yeats to Eulabee Dix, April 25, 1916, Princeton University Libraries Collection.
13. J. B. Yeats to Eulabee Dix, May 30, 1916, Princeton University Libraries Collection.
14. J. B. Yeats to Eulabee Dix, February 7, 1917, Princeton University Libraries Collection.
15. Ibid.
16. John Butler Yeats to Eulabee Dix, March 8, 1917, Princeton University Libraries Collection.

Chapter 11. NEW YORK, AT LAST (1918–1925)

1. Gaines to author (interview), November 18, 1994.
2. Gaines, *Exhuming Eulabee.*
3. Ibid.
4. J. B. Yeats to Eulabee Dix, June 18, 1918, Princeton University Libraries Collection.
5. Murphy, *Prodigal Father,* p. 496.
6. J. B. Yeats to Eulabee Dix, December 20, 1918, Princeton University Libraries Collection.
7. Gaines, *Exhuming Eulabee.*
8. Philip Dix Becker family papers.
9. Gaines, *Exhuming Eulabee.*
10. Samuel M. Dix to author (interview), October 23, 1994.
11. Gaines, *Exhuming Eulabee.*
12. J. B. Yeats to Eulabee Dix, June 23, 1919, Princeton University Libraries Collection.
13. J. B. Yeats to Eulabee Dix, August 18, 1919, Princeton University Libraries Collection.
14. J. B. Yeats to Eulabee Dix, December 28, 1919, Princeton University Libraries Collection.
15. J. B. Yeats to Eulabee Dix, December 31, 1919, Princeton University Libraries Collection.
16. Murphy, *Prodigal Father,* p. 441.
17. J. B. Yeats to Eulabee Dix, December 24, 1920, Princeton University Libraries Collection.
18. Murphy, *Prodigal Father,* p. 536.
19. J. B. Yeats to Eulabee Dix, January 20, 1922, Princeton University Libraries Collection.

Chapter 12. LET THE SHIP SAIL ON (1925–1928)

1. Gaines, *Exhuming Eulabee.*
2. Ibid.
3. Ibid.
4. Ewa Bobrowska-Jakubowska, "Olga Boznanska", Art & Business, No. 3/4, 1984.
5. Gaines, *Exhuming Eulabee.*

Chapter 13. BEGINNING ANEW (1928–1931)

1. Eulabee Dix to Margaretta Archambault (letter), August 26, 1928, Margaretta Archambault Collection, Archives of American Art, Smithsonian Institution, Washington, D.C.
2. Gaines, *Exhuming Eulabee.*
3. Gaines to author (interview), August 26, 1995.

4. Gaines, *Exhuming Eulabee.*
5. Ibid.
6. Ibid.

Chapter 14. ROSES (1932–1941)
1. Philip Dix Becker family papers.
2. Gaines, *Exhuming Eulabee.*
3. Ibid.
4. Ibid.
5. Ibid.
6. Rabbage and Gaines to author (interviews), 1993.
7. Paul Barker, Warwick Castle to author (letter), November 20, 1996.
8. Gaines, *Exhuming Eulabee.*
9. David Gaines to author (interview), January 11, 1995.
10. Gaines, *Exhuming Eulabee.*

Chapter 15. CALIFORNIA (1941–1945)
1. Sally and L. William Lisle to author (telephone interview), October 7, 1995.
2. *The Ojai*, April 18, May 2, 1941.
3. Swami Paramananda, *Principles and Purpose of Vedanta,* Ninth Edition, p. 34.
4. Lisles to author (telephone interview), October 17, 1995.
5. Lisles and Gaines to author (telephone interviews), October 17, 1995.
6. Gaines, *Exhuming Eulabee.*
7. Brooke Hayward Duchin to author (letter), February 15, 1995.
8. Gaines, *Exhuming Eulabee.*
9. Ibid.
10. *Hold Aloft the Light, The Story of Ananda Ashrama, 1923–1973,* (Ananda Ashrama, La Crescenta, California), unpaginated.

Chapter 16. UNDER THE "EL" (1945–1956)
1. Philip Dix Becker diary entry February 12, 1945.
2. Philip Dix Becker family papers.
3. Gaines, *Exhuming Eulabee.*
4. David Gaines to author (interview), January 11, 1995.
5. Gaines, *Exhuming Eulabee.*
6. Talpai to Gaines (tape recorded interview), 1986.
7. Samuel M. Dix to author (interview), October 16, 1993.
8. Ibid.
9. Gaines, *Exhuming Eulabee.*
10. Ibid.
11. Ibid.
12. Ibid.
13. Publication *Esse,* C. A. Stock, 790 Riverside Drive, New York, No. 5, May, 1959.
14. David Gaines to author (interview), January 12, 1995.
15. Gaines, *Exhuming Eulabee.*

Chapter 17. L'ENVOI (1956–1961)
1. Gaines, *Exhuming Eulabee.*
2. David Gaines to author (interview), January 12, 1995.
3. Talpai to Gaines (tape recorded interview), 1986.
4. Gaines, *Exhuming Eulabee.*
5. Ibid.

INDEX

Illustrations and the pages upon which they appear are indicated in boldface type.